編者的話

　　「學科能力測驗」是「指定科目考試」的前哨站，雖然難度較「指考」低，但是考試內容以及成績，仍然非常具有參考價值，而且「學測」考得好的同學，還可以甄選入學的方式，比別人早一步進入理想的大學，提前放暑假。

　　為了協助考生以最有效率的方式準備大學入學考試，我們特別蒐集了 103 年度「學測」各科試題，包括英文、數學、社會、自然和國文，做成「**103 年學科能力測驗各科試題詳解**」，書後並附有大考中心所公佈的各科選擇題答案、成績統計表，以及國文、英文兩科非選擇題閱卷評分原則說明。另外，在英文科詳解後面，還附上了英文試題修正意見及英文考科選文出處，讀者可利用空檔時間，上網瀏覽那些網站，增進自己的課外知識，並了解出題方向。

　　這本書的完成，要感謝各科名師全力協助解題：

　　英文 / 謝靜芳老師・蔡琇瑩老師・林工富老師
　　　　　蔡世偉老師・李冠勳老師・葉哲榮老師
　　　　　黃政翔老師
　　　　　美籍老師 Laura E. Stewart
　　　　　　　　　　 Christain A. Brieske

　　數學 / 高　鳴老師

　　社會 / 李　曄老師・王念平老師・李　易老師

　　國文 / 李雅清老師

　　自然 / 林清華老師・邱炳華老師・游　夏老師
　　　　　柯　舜老師

　　本書編校製作過程嚴謹，但仍恐有缺失之處，尚祈各界先進不吝指正。

劉　毅

CONTENTS

103 年大學入學學科能力測驗試題
英文考科

第壹部分：單選題（占 72 分）

一、詞彙（占 15 分）

說明：第 1 題至第 15 題，每題有 4 個選項，其中只有一個是正確或最適當的選項，請畫記在答案卡之「選擇題答案區」。各題答對者，得 1 分；答錯、未作答或畫記多於一個選項者，該題以零分計算。

1. Lost and scared, the little dog _____ along the streets, looking for its master.
   (A) dismissed　　(B) glided　　(C) wandered　　(D) marched

2. On a sunny afternoon last month, we all took off our shoes and walked on the grass with _____ feet.
   (A) bare　　(B) raw　　(C) tough　　(D) slippery

3. It is both legally and _____ wrong to spread rumors about other people on the Internet.
   (A) morally　　(B) physically　　(C) literarily　　(D) commercially

4. These warm-up exercises are designed to help people _____ their muscles and prevent injuries.
   (A) produce　　(B) connect　　(C) broaden　　(D) loosen

5. Mei-ling has a very close relationship with her parents. She always _____ them before she makes important decisions.
   (A) impresses　　(B) advises　　(C) consults　　(D) motivates

6. The restaurant has a _____ charge of NT$250 per person. So the four of us need to pay at least NT$1,000 to eat there.
   (A) definite　　(B) minimum　　(C) flexible　　(D) numerous

7. At the Book Fair, exhibitors from 21 countries will _____ textbooks, novels, and comic books.
   (A) predict　　(B) require　　(C) display　　(D) target

8. Before John got on the stage to give the speech, he took a deep
　　_____ to calm himself down.
　　(A) order　　　(B) rest　　　(C) effort　　　(D) breath

9. Most young people in Taiwan are not satisfied with a high school
　　_____ and continue to pursue further education in college.
　　(A) maturity　　(B) diploma　　(C) foundation　　(D) guarantee

10. Residents are told not to dump all household waste _____ into
　　the trash can; reusable materials should first be sorted out and
　　recycled.
　　(A) shortly　　(B) straight　　(C) forward　　(D) namely

11. Kevin had been standing on a ladder trying to reach for a book on
　　the top shelf when he lost his and fell to the ground.
　　(A) volume　　(B) weight　　(C) balance　　(D) direction

12. If student enrollment continues to drop, some programs at the
　　university may be _____ to reduce the operation costs.
　　(A) relieved　　(B) eliminated　　(C) projected　　(D) accounted

13. People in that remote village feed themselves by hunting and
　　engaging in _____ forms of agriculture. No modern agricultural
　　methods are used.
　　(A) universal　　(B) splendid　　(C) primitive　　(D) courteous

14. The government issued a travel _____ for Taiwanese in response
　　to the outbreak of civil war in Syria.
　　(A) alert　　(B) monument　　(C) exit　　(D) circulation

15. The baby panda Yuan Zai at the Taipei Zoo was separated from her
　　mother because of a minor injury that occurred during her birth.
　　She was _____ by zookeepers for a while.
　　(A) departed　　(B) jailed　　(C) tended　　(D) captured

二、綜合測驗（占 15 分）

說明：　第 16 題至第 30 題，每題一個空格，請依文意選出最適當的一個選項，
　　　　請畫記在答案卡之「選擇題答案區」。各題答對者，得 1 分；答錯、未
　　　　作答或畫記多於一個選項者，該題以零分計算。

第 16 至 20 題爲題組

　　Aesop, the Greek writer of fables, was sitting by the roadside one day when a traveler asked him what sort of people lived in Athens. Aesop replied, "Tell me where you come from and what sort of people live there, and I'll tell you what sort of people you'll find in Athens." ___16___, the man answered, "I come from Argos, and there the people are all friendly, generous, and warm-hearted. I love them."　___17___ this, Aesop answered, "I'm happy to tell you, my dear friend, that you'll find the people of Athens much the same."

　　A few hours later, ___18___ traveler came down the road. He too stopped and asked Aesop the same question.　___19___, Aesop made the same request. But frowning, the man answered, "I'm from Argos and there the people are unfriendly, ___20___, and vicious. They're thieves and murderers, all of them." "Well, I'm afraid you'll find the people of Athens much the same," replied Aesop.

16. (A) Amazing　　　(B) Smiling　　　(C) Deciding　　　(D) Praying
17. (A) At　　　(B) By　　　(C) For　　　(D) Into
18. (A) a　　　(B) the　　　(C) other　　　(D) another
19. (A) Again　　　(B) Indeed　　　(C) Together　　　(D) Moreover
20. (A) brave　　　(B) lonely　　　(C) mean　　　(D) skinny

第 21 至 25 題爲題組

　　Every year tens of thousands of tourists visit Mount Kilimanjaro, the highest mountain in Tanzania, Africa, to witness the scenes depicted in Earnest Hemingway's *The Snows of Kilimanjaro*. They are attracted by the American writer's ___21___ of the millennia-old glaciers. However, this tourist attraction will soon ___22___. According to the Climate Change Group, formed by environmentalists worldwide to document the effects of global warming, Mount Kilimanjaro's snows and glaciers are melting and are ___23___ to disappear by 2020. Not only will the summit lose its tourist attraction, but the disappearance of the snows will also cause major damage to the ecosystem on the dry African plains at its base. __24__ the snow covering the peak, there will not be enough moisture and water to nourish the plants and animals below. Rising temperatures, an effect of global warming, __25__ threaten the ecosystem of this mountain area. The loss of snows on the 5,892m peak, which have been there for about 11,700 years, could have disastrous effects on Tanzania.

21. (A) situations   (B) descriptions   (C) translations   (D) calculations
22. (A) operate   (B) expand   (C) recover   (D) vanish
23. (A) capable   (B) ready   (C) likely   (D) horrible
24. (A) Among   (B) Besides   (C) Inside   (D) Without
25. (A) thus   (B) just   (C) instead   (D) otherwise

第 26 至 30 題為題組

Most human beings actually decide before they think. When people encounter a complex issue and form an opinion, how thoroughly have they __26__ all the important factors involved before they make their decisions? The answer is: not very thoroughly, __27__ they are executives, specialized experts, or ordinary people in the street. Very few people, no matter how intelligent or experienced, can __28__ all the possibilities or outcomes of a policy or a course of action within just a short period of time. Those who take pride in being decisive often try their best to consider all the factors beforehand. __29__, it is not unusual for them to come up with a decision before they have the time to do so. And __30__ an opinion is formed, most of their thinking then is simply trying to find support for it.

26. (A) conveyed   (B) examined   (C) solved   (D) implied
27. (A) whoever   (B) because   (C) whether   (D) rather
28. (A) set out   (B) turn out
    (C) put into practice   (D) take into account
29. (A) However   (B) Furthermore   (C) Conditionally   (D) Similarly
30. (A) though   (B) unless   (C) once   (D) even

三、文意選填（占 10 分）

說明：　第 31 題至第 40 題，每題一個空格，請依文意在文章後所提供的 (A) 到
　　　　(J) 選項中分別選出最適當者，並將其英文字母代號畫記在答案卡之「選
　　　　擇題答案區」。各題答對者，得 1 分；答錯、未作答或畫記多於一個選
　　　　項者，該題以零分計算。

第 31 至 40 題為題組

　　In English-speaking cultures, the choice of first names for children
can be prompted by many factors: tradition, religion, nature, culture,
and fashion, to name just a few.

　　Certain people like to give a name that has been handed down in the
family to show ＿＿31＿＿ for or to remember a relative whom they love
or admire.　Some families have a tradition of ＿＿32＿＿ the father's first
name to the first born son.　In other families, a surname is included in
the selection of a child's given name to ＿＿33＿＿ a family surname going.
It may be the mother's maiden name, for instance.

　　For a long time, ＿＿34＿＿ has also played an important role in
naming children.　Boys' names such as John, Peter, and Thomas are
chosen from the Bible.　Girls' names such as Faith, Patience, and
Sophie (wisdom) are chosen because they symbolize Christian qualities.
However, for people who are not necessarily religious but are fond of
nature, names ＿＿35＿＿ things of beauty are often favored.　Flower and
plant names like Heather, Rosemary, and Iris ＿＿36＿＿ this category.

　　Another factor that has had a great ＿＿37＿＿ on the choice of names
is the spread of culture through the media.　People may choose a name
because they are strongly ＿＿38＿＿ a character in a book or a television
series; they may also adopt names of famous people or their favorite
actors and actresses.　Sometimes, people pick foreign names for their
children because those names are unusual and will thus make their
children more ＿＿39＿＿ and distinctive.

　　Finally, some people just pick a name the sound of which they like,

_____40_____ of its meaning, its origins, or its popularity. However, even these people may look at the calendar to pick a lucky day when they make their choice.

(A) drawn to   (B) fall into   (C) impact   (D) involving

(E) keep   (F) passing down   (G) regardless   (H) religion

(I) respect   (J) unique

四、閱讀測驗（占 32 分）

說明： 第 41 題至第 56 題，每題請分別根據各篇文章之文意選出最適當的一個
選項，請畫記在答案卡之「選擇題答案區」。各題答對者，得 2 分；答
錯、未作答或畫記多於一個選項者，該題以零分計算。

第 41 至 44 題為題組

American writer Toni Morrison was born in 1931 in Ohio. She was raised in an African American family filled with songs and stories of Southern myths, which later shaped her prose. Her happy family life led to her excellent performance in school, despite the atmosphere of racial discrimination in the society.

After graduating from college, Morrison started to work as a teacher and got married in 1958. Several years later, her marriage began to fail. For a temporary escape, she joined a small writers' group, in which each member was required to bring a story or poem for discussion. She wrote a story based on the life of a girl she knew in childhood who had prayed to God for blue eyes. The story was well received by the group, but then she put it away, thinking she was done with it.

In 1964, Morrison got divorced and devoted herself to writing. One day, she dusted off the story she had written for the writers' group and decided to make it into a novel. She drew on her memories from childhood and expanded upon them using her imagination so that the characters developed a life of their own. *The Bluest Eye* was eventually published in 1970. From 1970 to 1992, Morrison published five more novels.

In her novels, Morrison brings in different elements of the African American past, their struggles, problems and cultural memory. In *Song of Solomon*, for example, Morrison tells the story of an African American man and his search for identity in his culture. The novels and other works won her several prizes. In 1993, Morrison received the Nobel Prize in Literature. She is the eighth woman and the first African American woman to win the honor.

41. What is the passage mainly about?
    (A) The life of black people in the U.S.
    (B) The life of an African American writer.
    (C) The history of African American culture.
    (D) The history of the Nobel Prize in Literature.

42. Why did Morrison join the writers' group?
    (A) She wanted to publish *The Bluest Eye*.
    (B) She wanted to fight racial discrimination.
    (C) She wanted to be a professional writer.
    (D) She wanted to get away from her unhappy marriage.

43. According to the passage, what is one of the themes in Morrison's works?
    (A) A search for African American values.
    (B) Divorced black women in American society.
    (C) Songs and stories of African Americans in Ohio.
    (D) History of African Americans from the 1970s through the 1990s.

44. Which of the following statements is true about Toni Morrison?
    (A) She has been writing a lot since her adolescent years.
    (B) She suffered from severe racial discrimination in her family.
    (C) What she wrote in her novels are true stories of African Americans.
    (D) No African American woman ever received a Nobel Prize in Literature before her.

第 45 至 48 題爲題組

Below is an excerpt from an interview with Zeke Emanuel, a health-policy expert, on his famous brothers.

Interviewer: You're the older brother of Rahm, the mayor of Chicago, and Ari, an extremely successful talent agent. And you're a bioethicist and one of the architects of Obamacare. Isn't writing a book about how great your family is a bit odd?

Zeke: I don't write a book about how great my family is. There are lots of idiocies and foolishness—a lot to make fun of in the book. I wrote *Brothers Emanuel* because I had begun jotting stories for my kids. And then we began getting a lot of questions: What did Mom put in the cereal? Three successful brothers, all different areas.

I: To what do you attribute the Emanuel brothers' success?

Z: I would put success in quotes. We strive. First, I think we got this striving from our mother to make the world a better place. A second important thing is you never rest on the last victory. There's always more to do. And maybe the third important thing is my father's admonition that offense is the best defense. We don't give up.

I: Do you still not have a TV?

Z: I don't own a TV. I don't own a car. I don't Facebook. I don't tweet.

I: But you have four cell phones.

Z: I'm down to two, thankfully.

I: Your brothers are a national source of fascination. Where do you think they'll be in five years?

Z: Ari will be a superagent running the same company. Rahm would still be mayor of Chicago. I will probably continue to be my academic self. The one thing I can guarantee is none of us will have taken a cruise, none of us will be sitting on a beach with a pina colada.

45. What does Zeke Emanuel have in mind when saying "What did Mom put in the cereal?"
(A) The secret to bringing up successful kids.
(B) The recipe for a breakfast food.
(C) The difference among the brothers.
(D) The questions from his kids.

46. What does Zeke Emanuel think of the modern conveniences mentioned in the interview?
(A) Better late than never.
(B) Practice makes perfect.
(C) One can live without many of them.
(D) They are great inventions.

47. According to Zeke Emanuel, which of the following is a reason for the brothers' success?
(A) They defend themselves by attacking others.
(B) They learn a lot from great people's quotes.
(C) They are committed to glorifying their parents.
(D) They keep moving forward even after a big success.

48. Which of the following best summarizes Zeke Emanuel's response to the last question?
(A) The brothers look forward to a family trip on a cruise.
(B) Nothing much will change in the near future for them.
(C) Higher positions and more power will be their goals.
(D) None of the brothers will go to the beach.

第 49 至 52 題為題組

　　MOOC, a massive open online course, aims at providing large-scale interactive participation and open access via the web. In addition to traditional course materials such as videos, readings, and problem sets, MOOCs provide interactive user forums that help build a community for the students, professors, and teaching assistants.

MOOCs first made waves in the fall of 2011, when Professor Sebastian Thrun from Stanford University opened his graduate-level artificial intelligence course up to any student anywhere, and 160,000 students in more than 190 countries signed up. This new breed of online classes is shaking up the higher education world in many ways. Since the courses can be taken by hundreds of thousands of students at the same time, the number of universities might decrease dramatically. Professor Thrun has even envisioned a future in which there will only need to be 10 universities in the world. Perhaps the most striking thing about MOOCs, many of which are being taught by professors at prestigious universities, is that they're free. This is certainly good news for **cash-strapped** students.

There is a lot of excitement and fear surrounding MOOCs. While some say free online courses are a great way to increase the enrollment of minority students, others have said they will leave many students behind. Some critics have said that MOOCs promote an unrealistic one-size-fits-all model of higher education and that there is no replacement for true dialogues between professors and their students. After all, a brain is not a computer. We are not blank hard drives waiting to be filled with data. People learn from people they love and remember the things that arouse emotion. Some critics worry that online students will miss out on the social aspects of college.

49. What does the word "**cash-strapped**" in the second paragraph mean?
   (A) Making a lot of money.
   (B) Being short of money.
   (C) Being careful with money.
   (D) Spending little money.

50. Which of the following is **NOT** one of the features of MOOCs?
   (A) It is free to take the courses.
   (B) Many courses are offered by famous universities.
   (C) Most courses address artificial intelligence.
   (D) Many students can take the course at the same time.

51. What is the second paragraph mainly about?
   (A) The impact of MOOCs.
   (B) The goal of MOOCs.
   (C) The size of MOOC classes.
   (D) The cost of MOOC courses.

52. Which of the following is a problem of MOOCs mentioned in the passage?
   (A) The disappearance of traditional course materials.
   (B) The limited number of courses offered around the world.
   (C) The overreliance on professors from prestigious universities.
   (D) The lack of social interaction among students and professors.

第 53 至 56 題爲題組

Today the car seems to make periodic leaps in progress. A variety of driver assistance technologies are appearing on new cars. A developing technology called Vehicle-to-Vehicle communication, or V2V, is being tested by automotive manufacturers as a way to help reduce the number of accidents. V2V works by using wireless signals to send information back and forth between cars about their location, speed and direction, so that they keep safe distances from each other. Another new technology being tested is Vehicle-to-Infrastructure communication, or V2I. V2I would allow vehicles to communicate with road signs or traffic signals and provide information to the vehicle about safety issues. V2I could also request traffic information from a traffic management system and access the best possible routes. Both V2V and V2I have the potential to reduce around 80 percent of vehicle crashes on the road.

More and more new cars can reverse-park, read traffic signs, maintain a safe distance in steady traffic and brake automatically to avoid crashes. Moreover, a number of firms are creating cars that drive themselves to a chosen destination without a human at the controls. It is predicted that driverless cars will be ready for sale within five years. If and when cars go completely driverless, the benefits will be enormous. Google, which already uses prototypes of such cars to ferry its staff along Californian freeways, once put a blind man in a prototype and filmed him being driven off to buy takeaway hamburgers. If this works, huge numbers of elderly and disabled people can regain their personal mobility. The young will not have to pay crippling motor insurance, because their reckless hands and feet will no longer touch the wheel or the accelerator. People who commute by car will gain hours each day to work, rest, or read a newspaper.

53. Which of the following statements is true about V2V?
    (A) V2V communication has been very well developed.
    (B) Through V2V, drivers can chat with each other on the road.
    (C) V2V is designed to decrease crashes by keeping safe distances.
    (D) Through V2V, a car can warn cyclists nearby of its approach.

54. What does "**infrastructure**" in Vehicle-to-Infrastructure refer to?
    (A) Traffic facilities and information systems.
    (B) The basic structure of roads and bridges.
    (C) Knowledge and regulations about safe driving.
    (D) The traffic department of the government.

55. Which of the following is **NOT** a potential benefit of driverless cars?
    (A) The elderly will become more mobile.
    (B) "Drivers" can sleep in cars all the way to work.
    (C) People can race cars to their heart's content.
    (D) A blind man can get into a car and travel safely.

56. What can be inferred from the passage?
    (A) Cars will refuse to start if the driver is drunk.
    (B) The future may be a vehicle-accident-free era.
    (C) Everyone, including children, can afford a car.
    (D) The production of driverless cars is still far away.

第貳部份：非選擇題（占 28 分）

說明： 本部分共有二題，請依各題指示作答，答案必須寫在「答案卷」上，並標明大題號（一、二）。作答務必使用筆尖較粗之黑色墨水的筆書寫，且不得使用鉛筆。

一、中譯英（占 8 分）

說明： 1. 請將以下中文句子譯成正確、通順、達意的英文，並將答案寫在「答案卷」上。
　　　 2. 請依序作答，並標明題號。每題 4 分，共 8 分。

1. 有些年輕人辭掉都市裡的高薪工作，返回家鄉種植有機蔬菜。

2. 藉由決心與努力，很多人成功了，不但獲利更多，還過著更健康的生活。

二、英文作文（占 20 分）

說明： 1. 依提示在「答案卷」上寫一篇英文作文。
　　　 2. 文長至少 120 個單詞（words）。

提示： 請仔細觀察以下三幅連環圖片的內容，並想像第四幅圖片可能的發展，寫一篇涵蓋所有連環圖片內容且有完整結局的故事。

103年度學科能力測驗英文科試題詳解

第壹部分：單選題

一、詞彙題：

1. (**C**) Lost and scared, the little dog <u>wandered</u> along the streets, looking for its master.
   迷路而受驚嚇的小狗，沿著街道<u>徘徊</u>，尋找牠的主人。
   (A) dismiss〔dɪsˈmɪs〕*v.* 解散　　(B) glide〔glaɪd〕*v.* 滑行
   (C) ***wander***〔ˈwɑndɚ〕*v.* 徘徊　(D) march〔mɑrtʃ〕*v.* 行進
   lost〔lɔst〕*adj.* 迷路的；不知所措的　　scared〔skɛrd〕*adj.* 害怕的
   look for 尋找　　master〔ˈmæstɚ〕*n.* 主人

2. (**A**) On a sunny afternoon last month, we all took off our shoes and walked on the grass with <u>bare</u> feet.
   在上個月一個晴朗的下午，我們都脫下了鞋子，<u>赤裸</u>著腳走在草地上。
   (A) ***bare***〔bɛr〕*adj.* 赤裸的　　(B) raw〔rɔ〕*adj.* 生的
   (C) tough〔tʌf〕*adj.* 困難的　　(D) slippery〔ˈslɪpərɪ〕*adj.* 滑的
   sunny〔ˈsʌnɪ〕*adj.* 晴朗的　　***take off*** 脫下
   grass〔græs〕*n.* 草；草坪

3. (**A**) It is both legally and <u>morally</u> wrong to spread rumors about other people on the Internet. 在網路上散播有關他人的謠言，在法律上和<u>道德</u>上兩方面，都是錯的。
   (A) ***morally***〔ˈmɔrəlɪ〕*adv.* 道德上
   (B) physically〔ˈfɪzɪklɪ〕*adv.* 身體上
   (C) literarily〔ˈlɪtəˌrɛrəlɪ〕*adv.* 文學上
   (D) commercially〔kəˈmɝʃəlɪ〕*adv.* 商業上
   legally〔ˈligl̩ɪ〕*adv.* 法律上　　spread〔sprɛd〕*v.* 散播
   rumor〔ˈrumɚ〕*n.* 謠言

4. (**D**) These warm-up exercises are designed to help people <u>loosen</u> their muscles and prevent injuries.
   這些暖身運動是要幫助人們<u>放鬆</u>肌肉，避免受傷。

(A) produce〔prə'djus〕*v.* 生產；製造
(B) connect〔kə'nɛkt〕*v.* 連接
(C) broaden〔'brɔdn̩〕*v.* 加寬；拓寬
(D) *loosen*〔'lusn̩〕*v.* 鬆開；放鬆
warm-up〔'wɔrm͵ʌp〕*n.* 暖身　　*be designed to V.* 目的是爲了…
muscle〔'mʌsl̩〕*n.* 肌肉　　prevent〔prɪ'vɛnt〕*v.* 預防
injury〔'ɪndʒərɪ〕*n.* 傷害

5. (**C**) Mei-ling has a very close relationship with her parents. She always <u>consults</u> them before she makes important decisions.
美玲與父母的關係非常親近。她在做重要的決定之前，總是會<u>請教</u>他們。
(A) impress〔ɪm'prɛs〕*v.* 使印象深刻
(B) advise〔əd'vaɪz〕*v.* 勸告
(C) *consult*〔kən'sʌlt〕*v.* 請教；查閱
(D) motivate〔'motə͵vet〕*v.* 激勵
close〔klos〕*adj.* 親近的　　*make a decision* 做決定

6. (**B**) The restaurant has a <u>minimum</u> charge of NT$250 per person. So the four of us need to pay at least NT$1,000 to eat there.
該餐廳有每人新台幣 250 元的<u>最低</u>消費。所以我們四個人在那邊用餐至少要付新台幣 1,000 元。
(A) definite〔'dɛfənɪt〕*adj.* 明確的；確定的
(B) *minimum*〔'mɪnəməm〕*adj.* 最低的；最小的
(C) flexible〔'flɛksəbl̩〕*adj.* 有彈性的
(D) numerous〔'njumərəs〕*adj.* 許多的
charge〔tʃɑrdʒ〕*n.* 費用　　per〔pɚ〕*prep.* 每…　　*at least* 至少

7. (**C**) At the Book Fair, exhibitors from 21 countries will <u>display</u> textbooks, novels, and comic books.
在書展上，來自二十一個國家的展覽商將會<u>展出</u>教科書、小說，和漫畫。
(A) predict〔prɪ'dɪkt〕*v.* 預測　　(B) require〔rɪ'kwaɪr〕*v.* 要求
(C) *display*〔dɪ'sple〕*v.* 展示　　(D) target〔'tɑrgɪt〕*v.* 將…定作目標
fair〔fɛr〕*n.* 展覽會　　exhibitor〔ɪg'zɪbɪtɚ〕*n.* 展覽者
textbook〔'tɛkst͵bʊk〕*n.* 教科書　　novel〔'nɑvl̩〕*n.* 小說
comic book 漫畫

8. (**D**) Before John got on the stage to give the speech, he took a deep <u>breath</u> to calm himself down.

約翰在上台發表演說前，做個深<u>呼吸</u>，讓自己冷靜下來。

(A) order〔'ɔrdɚ〕*n.* 順序；命令　　(B) rest〔rɛst〕*n.* 休息

(C) effort〔'ɛfɚt〕*n.* 努力

(D) ***breath***〔brɛθ〕*n.* 呼吸　　***take a deep breath*** 做個深呼吸

stage〔stedʒ〕*n.* 舞台　　speech〔spitʃ〕*n.* 演講

give a speech 發表演說

calm〔kɑm〕*v.* 使平靜　　***calm sb. down*** 使某人冷靜下來

9. (**B**) Most young people in Taiwan are not satisfied with a high school <u>diploma</u> and continue to pursue further education in college.

在台灣大多數的年輕人對高中<u>文憑</u>感到不滿意，會繼續讀大學，接受更進一步的教育。

(A) maturity〔mə'tʃurətɪ〕*n.* 成熟

(B) ***diploma***〔dɪ'plomə〕*n.* 文憑；畢業證書

(C) foundation〔faʊn'deʃən〕*n.* 創立；基礎

(D) guarantee〔͵gærən'ti〕*n.* 保證；保證書

satisfy〔'sætɪs͵faɪ〕*v.* 使滿足　　***be satisfied with*** 對…感到滿意

pursue〔pɚ'su〕*v.* 追求；從事　　further〔'fɝðɚ〕*adj.* 更進一步的

10. (**B**) Residents are told not to dump all household waste <u>straight</u> into the trash can; reusable materials should first be sorted out and recycled. 居民被告知不要<u>直接</u>將所有的家庭廢棄物丟到垃圾桶；可再使用的物質應先被挑出來回收再利用。

(A) shortly〔'ʃɔrtlɪ〕*adv.* 不久　　(B) ***straight***〔stret〕*adv.* 直接地

(C) forward〔'fɔrwɚd〕*adv.* 往前　　(D) namely〔'nemlɪ〕*adv.* 也就是

resident〔'rɛzədənt〕*n.* 居民　　dump〔dʌmp〕*v.* 丟棄

household〔'haʊs͵hold〕*adj.* 家庭的　　waste〔west〕*n.* 廢棄物

trash can 垃圾筒　　reusable〔ri'juzəbḷ〕*adj.* 可再使用的

material〔mə'tɪrɪəl〕*n.* 物質　　sort〔sɔrt〕*v.* 分類

sort out 分類；挑出　　recycle〔ri'saɪkḷ〕*v.* 回收再利用

11. (**C**) Kevin had been standing on a ladder trying to reach for a book on the top shelf when he lost his <u>balance</u> and fell to the ground.

當凱文站在梯子上想伸手去拿放在架子最上層的書時，失去<u>平衡</u>跌倒在地。

(A) volume〔'vɑljəm〕*n.* 書籍；冊
(B) weight〔wet〕*n.* 重量
(C) ***balance***〔'bæləns〕*n.* 平衡
(D) direction〔də'rɛkʃən〕*n.* 方向

ladder〔'lædɚ〕*n.* 梯子　　***reach for*** 伸手去拿
top shelf 架子的最上層

12. (**B**) If student enrollment continues to drop, some programs at the university may be <u>eliminated</u> to reduce the operation costs.
如果學生的註冊人數持續下降，有些大學的課程可能要刪除，以降低營運成本。

(A) relieve〔rɪ'liv〕*v.* 減輕；使放心
(B) ***eliminate***〔ɪ'lɪmə,net〕*v.* 除去
(C) project〔prə'dʒɛkt〕*v.* 投射
(D) account〔ə'kaʊnt〕*v.* 說明；解釋 <*for*>

enrollment〔ɪn'rolmənt〕*n.* 註冊人數　　drop〔drɑp〕*v.* 下降
program〔'progræm〕*n.* 課程　　reduce〔rɪ'djus〕*v.* 降低；減少
operation〔,ɑpə'reʃən〕*n.* 運作；經營

13. (**C**) People in that remote village feed themselves by hunting and engaging in <u>primitive</u> forms of agriculture. No modern agricultural methods are used. 在那個偏遠村莊的人，靠打獵和從事<u>原始</u>型態的農業養活自己。沒有使用現代的農業技術。

(A) universal〔,junə'vɝsḷ〕*adj.* 普遍的；一般的
(B) splendid〔'splɛndɪd〕*adj.* 壯觀的；輝煌的
(C) ***primitive***〔'prɪmətɪv〕*adj.* 原始的
(D) courteous〔'kɝtɪəs〕*adj.* 有禮貌的

remote〔rɪ'mot〕*adj.* 遙遠的；偏僻的　　village〔'vɪlɪdʒ〕*n.* 村莊
feed〔fid〕*v.* 餵；養活　　hunting〔'hʌntɪŋ〕*n.* 打獵
engage in 從事　　form〔fɔrm〕*n.* 形式；型態
agriculture〔'ægrɪ,kʌltʃɚ〕*n.* 農業
agricultural〔,ægrɪ'kʌltʃərəl〕*adj.* 農業的
method〔'mɛθəd〕*n.* 方法

14. (**A**) The government issued a travel <u>alert</u> for Taiwanese in response to the outbreak of civil war in Syria.
政府因應敘利亞內戰的爆發，對台灣人民發佈了旅遊<u>警報</u>。

(A) *alert*〔ə'lɜt〕 *n.* 警報；留意
(B) monument〔'mɑnjəmənt〕 *n.* 紀念碑
(C) exit〔'ɛgzɪt〕 *n.* 出口
(D) circulation〔,sɜkjə'leʃən〕 *n.* 循環；流通
issue〔'ɪʃʊ〕 *v.* 發佈   *in response to* 回應
outbreak〔'aʊt,brek〕 *n.* 爆發   *civil war* 內戰
Syria〔'sɪrɪə〕 *n.* 敘利亞【位於地中海東岸】

15. (**C**) The baby panda Yuan Zai at the Taipei Zoo was seperated from
    her mother because of a minor injury that occurred during her
    birth. She was <u>tended</u> by zookeepers for a while.
    台北市立動物園的貓熊寶寶圓仔和牠的母親分開，因爲牠出生時
    有輕微的受傷，有一段時間是由動物園管理員負責照顧。
    (A) depart〔dɪ'pɑrt〕 *v.* 離開；出發   (B) jail〔dʒel〕 *v.* 監禁
    (C) *tend*〔tɛnd〕 *v.* 照顧   (D) capture〔'kæptʃɚ〕 *v.* 捕捉
    panda〔'pændə〕 *n.* 貓熊   separate〔'sɛpə,ret〕 *v.* 使分開 <*from*>
    minor〔'maɪnɚ〕 *adj.* 輕微的   birth〔bɜθ〕 *n.* 出生
    zookeeper〔'zu,kipɚ〕 *n.* 動物園管理員

二、綜合測驗：

<u>第 16 至 20 題爲題組</u>

Aesop, the Greek writer of fables, was sitting by the roadside one day
when a traveler asked him what sort of people lived in Athens. Aesop replied,
"Tell me where you come from and what sort of people live there, and I'll tell
you what sort of people you'll find in Athens." <u>Smiling</u>, the man answered,
                                                        16
"I come from Argos, and there the people are all friendly, generous, and
warm-hearted. I love them." <u>At</u> this, Aesop answered, "I'm happy to tell
                                 17
you, my dear friend, that you'll find the people of Athens much the same."

　　希臘的寓言作家伊索有一天坐在路邊時，一名旅行者問他，什麼樣的人會
住在雅典。伊索回答說：「告訴我你從哪裡來，以及什麼樣的人住在那裏，我便
會告訴你在雅典會發現什麼樣的人。」男士笑著回答說：「我來自阿哥斯，那裏
的人很友善、很慷慨、很熱心，我很喜歡他們。」一聽到他這樣說，伊索回答：
「親愛的朋友，我很高興告訴你，你會發現和雅典的人大致一樣。」

Aesop〔'isɑp〕*n.* 伊索【古希臘的寓言作家】
Greek〔grik〕*adj.* 希臘的　　fable〔'febl̩〕*n.* 寓言
roadside〔'rod͵saɪd〕*n.* 路邊
Athens〔'æθɪnz〕*n.* 雅典【希臘的首都】
reply〔rɪ'plaɪ〕*v.* 回答　　Argos〔'ɑrgos〕*n.* 阿哥斯【古希臘國】
warm-hearted〔'wɔrm'hɑrtɪd〕*adj.* 熱心的；慈愛的
generous〔'dʒɛnərəs〕*adj.* 慷慨的

16. (**B**) 依句意，應選 (B) *Smiling*，且現在分詞的結構表示主動的概念，描
　　　述男士帶著微笑回答。而 (A) amazing〔ə'mezɪŋ〕*adj.* 令人驚訝的，
　　　(C) decide〔dɪ'saɪd〕*v.* 決定，(D) pray〔pre〕*v.* 祈禱，則不合句意。

17. (**A**) 依句意，應選 (A) *At*「一聽到」。

A few hours later, <u>another</u> traveler came down the road. He too
　　　　　　　　　　　18
stopped and asked Aesop the same question. <u>Again</u>, Aesop made the
　　　　　　　　　　　　　　　　　　　　　19
same request. But frowning, the man answered, "I'm from Argos and there
the people are unfriendly, <u>mean</u>, and vicious. They're thieves and
　　　　　　　　　　　　　20
murderers, all of them." "Well, I'm afraid you'll find the people of Athens
much the same," replied Aesop.

　　　幾個小時過後，另一位旅行者沿路走來，他也停下來問伊索同樣的問題。
伊索提出同樣的要求，但男士皺著眉回答說：「我來自阿哥斯，那裏的人很不友
善、很卑劣、很邪惡，他們全都是小偷跟兇手，所有都是。」伊索回答說：「嗯，
恐怕你會發現雅典的人大致一樣。」

down〔daʊn〕*prep.* 沿著　　request〔rɪ'kwɛst〕*n.* 要求
frown〔fraʊn〕*v.* 皺眉　　unfriendly〔ʌn'frɛndlɪ〕*adj.* 不友善的
vicious〔'vɪʃəs〕*adj.* 邪惡的　　thief〔θif〕*n.* 小偷
murderer〔'mɝdərɚ〕*n.* 兇手　　***much the same*** 大致相同

18. (**D**) 依句意，選 (D) *another*「另一位」。而 (C) other「其他的」，通常接
　　　複數名詞，如 other people（其他的人），在此用法不合。

19. (**A**) 依句意，選 (A) *again*〔ə'gɛn〕*adv.* 再一次。而 (B) indeed
　　　〔ɪn'did〕*adv.* 的確，(C) together〔tə'gæðɚ〕*adv.* 一起，
　　　(D) moreover〔mor'ovɚ〕*adv.* 此外，皆不合句意。

20. (**C**) 依句意，選 (C) *mean* 〔 min 〕 *adj.* 卑劣的。而 (A) brave 〔 brev 〕 *adj.*
勇敢的，(B) lonely 〔'lonlı 〕 *adj.* 寂寞的，(D) skinny 〔'skını 〕 *adj.* 骨
瘦如柴的，皆不合句意。

第 21 至 25 題爲題組

　　Every year tens of thousands of tourists visit Mount Kilimanjaro, the
highest mountain in Tanzania, Africa, to witness the scenes depicted in
Earnest Hemingway's *The Snows of Kilimanjaro*. They are attracted by the
American writer's <u>description</u> of the millennia-old glaciers. However, this
　　　　　　　　　　　　21
tourist attraction will soon <u>vanish</u>. According to the Climate Change
　　　　　　　　　　　　　　　22
Group, formed by environmentalists worldwide to document the effects of
global warming, Mount Kilimanjaro's snows and glaciers are melting and
are <u>likely</u> to disappear by 2020.
　　23

　　每年有數以萬計的觀光客，造訪位在坦尙尼亞的非洲最高峰吉利馬扎羅
山，爲的是要一睹海明威在「雪山盟」中所描述的景象。他們是受到這位美國
作家對百萬年冰河描述的吸引。然而，這個觀光勝地將會很快消失。根據「氣
候變遷小組」，它是由世界各地的環保人士爲記錄全球暖化影響所組成的，吉利
馬扎羅山的雪和冰河正在融化，而且有可能在 2020 年以前消失。

　　tens of thousands of 數以萬計的　　　tourist 〔'turıst 〕 *n.* 觀光客
　　Mount Kilimanjaro 吉利馬扎羅山
　　Tanzania 〔ˌtænzə'niə 〕 *n.* 坦尙尼亞【位於東非赤道以南的國家】
　　Africa 〔'æfrıkə 〕 *n.* 非洲　　witness 〔'wıtnıs 〕 *v.* 目睹
　　scene 〔 sin 〕 *n.* 景象　　depict 〔 dı'pıkt 〕 *v.* 描述
　　Earnest Hemingway 厄尼斯特・海明威【美國著名作家】
　　The Snows of Kilimanjaro 雪山盟【美國著名作家海明威作品】
　　attract 〔 ə'trækt 〕 *v.* 吸引
　　millennia 〔 mə'lɛnıə 〕 *n. pl.* 千年【單數爲 millennium】
　　glacier 〔'gleʃɚ 〕 *n.* 冰河　　**tourist attraction** 觀光勝地
　　Climate Change Group 氣候變遷小組
　　form 〔 fɔrm 〕 *v.* 組成；成立
　　environmentalist 〔 ınˌvaırən'mɛntl̩ıst 〕 *n.* 環保人士
　　worldwide 〔'wɝld'waıd 〕 *adv.* 在全世界
　　document 〔'dɑkjəˌmɛnt 〕 *v.* 記錄；證明　　effect 〔 ı'fɛkt 〕 *n.* 影響
　　global warming 全球暖化　　melt 〔 mɛlt 〕 *v.* 融化
　　disappear 〔ˌdısə'pır 〕 *v.* 消失

21. (**B**) 依句意，選 (B) *description* 〔 dɪs'krpʃən 〕 *n.* 描述。而 (A) situation
〔ˌsɪtʃʊ'eʃən 〕 *n.* 情況，(C) translation 〔 træns'leʃən 〕 *n.* 翻譯，
(D) calculation 〔ˌkælkjə'leʃən 〕 *n.* 計算，則不合句意。

22. (**D**) 依句意，選 (D) *vanish* 〔'vænɪʃ 〕 *v.* 消失。而 (A) operate 〔'ɑpəˌret 〕 *v.*
操作，(B) expand 〔 ɪks'pænd 〕 *v.* 擴大，(C) recover 〔 rɪ'kʌvɚ 〕 *v.* 恢
復，則不合句意。

23. (**C**) 依句意，選 (C) *likely* 〔'laɪklɪ 〕 *adj.* 可能的。
而 (A) capable 〔'kepəbl̩ 〕 *adj.* 能夠的，(B) ready 〔'rɛdɪ 〕 *adj.* 準備好
的，(D) horrible 〔'harəbl̩ 〕 *adj.* 可怕的，則不合句意。

Not only will the summit lose its tourist attraction, but the disappearance of
the snows will also cause major damage to the ecosystem on the dry African
plains at its base. <u>Without</u> the snow covering the peak, there will not be
　　　　　　　　24
enough moisture and water to nourish the plants and animals below. Rising
temperatures, an effect of global warming, <u>thus</u> threaten the ecosystem of
　　　　　　　　　　　　　　　　　　　　25
this mountain area. The loss of snows on the 5,892m peak, which have been
there for about 11,700 years, could have disastrous effects on Tanzania.

積雪消失不只是山峰無法成為觀光勝地，對山下乾燥的非洲平原生態系統也造
成重大的危害。若沒有積雪覆蓋山頂，就沒有足夠的濕度和水滋養山下的動植
物。全球暖化所造成的氣溫上升，便因此威脅了山區的生態系統。位在五千八
百九十二公尺高山上，已有一萬一千七百年歷史的積雪的消失，可能會對坦桑
尼亞造成災難性的影響。

   not only…but (also)~　不只…而且~
   summit 〔'sʌmɪt 〕 *n.* 山峰 major 〔'medʒɚ 〕 *adj.* 重大的
   ecosystem 〔'ɪkoˌsɪstəm 〕 *n.* 生態系統 plain 〔 plen 〕 *n.* 平原
   base 〔 bes 〕 *n.* 基部；底部 peak 〔 pik 〕 *n.* 山峰
   moisture 〔'mɔɪstʃɚ 〕 *n.* 濕度；水氣 nourish 〔'nɝɪʃ 〕 *v.* 滋養
   rise 〔 raɪz 〕 *v.* 上升
   temperature 〔'tɛmpərətʃɚ 〕 *n.* 氣溫 threaten 〔'θrɛtn̩ 〕 *v.* 威脅
   disastrous 〔 dɪ'zæstrəs 〕 *adj.* 災難性的 effect 〔 ɪ'fɛkt 〕 *n.* 影響

24. (**D**) 依句意,「如果沒有」積雪覆蓋山頂,選 (D) *Without*。

25. (**A**) 依句意,選 (A) *thus*〔ðʌs〕*adv.* 因此。而 (B) just〔dʒʌst〕*adv.* 只是;
僅僅,(C) instead〔ɪn'stɛd〕*adv.* 反而,(D) otherwise〔'ʌðə,waɪz〕
adv. 否則,則不合句意。

第 26 至 30 題為題組

Most human beings actually decide before they think. When people
encounter a complex issue and form an opinion, how thoroughly have they
examined all the important factors involved before they make their decisions?
　　26

　　大部分的人都在思考之前做決定。當人們遭遇複雜的議題並且在腦中形成
意見,做出決定之前,他們對於相關重要因素的檢驗有多全面?

> ***human being*** 人類　　actually〔'æktʃuəlɪ〕*adv.* 實際上;真地
> encounter〔ɪn'kauntə〕*v.* 遭遇
> complex〔kəm'plɛks , 'kɑmplɛks〕*adj.* 複雜的
> issue〔'ɪʃju〕*n.* 議題;問題　　form〔fɔrm〕*v.* 形成
> opinion〔ə'pɪnjən〕*n.* 意見;看法
> thoroughly〔'θɜolɪ〕*adv.* 完全地;徹底地
> factor〔'fæktə〕*n.* 因素
> involved〔ɪn'valvd〕*adj.* 牽涉在內的;有關係的

26. (**B**) 依句意,選 (B) *examined*。　examine〔ɪg'zæmɪn〕*v.* 檢查;審查
而 (A) convey〔kən've〕*v.* 傳達,(C) solve〔salv〕*v.* 解決,
(D) imply〔ɪm'plaɪ〕*v.* 暗示,則不合句意。

The answer is: not very thoroughly, whether they are executives, specialized
　　　　　　　　　　　　　　　　　　27
experts, or ordinary people in the street. Very few people, no matter how
intelligent or experienced, can take into account all the possibilities or
　　　　　　　　　　　　　　　　　　28
outcomes of a policy or a course of action within just a short period of time.
答案是:不很全面,無論他們是主管、專家,或是街上的一般人。不管多聰明
或多有經驗,很少人可以在短時間之內,將一個政策或是行為過程中的所有可
能性與產生的結果都納入考量。

executive〔ɪgˈzɛkjʊtɪv〕*n.* 主管
specialized〔ˈspɛʃəlˌaɪzd〕*adj.* 專門的；專業的
expert〔ˈɛkspɝt〕*n.* 專家　　ordinary〔ˈɔrdnˌɛrɪ〕*adj.* 普通的；平常的
intelligent〔ɪnˈtɛlədʒənt〕*adj.* 聰明的
experienced〔ɪkˈspɪrɪənst〕*adj.* 有經驗的；經驗豐富的
possibilities〔ˌpɑsəˈbɪlətɪz〕*n. pl.* 可能性
outcome〔ˈaʊtˌkʌm〕*n.* 結果　　policy〔ˈpɑləsɪ〕*n.* 政策
course〔kors〕*n.* 做法；策略　　***course of action*** 行動策略
within〔wɪðˈɪn〕*prep.* 在…之內　　period〔ˈpɪrɪəd〕*n.* 期間

27. (**C**) 依句意，選 (C) ***whether***「無論」。　***whether A or B*** 無論 A 或 B
而 (A) whoever「無論是誰」，(B) because「因爲」，(D) rather「更確
切地說」，則不合句意。

28. (**D**) 依句意，選 (D) ***take into account***「把…考慮在內」(= *take into
consideration*)。而 (A) set out「出發」，(B) turn out「結果（成爲）」，
(C) put into practice「把…付諸實行」，則不合句意。

Those who take pride in being decisive often try their best to consider all the
factors beforehand. However, it is not unusual for them to come up with a
　　　　　　　　　　　　　29
decision before they have the time to do so. And once an opinion is formed,
　　　　　　　　　　　　　　　　　　　　　　30
most of their thinking then is simply trying to find support for it.
那些以果斷自豪的人們通常會盡力預先考量所有的因素。然而，在來不及做這
些工作之前就必須做出決定的情形，對他們而言也並不罕見。意見一旦被形塑，
之後所有的思考，其實都只是試圖支持自己的意見而已。

　　take pride in 以…爲榮（ = *be proud of* ）
　　decisive〔dɪˈsaɪsɪv〕*adj.* 有決斷力的；果斷的
　　try one's ***best*** 盡力　　consider〔kənˈsɪdɚ〕*v.* 考慮
　　beforehand〔bɪˈforˌhænd〕*adv.* 事先
　　unusual〔ʌnˈjuʒʊəl〕*adj.* 不尋常的
　　come up with 提出；想出　　thinking〔ˈθɪŋkɪŋ〕*n.* 思想；思考
　　support〔səˈport〕*n.* 支持

29. (**A**) 依句意，選 (A) ***However***「然而」。
　　(B) furthermore〔ˈfɝðɚˌmor〕*adv.* 此外

(C) conditionally〔kən'dıʃənlı〕*adv.* 有條件地

(D) similarly〔'sımələlı〕*adv.* 同樣地

30. (**C**) 依句意，意見「一旦」被形塑，選 (C) *once*。而 (A) though「雖然」，
(B) unless「除非」，(D) even「甚至；即使」，則不合句意。

三、文意選填：

第 31 至 40 題爲題組

　　In English-speaking cultures, the choice of first names for children
can be prompted by many factors: tradition, religion, nature, culture, and
fashion, to name just a few.

　　英語系國家之中，小孩子名字的選擇，受到諸多因素影響：傳統、宗教、
自然、文化、還有流行等等。

> culture〔'kʌltʃɚ〕*n.* 文化　　***first name*** 名字【last name　姓】
> prompt〔prɑmpt〕*v.* 促使；推動
> tradition〔trə'dıʃən〕*n.* 傳統　　religion〔rı'lıdʒən〕*n.* 宗教
> fashion〔'fæʃən〕*n.* 流行
> ***to name just a few*** 只舉出其中幾個例子；等等

　　Certain people like to give a name that has been handed down in the
family to show ³¹· **(I) respect** for or to remember a relative whom they love
or admire. Some families have a tradition of ³²· **(F) passing down** the father's
first name to the first born son. In other families, a surname is included in the
selection of a child's given name to ³³· **(E) keep** a family surname going. It
may be the mother's maiden name, for instance.

　　有些人喜歡幫小孩取家傳的名字，以緬懷自己所深愛或欣賞的親戚，並且
對他們獻上敬意。有些家庭有把父親名字傳承給長子的傳統。在某些其他的家
庭當中，姓氏也在小孩名字的選項之列，目的是讓家族的姓氏能夠繼續流傳下
去，例如母親的娘家姓，就是常見的選擇。

> certain〔'sɝtṇ〕*adj.* 某些　　***give a name*** 取名字
> ***hand down*** 傳下　　respect〔rı'spɛkt〕*n.* 尊敬
> remember〔rı'mɛmbɚ〕*v.* 記得；紀念
> relative〔'rɛlətıv〕*n.* 親戚　　admire〔əd'maır〕*v.* 讚賞；欽佩

pass down 將⋯傳給
surname〔'sɜ,nem〕*n.* 姓（= *last name* = *family name*）
include〔ɪn'klud〕*v.* 包括　　selection〔sə'lɛkʃən〕*n.* 選擇
given name 名字（= *first name*）　　keep〔kip〕*v.* 使保持
go〔go〕*v.* 流傳
maiden〔'medn̩〕*adj.* 處女的；未婚的
maiden name （女子未婚前之）娘家姓氏
for instance 例如（= *for example*）

For a long time, ^{34.} **(H) religion** has also played an important role in
naming children. Boys' names such as John, Peter, and Thomas are chosen
from the Bible. Girls' names such as Faith, Patience, and Sophie (wisdom)
are chosen because they symbolize Christian qualities. However, for
people who are not necessarily religious but are fond of nature, names
^{35.} **(D) involving** things of beauty are often favored. Flower and plant names
like Heather, Rosemary, and Iris ^{36.} **(B) fall into** this category.

　　長久以來，宗教也在小孩的命名中扮演很重要的角色。男生的名字像是
John、Peter 以及 Thomas 都出自聖經。女生的名字像是 Faith、Patience，以
及 Sophie（智慧），都是因爲象徵基督教標榜的特質而被選擇。然而，並不篤
信宗教但卻熱愛大自然的人，往往偏好那些與美好事物有關的名字。花朵和植
物的名稱，像是 Heather、Rosemary，或是 Iris 當屬此類。

　　play an important role 扮演一個重要的角色
　　name〔nem〕*v.* 給⋯命名　　*such as* 像是
　　Bible〔'baɪbl̩〕*n.* 聖經　　faith〔feθ〕*n.* 信念；信仰
　　patience〔'peʃəns〕*n.* 耐心　　Sophie〔'sofɪ〕*n.* 蘇菲【Sofia 的暱稱】
　　wisdom〔'wɪzdəm〕*n.* 智慧　　symbolize〔'sɪmbl̩,aɪz〕*v.* 象徵
　　Christian〔'krɪstʃən〕*adj.* 基督教的
　　quality〔'kwɑlətɪ〕*n.* 特質；特性
　　not necessarily 未必；不一定　　religious〔rɪ'lɪdʒəs〕*adj.* 虔誠的
　　be fond of 喜歡　　nature〔'netʃɚ〕*n.* 大自然
　　involve〔ɪn'vɑlv〕*v.* 和⋯有關　　beauty〔'bjutɪ〕*n.* 美
　　favor〔'fevɚ〕*v.* 偏愛　　heather〔'hɛðɚ〕*n.* 石楠屬植物
　　rosemary〔'roz,mɛrɪ〕*n.* 迷迭香　　iris〔'aɪrɪs〕*n.* 鳶尾科植物
　　fall into 屬於　　category〔'kætə,gorɪ〕*n.* 類別；範疇

Another factor that has had a great [37.] (C) impact on the choice of names is the spread of culture through the media. People may choose a name because they are strongly [38.] (A) drawn to a character in a book or a television series; they may also adopt names of famous people or their favorite actors and actresses. Sometimes, people pick foreign names for their children because those names are unusual and will thus make their children more [39.] (J) unique and distinctive.

　　另外一個在名字選擇上有強大影響力的因素，是媒體所散播的文化。人們可能會因為深受某本書，或是某個電視影集裡面的角色吸引而選擇名字；他們可能採用某個名人，或是自己最愛的男女演員的名字。有時候，人們會刻意為自己的小孩選擇異國的名字，因為那些名字很少見，所以可以讓他們的小孩更特別，也更有辨識度。

> impact〔'ɪmpækt〕n. 影響
> ***have a great impact on*** 對⋯有很大的影響
> spread〔sprɛd〕n. 散播；流傳　　media〔'midɪə〕n. pl. 媒體
> strongly〔'strɔŋlɪ〕adv. 強烈地　　draw〔drɔ〕v. 吸引
> character〔'kærɪktɚ〕n. 人物
> series〔'sɪrɪz , 'siriz〕n.（電視、電影等的）影集
> adopt〔ə'dɑpt〕v. 採用　　favorite〔'fevərɪt〕adj. 最喜愛的
> actor〔'æktɚ〕n. 演員　　actress〔'æktrɪs〕n. 女演員
> pick〔pɪk〕v. 挑選　　thus〔ðʌs〕adv. 因此
> unique〔ju'nik〕adv. 獨特的
> distinctive〔dɪ'stɪŋktɪv〕adj. 獨特的；有特色的

　　Finally, some people just pick a name the sound of which they like, [40.] (G) regardless of its meaning, its origins, or its popularity. However, even these people may look at the calendar to pick a lucky day when they make their choice.

　　最後，有些人選擇名字，只管聽起來順不順耳，完全不考慮名字的意義、起源，或是流行程度。然而，連這樣的人都可能會在日曆上挑出一個黃道吉日，再為小孩命名。

> ***regardless of*** 不管；不論　　origin〔'ɔrədʒɪn〕n. 起源
> popularity〔ˌpɑpjə'lærətɪ〕n. 受歡迎
> calendar〔'kæləndɚ〕n. 日曆　　***make one's choice*** 做選擇

四、閱讀測驗：

第 41 至 44 題為題組

American writer Toni Morrison was born in 1931 in Ohio. She was raised in an African American family filled with songs and stories of Southern myths, which later shaped her prose. Her happy family life led to her excellent performance in school, despite the atmosphere of racial discrimination in the society.

美國作家托妮‧莫里森在1931年出生於俄亥俄州。養育她的是個非裔美國家庭，充滿著關於南方神話的歌曲與故事，為她日後的文章塑型。她快樂的家庭生活使她在校表現優秀，即使社會上有種族歧視的氛圍。

Ohio〔oˈhaɪo〕*n.* (美國) 俄亥俄州　　raise〔rez〕*v.* 養育
African American 非裔美國人的
be filled with 充滿了　　myth〔mɪθ〕*n.* 神話
later〔ˈletɚ〕*adv.* 後來　　shape〔ʃep〕*v.* 塑造
prose〔proz〕*n.* 散文　　***lead to*** 導致
performance〔pɚˈfɔrməns〕*n.* 表現
despite〔dɪˈspaɪt〕*prep.* 儘管
atmosphere〔ˈætməsˌfɪr〕*n.* 氣氛　　racial〔ˈreʃəl〕*adj.* 種族的
discrimination〔dɪˌskrɪməˈneʃən〕*n.* 歧視

After graduating from college, Morrison started to work as a teacher and got married in 1958. Several years later, her marriage began to fail. For a temporary escape, she joined a small writers' group, in which each member was required to bring a story or poem for discussion. She wrote a story based on the life of a girl she knew in childhood who had prayed to God for blue eyes. The story was well received by the group, but then she put it away, thinking she was done with it.

從大學畢業後，莫里森開始任職教師，並在1958年結婚。幾年後，她的婚姻開始出問題。為了暫時逃避，她加入了一個小型的寫作團體，團體中每個成員都被要求帶一則故事或詩文來討論。她寫了一則故事，是關於她兒時認識的一個女孩的生活，那女孩向上帝祈求一雙藍色的眼睛。那則故事在寫作團體中相當受歡迎，但她接著就把故事放在一旁，覺得已經了結了。

graduate〔'grædʒʊˌet〕*v.* 畢業
temporary〔'tɛmpəˌrɛrɪ〕*adj.* 暫時的
escape〔ə'skep〕*n.* 逃避　　member〔'mɛmbɚ〕*n.* 成員
require〔rɪ'kwaɪr〕*v.* 要求　　***based on*** 以…爲基礎；根據
pray to sb. ***for*** sth. 向某人祈求某物
put sth. ***away*** 把某物放在一旁　　***be done with*** sth. 已了結某物

In 1964, Morrison got divorced and devoted herself to writing. One day, she dusted off the story she had written for the writers' group and decided to make it into a novel. She drew on her memories from childhood and expanded upon them using her imagination so that the characters developed a life of their own. *The Bluest Eye* was eventually published in 1970. From 1970 to 1992, Morrison published five more novels.

在1964年，莫里森離婚後投入寫作。有一天，她重拾了那則爲參加寫作團體而寫的故事，決定將它寫成小說。她憑藉著童年的記憶，並用想像力將它擴展，使得裡面的角色發展出自己的生命。終於在1970年，《最藍的眼睛》出版。從1970年到1992年，莫里森又出版了五本小說。

divorce〔də'vors〕*n.v.* 離婚　　***devote*** oneself ***to*** 致力於
dust off 拍掉灰塵；重拾　　***draw on*** 憑藉著
expand〔ɪk'spænd〕*v.* 擴大
imagination〔ɪˌmædʒə'neʃən〕*n.* 想像力
character〔'kærɪktɚ〕*n.* 角色；人物　　***of*** one's ***own*** 自己的
eventually〔ɪ'vɛntʃʊəlɪ〕*adv.* 最後　　publish〔'pʌblɪʃ〕*v.* 出版

In her novels, Morrison brings in different elements of the African American past, their struggles, problems and cultural memory. In *Song of Solomon*, for example, Morrison tells the story of an African American man and his search for identity in his culture. The novels and other works won her several prizes. In 1993, Morrison received the Nobel Prize in Literature. She is the eighth woman and the first African American woman to win the honor.

在她的小說裡，莫里森帶入了來自非裔美國人的不同元素，包括他們的過去、奮鬥、難題，以及文化記憶。例如在《所羅門之歌》一書中，莫里森述說

了一位非裔美國男性尋找在他文化中的認同的故事。這些小說和其他作品爲她贏得了一些獎項。1993年，莫里森獲得了諾貝爾文學獎。她是獲得該獎的第八位女性，而且是首位非裔美國女性。

> element〔ˈɛləmənt〕*n.* 要素　　struggle〔ˈstrʌgl̩〕*n.* 奮鬥
> cultural〔ˈkʌltʃərəl〕*adj.* 文化的　　search〔sɝtʃ〕*n.* 搜尋；追求
> identity〔aɪˈdɛntətɪ〕*n.* 認同；身分
> work〔wɝk〕*n.* 作品　　*win sb. sth.* 爲某人贏得某物
> *Nobel Prize in Literature* 諾貝爾文學獎　　honor〔ˈɑnɚ〕*n.* 光榮

41. (**B**) 本文的主旨爲何？
    (A) 美國黑人的生活。
    (B) <u>一位非裔美國作家的一生。</u>
    (C) 非裔美國文化的歷史。
    (D) 諾貝爾文學獎的歷史。

42. (**D**) 莫里森爲什麼要加入寫作團體？
    (A) 她想要出版《最藍的眼睛》。
    (B) 她想要對抗種族歧視。
    (C) 她想要成爲專業作家。
    (D) <u>她想要逃離她不快樂的婚姻。</u>

43. (**A**) 根據本文，哪一項是莫里森作品的主題之一？
    (A) <u>非裔美國人對於價值觀的追尋。</u>
    (B) 在美國社會中離婚的黑人女性。
    (C) 俄亥俄州非裔美國人的歌曲和故事。
    (D) 非裔美國人自 1970 年代至 1990 年代的歷史。

44. (**D**) 下列哪一項關於托妮‧莫里森的敘述是正確的？
    (A) 她從青少年時期就開始大量寫作。
    (B) 她在家庭中遭到嚴重的種族歧視。
    (C) 她在小說中寫的是非裔美國人的眞實故事。
    (D) <u>在她之前，沒有任何一位非裔美國女性得到諾貝爾文學獎。</u>

    > adolescent〔͵ædl̩ˈɛsnt〕*n.* 青少年
    > suffer〔ˈsʌfɚ〕*v.* 受苦；罹患 <*from*>
    > severe〔səˈvɪr〕*adj.* 嚴重的

第 45 至 48 題爲題組

Below is an excerpt from an interview with Zeke Emanuel, a health-policy expert, on his famous brothers.

以下摘錄自和衛生政策專家紀克・伊曼紐爾的專訪，主題是關於他著名的兄弟。

Interviewer: You're the older brother of Rahm, the mayor of Chicago, and Ari, an extremely successful talent agent. And you're a bioethicist and one of the architects of Obamacare. Isn't writing a book about how great your family is a bit odd?

訪問者：你是芝加哥市長拉姆和非常成功的星探阿里的哥哥。而你是一位生物倫理學者，也是歐巴馬健保的設計者之一。寫一本關於你家族有多偉大的書不是有點奇怪嗎？

Zeke: I don't write a book about how great my family is. There are lots of idiocies and foolishness—a lot to make fun of in the book. I wrote *Brothers Emanuel* because I had begun jotting stories for my kids. And then we began getting a lot of questions: What did Mom put in the cereal? Three successful brothers, all different areas.

紀克：我不是寫一本關於我家人有多偉大的書。書裡有很多白癡和愚蠢的事—有很多的嘲弄。我寫《伊曼紐爾兄弟》是因爲我已經開始爲我的孩子們記下故事。而我們開始有很多問題：媽媽在早餐裡放了什麼？造就了三個成功的兄弟，而且全都是不同的領域。

I: To what do you attribute the Emanuel brothers' success?
訪問者：你把伊曼紐爾兄弟的成功歸因於什麼？

Z: I would put success in quotes. We strive. First, I think we got this striving from our mother to make the world a better place. A second important thing is you never rest on the last victory. There's always more to do. And maybe the third important thing is my father's admonition that offense is the best defense. We don't give up.

紀克：我會把「成功」加上引號。我們非常努力。首先，我認爲這個努力
來自於我們的母親，她讓這個世界變成一個更好的地方。第二件重
要的事，就是你絕不能滿足於上一次的勝利。總是有更多的事要做。
還有可能是第三重要的事，那就是我父親的訓誡，他說攻擊就是最
好的防禦。我們都不會放棄。

I: Do you still not have a TV?

訪問者：你還是沒有電視嗎？

Z: I don't own a TV. I don't own a car. I don't Facebook. I don't
tweet.

紀克：我沒有電視。我沒有車。我不上臉書。我不用推特。

I: But you have four cell phones.

訪問者：可是你有四隻手機。

Z: I'm down to two, thankfully.

紀克：謝天謝地，我剩下兩隻。

I: Your brothers are a national source of fascination. Where do you
think they'll be in five years?

訪問者：你的兄弟是全國矚目的焦點。你認爲五年後他們會在哪裡？

Z: Ari will be a superagent running the same company. Rahm
would still be mayor of Chicago. I will probably continue to be
my academic self. The one thing I can guarantee is none of us
will have taken a cruise, none of us will be sitting on a beach with
a pina colada.

紀克：阿里將會是經營同一間公司的超級星探。拉姆還會是芝加哥市長。
我可能繼續當學者。我能保證的一件事，就是我們都不會去坐遊輪，
我們都不會坐在海灘喝鳳梨可樂達雞尾酒。

---

below〔bə'lo〕*adv.* 以下　　excerpt〔'ɛksɝpt〕*n.* 摘錄
interview〔'ɪntɚˏvju〕*n.* 訪談
Zeke Emanuel 紀克·伊曼紐爾【美國科學家】
health〔hɛlθ〕*n.* 健康；衛生　　policy〔'pɑləsɪ〕*n.* 政策
expert〔'ɛkspɝt〕*n.* 專家　　famous〔'feməs〕*adj.* 有名的
Rahm Emanuel 拉姆·伊曼紐爾【美國芝加哥市長】

mayor〔'meɚ〕*n.* 市長　　Chicago〔ʃɪ'kago〕*n.* 芝加哥【美國第二大城】
Ari Emanuel 阿里・伊曼紐爾【美國著名星探】
extremely〔ɪk'strimlɪ〕*adv.* 非常地
talent〔'tælənt〕*n.* 演藝圈人才　　agent〔'edʒənt〕*n.* 經紀人
talent agent 星探　　bioethicist〔ˌbaɪo'ɛθəsɪst〕*n.* 生物倫理學家
architect〔'ɑrkəˌtɛkt〕*n.* 設計者；建築師
Obamacare 歐巴馬健保【美國總統歐巴馬所簽署的醫療法案，故得其名】
a bit 有些　　odd〔ɑd〕*adj.* 奇怪的
idiocy〔'ɪdɪəsɪ〕*n.* 白癡（的言行）
foolishness〔'fulɪʃnɪs〕*n.* 愚蠢（的言行）
make fun of 嘲笑　　jot〔dʒɑt〕*v.* 記下
cereal〔'sɪrɪəl〕*n.* 穀類食品【尤指早餐時吃的，如玉米片等】
area〔'ɛrɪə〕*n.* 領域　　attribute〔ə'trɪbjut〕*v.* 將…歸因於
quote〔kwot〕*n.* 引號；引文　　***put sth. in quotes*** 把某物加上引號
strive〔straɪv〕*v.* 努力　　***rest on*** 停留在
admonition〔ˌædmə'nɪʃən〕*n.* 訓誡
offense〔ə'fɛns〕*n.* 攻擊　　defense〔dɪ'fɛns〕*n.* 防禦
give up 放棄　　thankfully〔'θæŋkfəlɪ〕*adv.* 感謝地
national〔'næʃənḷ〕*adj.* 全國的　　source〔sors〕*n.* 來源
fascination〔ˌfæsn'eʃən〕*n.* 魅力；令人著迷的事物
run〔rʌn〕*v.* 經營　　academic〔ˌækə'dɛmɪk〕*n.* 學者
guarantee〔ˌgærən'ti〕*v.* 保證　　cruise〔kruz〕*n.* 乘船旅行；遊輪
pina colada 鳳梨可樂達雞尾酒

45. (**A**) 當紀克・伊曼紐爾說「媽媽在早餐裡放了什麼？」時，他腦海中在想什麼？
    (A) 養育出成功的小孩的秘訣。　　(B) 做早餐的食譜。
    (C) 三兄弟的不同之處。　　(D) 他小孩的問題。
    secret〔'sikrɪt〕*n.* 秘訣　　***bring up*** 養育
    recipe〔'rɛsəpɪ〕*n.* 食譜

46. (**C**) 在這個訪談中提到的現代便利的設備，紀克・伊曼紐爾有什麼想法？
    (A) 遲做總比不做好。　　(B) 熟能生巧。
    (C) 沒有這些東西也沒關係。　　(D) 它們是偉大的發明。
    conveniences〔kən'vinjənsɪz〕*n. pl.* 便利的設備
    mention〔'mɛnʃən〕*v.* 提到
    Better late than never.【諺】遲做總比不做好。
    Practice makes perfect.【諺】熟能生巧。
    invention〔ɪn'vɛnʃən〕*n.* 發明

47. (**D**) 根據紀克‧伊曼紐爾，以下何者是三兄弟成功的原因？
　　(A) 他們藉由攻擊別人來防衛自己。
　　(B) 他們從偉人的引用文句中學到很多。
　　(C) 他們致力於榮耀父母。
　　(D) 即使在非常成功之後，他們也會持續前進。
　　be committed to V-ing 致力於…　　glorify〔'glorə,faɪ〕*v.* 使榮耀

48. (**B**) 以下何者最能總結紀克‧伊曼紐爾對最後一個問題的回應？
　　(A) 三兄弟期待全家人可以搭遊輪旅行。
　　(B) 在不久的將來，他們不會有什麼改變。
　　(C) 更高的地位和更多的權力將是他們的目標。
　　(D) 三兄弟都不會去海灘。
　　summarize〔'sʌmə,raɪz〕*v.* 總結　　response〔rɪ'spɑns〕*n.* 回應
　　look forward to 期待　　　*in the near future* 在不久的將來
　　position〔pə'zɪʃən〕*n.* 地位　　power〔'pauɚ〕*n.* 權力
　　goal〔gol〕*n.* 目標

第 49 至 52 題為題組

　　MOOC, a massive open online course, aims at providing large-scale interactive participation and open access via the web. In addition to traditional course materials such as videos, readings, and problem sets, MOOCs provide interactive user forums that help build a community for the students, professors, and teaching assistants.

　　MOOC是一個大型的開放式線上課程，目標是提供大規模的互動參與，和網路上的開放途徑。除了傳統的課程資料，像是影片、文章，和問題集，MOOC也提供使用者互動論壇來幫助建立一個社群，供學生、教授和教學助理使用。

　　massive〔'mæsɪv〕*adj.* 大型的　　open〔'opən〕*adj.* 公開的
　　online〔,ɑn'laɪn〕*adj.* 線上的　　course〔kors〕*n.* 課程
　　aim at 目標是　　provide〔prə'vaɪd〕*v.* 提供
　　scale〔skel〕*n.* 規模　　interactive〔,ɪntɚ'æktɪv〕*adj.* 互動的
　　participation〔pɚ,tɪsə'peʃən〕*n.* 參與
　　access〔'æksɛs〕*n.* 接觸；途徑
　　via〔'vaɪə〕*prep.* 經由；透過　　web〔wɛb〕*n.* 網路
　　in addition to 除了…之外（還有）

traditional〔trə'dɪʃənḷ〕*adj.* 傳統的
material〔mə'tɪrɪəl〕*n.* 材料；資料　　***problem set*** 問題集；問題組
forum〔'fɔrəm〕*n.* 論壇　　community〔kə'mjunətɪ〕*n.* 社區；社群
professor〔prə'fɛsɚ〕*n.* 教授　　***teaching assistant*** 教學助理

MOOCs first made waves in the fall of 2011, when Professor Sebastian Thrun from Stanford University opened his graduate-level artificial intelligence course up to any student anywhere, and 160,000 students in more than 190 countries signed up. This new breed of online classes is shaking up the higher education world in many ways. Since the courses can be taken by hundreds of thousands of students at the same time, the number of universities might decrease dramatically. Professor Thrun has even envisioned a future in which there will only need to be 10 universities in the world. Perhaps the most striking thing about MOOCs, many of which are being taught by professors at prestigious universities, is that they're free. This is certainly good news for **cash-strapped** students.

MOOC第一次在2011年的秋天造成轟動，當時史丹佛大學教授，塞巴斯蒂安‧特隆，開放他的研究所程度的人工智慧課程，給任何地方的學生，所以有超過190個國家的十六萬名學生報名。這種新的線上課程在很多方面都撼動了高等教育界。因爲有好幾十萬的學生可以同時上課，大學的數量可能會大大地減少。特隆教授甚至預視未來全世界只需要十所大學。因爲MOOCs很多課程是由知名大學的教授所傳授，或許最引人注意的地方是，它們都免費的。這對經濟困難的學生來說，的確是個好消息。

make waves 引起轟動　　***Stanford University*** 史丹佛大學
graduate〔'grædʒuɪt〕*adj.* 研究所的；研究生的
open up to 開放給⋯　　artificial〔ˌɑrtə'fɪʃəl〕*adj.* 人工的
intelligence〔ɪn'tɛlədʒəns〕*n.* 智力；智能　　***sign up*** 報名；註册
breed〔brid〕*n.* 種類　　***shake up*** 撼動
higher education 高等教育　　world〔wɝld〕*n.* ⋯界
hundreds of thousands of 數十萬的　　decrease〔dɪ'kris〕*v.* 減少
dramatically〔drə'mætɪkḷɪ〕*adv.* 大大地
envision〔ɛn'vɪʒən〕*v.* 想像；預見
striking〔'straɪkɪŋ〕*adj.* 醒目的；引人注意的
prestigious〔prɛs'tɪdʒəs〕*adj.* 有名望的
free〔fri〕*adj.* 免費的　　strap〔stræp〕*v.* 用皮帶捆
cash-strapped　*adj.* 缺乏現金的；經濟困難的

　　There is a lot of excitement and fear surrounding MOOCs. While some say free online courses are a great way to increase the enrollment of minority students, others have said they will leave many students behind. Some critics have said that MOOCs promote an unrealistic one-size-fits-all model of higher education and that there is no replacement for true dialogues between professors and their students. After all, a brain is not a computer. We are not blank hard drives waiting to be filled with data. People learn from people they love and remember the things that arouse emotion. Some critics worry that online students will miss out on the social aspects of college.

　　關於MOOCs有很多興奮和恐懼。雖然有些人說，免費的線上課程是很好的方法，可增加少數族群學生的註冊人數，有些人說這些課程會使許多學生落後。一些批評者說，MOOCs 提倡了一個不切實際的高等教育通用模式，而且教授和學生之間真實的對話是無法取代的。畢竟，人腦不是電腦，我們不是空白的硬碟等著裝載資料。人從他們愛的人身上學習，並記得觸動感情的事物。有些批評者擔心，參與線上課程的學生，會錯過大學能提供的社交機會。

excitement〔ɪkˋsaɪtmənt〕*n.* 興奮　　fear〔fɪr〕*n.* 恐懼
surround〔səˋraʊnd〕*v.* 與…相關　　increase〔ɪnˋkris〕*v.* 增加
enrollment〔ɪnˋrolmənt〕*n.* 註冊人數
minority〔maɪˋnɔrətɪ〕*adj.* 少數的；少數名族的
leave…behind 使…落後　　critic〔ˋkrɪtɪk〕*n.* 批評者
promote〔prəˋmot〕*v.* 促進；提倡
unrealistic〔͵ʌnriəˋlɪstɪk〕*adj.* 不切實際的
one-size-fits-all *adj.* 通用的　　model〔ˋmɑdḷ〕*n.* 模型
replacement〔rɪˋplesmənt〕*n.* 取代
dialogue〔ˋdaɪə͵lɔg〕*n.* 對話
after all 畢竟　　blank〔blæŋk〕*adj.* 空白的
hard drive 硬碟　　***be filled with*** 充滿了　　data〔ˋdetə〕*n. pl.* 資料
arouse〔əˋraʊz〕*v.* 喚起　　emotion〔ɪˋmoʃən〕*n.* 感情；情緒
miss out on 錯過　　social〔ˋsoʃəl〕*adj.* 社會的；社交的
aspect〔ˋæspɛkt〕*n.* 方面；（事物的某一）面

49. (**B**) 第二段的 "**cash-strapped**" 是什麼意思？
　　(A) 賺很多錢。　　　　　　　　(B) 缺錢。
　　(C) 小心用錢。　　　　　　　　(D) 花很少的錢。
　　be short of 缺乏　　***be careful with*** 對…很小心；小心使用

50. (**C**) 以下何者不是 MOOCs 的特色之一？
    (A) 上課是免費的。   (B) 很多課程是知名大學所提供。
    (C) 大多數的課程是講人工智慧。   (D) 很多學生可以同時上課。
    feature〔'fitʃɚ〕 *n.* 特色
    address〔ə'drɛs〕 *v.* 演說；演講；處理 (= *deal with*)

51. (**A**) 第二段主要是關於什麼？
    (A) MOOCs 的影響。   (B) MOOCs 的目標。
    (C) MOOCs 班級的大小。   (D) MOOCs 課程的費用。
    impact〔'ımpækt〕 *n.* 影響

52. (**D**) 下列何者是本文所提到關於 MOOCs 的問題？
    (A) 傳統課程資料的消失。   (B) 全世界提供的課程數量有限。
    (C) 過度依賴知名大學的教授。
    (D) 缺乏學生和教授之間的社交互動。
    disappearance〔͵dısə'pırəns〕 *n.* 消失
    limited〔'lımıtıd〕 *adj.* 有限的   offer〔'ɔfɚ〕 *v.* 提供
    overreliance〔͵ovɚrı'laıəns〕 *n.* 過度依賴 < *on* >   lack〔læk〕 *n.* 缺乏

第 53 至 56 題為題組

　　Today the car seems to make periodic leaps in progress. A variety of driver assistance technologies are appearing on new cars. A developing technology called Vehicle-to-Vehicle communication, or V2V, is being tested by automotive manufacturers as a way to help reduce the number of accidents. V2V works by using wireless signals to send information back and forth between cars about their location, speed and direction, so that they keep safe distances from each other.

　　現今汽車似乎是不斷地在大幅進步。新款的車輛配備中,已經出現各式各樣的駕駛輔助科技。汽車製造商已經在測試,一項名為「車對車通訊」的研發中科技,希望藉此能夠降低汽車事故的數字。「車對車通訊」是藉由使用無線信號,在車輛間來回傳送地點、速度,和方向的訊息,如此車與車之間就能夠保持安全距離。

    periodic〔͵pırı'adık〕 *adj.* 週期性的;定期的
    leap〔lip〕 *n.* 跳躍;遽增   progress〔'pragrɛs〕 *n.* 進步
    variety〔və'raıətı〕 *n.* 多樣性   ***a variety of*** 各式各樣的
    vihicle〔'viıkl̩〕 *n.* 車輛   communication〔kə͵mjunə'keʃən〕 *n.* 通訊

automotive〔͵ɔtə'motɪv〕*adj.* 汽車的；自動的
manufacturer〔͵mænjə'fæktʃərə〕*n.* 製造商
number〔'nʌmbə〕*n.* 數目

Another new technology being tested is Vehicle-to-Infrastructure communication, or V2I. V2I would allow vehicles to communicate with road signs or traffic signals and provide information to the vehicle about safety issues. V2I could also request traffic information from a traffic management system and access the best possible routes. Both V2V and V2I have the potential to reduce around 80 percent of vehicle crashes on the road.

另外一項測試中的科技則稱為「車對基本設施通訊」，可以讓車輛與道路標誌和交通號誌連線，並且提供車輛安全問題的資訊。車對基本設施通訊系統也會讀取交通管裡系統的交通資訊，並取得最佳路線。車對車通訊和車對基本設施通訊都將可能減少百分之八十的道路交通事故。

wireless〔'waɪrlɪs〕*adj.* 無線的　　signal〔'sɪgnḷ〕*n.* 信號
back and forth 來回地
infrastructure〔'ɪnfrə͵strʌktʃə〕*n.* 基本設施　　sign〔saɪn〕*n.* 告示
issue〔'ɪʃu〕*n.* 問題　　management〔'mænɪdʒmənt〕*n.* 管理
access〔'æksɛs〕*v.* 取得　　route〔rut〕*n.* 路線
potential〔pə'tɛnʃəl〕*n.* 潛力；可能性　　crash〔kræʃ〕*n.* 相撞

More and more new cars can reverse-park, read traffic signs, maintain a safe distance in steady traffic and brake automatically to avoid crashes. Moreover, a number of firms are creating cars that drive themselves to a chosen destination without a human at the controls. It is predicted that driverless cars will be ready for sale within five years. If and when cars go completely driverless, the benefits will be enormous.

越來越多新的車子可以倒轉停車，讀取交通號誌，在穩定的車流中保持安全距離，並且可以自動煞車以避免相撞。此外，有一些公司正在製造無人駕駛，可以自動開往預定地點的車。一般預測，無人駕駛的車會在五年內量產上市。如果車子可以完全無人駕駛，那會有很多的好處。

reverse〔rɪ'vɚs〕*adj.* 倒轉的　　reverse-park *v.* 倒車停車
steady〔'stɛdɪ〕*adj.* 穩定的　　brake〔brek〕*v.* 煞車
automatically〔͵ɔtə'mætɪkḷɪ〕*adv.* 自動地
firm〔fɝm〕*n.* 公司　　chosen〔'tʃozn̩〕*adj.* 被選上的
destination〔͵dɛstə'neʃən〕*n.* 目的地

controls〔kən'trolz〕*n. pl.*（車輛的）操縱裝置
predict〔prɪ'dɪkt〕*v.* 預測　　go〔go〕*v.* 變得
benefit〔'bɛnəfɪt〕*n.* 利益；好處
enormous〔ɪ'nɔrməs〕*adj.* 巨大的

Google, which already uses prototypes of such cars to ferry its staff along Californian freeways, once put a blind man in a prototype and filmed him being driven off to buy takeaway hamburgers. If this works, huge numbers of elderly and disabled people can regain their personal mobility. The young will not have to pay crippling motor insurance, because their reckless hands and feet will no longer touch the wheel or the accelerator. People who commute by car will gain hours each day to work, rest, or read a newspaper.

谷歌公司已經使用無人駕駛車，載運自己的員工行駛加州高速公路，他們曾經讓一位盲人坐在原形車的駕駛座，拍攝車子載他離開去買外帶漢堡的影片。如果這項計畫可以成功，許多的年長者和殘障人士就可以重獲移動能力。年輕人也不用再買造成嚴重損害的汽車事故險，因為他們魯莽的手腳將不會再碰到方向盤或油門。坐車的通勤族以後每天可以多幾個小時工作、休息，或看報紙。

prototype〔'protə,taɪp〕*n.* 原型　　ferry〔'fɛrɪ〕*v.* 載運
staff〔stæf〕*n.* 全體員工　　freeway〔'fri,we〕*n.* 高速公路
film〔fɪlm〕*v.* 拍攝　　***drive off*** 開車離去
takeaway〔'tekə,we〕*adj.* 外帶的　　work〔wɜk〕*v.* 有效；行得通
elderly〔'ɛldəlɪ〕*adj.* 年長的　　disabled〔dɪs'eblḍ〕*adj.* 殘障的
regain〔rɪ'gen〕*v.* 恢復　　mobility〔mo'bɪlətɪ〕*n.* 機動性
crippling〔'krɪplḷŋ〕*adj.* 造成嚴重損害的
motor insurance 汽車險　　reckless〔'rɛklɪs〕*adj.* 魯莽的
wheel〔hwil〕*n.* 方向盤　　accelerator〔æk'sɛlə,retə〕*n.* 油門
commute〔kə'mjut〕*v.* 通勤　　gain〔gen〕*v.* 獲得

53.（**C**）以下對於 V2V 的敘述何者正確？
　　(A) V2V 通訊已經發展得很完備。
　　(B) 透過 V2V，駕駛人可以在路上互相聊天。
　　(C) <u>V2V 的設計是要藉由保持安全距離減少車禍。</u>
　　(D) 透過 V2V，車子可以警告在附近的腳踏車騎士車子正在靠近。
　　warn *sb.* ***of*** *sth.* 警告某人某事
　　cyclist〔'saɪklɪst〕*n.* 腳踏車騎士
　　nearby〔'nɪr,baɪ〕*adj.* 附近的　　approach〔ə'protʃ〕*n.* 接近

54. (**A**) 在 Vehicle-to-Infrastructure 中的 infrastructure 指的是什麼？
　　(A) 交通設施和資訊系統。　　　(B) 道路和橋樑的基礎結構。
　　(C) 安全駕駛的知識和規定。　　(D) 政府的交通部門。
　　facilities〔fə'sɪlətɪz〕*n. pl.* 設施　　structure〔'strʌktʃɚ〕*n.* 結構
　　regulation〔ˌrɛgjə'leʃən〕*n.* 規定
　　department〔dɪ'partmənt〕*n.* 部門

55. (**C**) 下列何者不是無人駕駛車輛可能的好處？
　　(A) 年長者會更有機動性。
　　(B)「駕駛人」可以在去上班途中一路睡覺。
　　(C) 人們可以盡情賽車。　　　(D) 盲人可以開車並且一路平安。
　　the elderly 老人（= *elderly people*）　　mobile〔'mobl̩〕*adj.* 機動的
　　content〔kən'tɛnt〕*n.* 滿足　　***race cars*** 賽車
　　to one's heart's content 盡情地　　travel〔'trævl̩〕*v.* 行進

56. (**B**) 從這篇文章可以推論出什麼？
　　(A) 駕駛人如果酒醉汽車會拒絕發動。
　　(B) 未來可能是沒有車禍的時代。
　　(C) 男女老幼都買得起車。　　(D) 無人駕駛車輛的生產還遙不可及。
　　start〔start〕*v.* 發動　　　drunk〔drʌŋk〕*adj.* 喝醉的
　　free〔fri〕*adj.* 無…的　　　era〔'ɪrə〕*n.* 時代
　　afford〔ə'ford〕*v.* 負擔得起

第貳部分：非選擇題

一、中譯英

1. 有些年輕人辭掉都市裡高薪的工作，返回家鄉種植有機蔬菜。

Some young people $\left\{ \begin{array}{l} \text{quit} \\ \text{resigned from} \end{array} \right\}$ their high-paying/well-paid jobs

in the city, and went back to their hometown to grow organic vegetables.

2. 藉由決心和努力，很多人成功了，不但獲利更多，還過著更健康的生活。

$\left\{ \begin{array}{l} \text{With} \\ \text{By means of} \end{array} \right\}$ determination and effort, many succeeded, not only

$\left\{ \begin{array}{l} \text{making more profit,} \\ \text{earning/making more money,} \end{array} \right\}$ but also $\left\{ \begin{array}{l} \text{leading} \\ \text{living} \end{array} \right\}$ a healthier life.

二、英文作文：

Steve's Lucky Day

Irene and Steve were walking home from school. They each had their own iPhone. Irene liked to text and chat with her friends, while Steve enjoyed listening to music. This afternoon, they took a shortcut through the park. It wasn't their usual route. As they entered the park, Irene was texting with her friends and not paying attention to the path, which took a sharp turn to the left. Blissfully unaware of her surroundings, Irene bumped her head on a tree, and dropped her iPhone. Lost in his music, Steve continued walking without notice.

Several minutes later, Steve had to cross a busy street. Still listening to music at a dangerously loud level, he didn't look before stepping out into the roadway. An oncoming driver honked his horn and slammed on his brakes, otherwise he would have hit Steve with his car. *However*, unaware of the danger, Steve continued on his merry way. *Of course*, the driver was furious, and began shouting and cursing, but it was to no avail. It must have been Steve's lucky day.

text〔tɛkst〕*v.* 傳簡訊　　chat〔tʃæt〕*v.* 聊天
shortcut〔'ʃɔrt͵kʌt〕*n.* 捷徑；近路　　route〔rut〕*n.* 路線
pay attention to 注意　　path〔pæθ〕*n.* 小道；小徑
sharp〔ʃɑrp〕*adj.* 急轉的　　***to the left*** 向左
blissfully〔'blɪsfəlɪ〕*adv.* 幸福地；極快樂地
unaware〔͵ʌnə'wɛr〕*adj.* 不注意的；未察覺的 < *of* >
surroundings〔sə'raʊndɪŋz〕*n. pl.* 周遭環境
bump〔bʌmp〕*v.* 使撞上 < *on / against* >
drop〔drɑp〕*v.* 掉落　　***be lost in*** 沈迷於　　level〔'lɛvl̩〕*n.* 程度
at a~level 以~程度　　step〔stɛp〕*v.* 步行；踏出一步
roadway〔'rod͵we〕*n.* 道路
oncoming〔'ɑn͵kʌmɪŋ〕*adj.* 即將到來的；接近的
honk** one's **horn 按喇叭 (= *sound one's horn*)
slam on** one's **brakes 緊急煞車 (= *hit the brakes*)
merry〔'mɛrɪ〕*adj.* 快樂的　　***on** one's **way*** 在路上
furious〔'fjʊrɪəs〕*adj.* 憤怒的　　curse〔kɝs〕*v.* 咒罵
to no avail 無效；枉然 (= *in vain*)　　***must have** + **p.p.*** 當時一定…

103 年學測英文科試題出題來源

題　　號	出　　　　　　　　　處
一、詞彙 第 1～15 題	所有各題對錯答案的選項，均出自大考中心編製的「高中常用 7000 字」。
二、綜合測驗 第 16～20 題	改寫自 Aesop's Fables（伊索寓言），敘述伊索和將去希臘旅遊的人的對話，表達他對希臘的觀點和評價。
第 21～25 題	改寫自 Global Warming Thaws Mount Kilimanjaro（全球暖化解凍吉力馬札羅山），全球暖化如何讓吉力馬札羅山失去長年以來的雪。
第 26～30 題	改寫自 Better Decision Making: From Who's Right to What's Right; A Computer-Aided Structured-Inquiry Method Offers a Better Way to Make Tough Decisions（做更好的決定：從誰是對的到什麼是對的；一個電腦輔助結構式探究方法提供更好的方式做困難的決定），敘述人們做決定的過程。
四、閱讀測驗 第 41～44 題	改寫自 Toni Morrison: biography（托妮‧莫里森：傳記），描述非裔美國女作家妮‧莫里森成為知名作家的經歷。
第 45～48 題	改寫自 10 Questions for Zeke Emanuel（十問齊克‧伊曼紐爾），為一訪談，描述齊克兄弟的成功和其家庭的關係。
第 49～52 題	改寫自 Massive open online course（大型開放型線上課程），描述線上免費課程的出現和其衍生的影響。
第 53～56 題	改寫自 Clean, safe and it drives itself（乾淨又安全，自己會開車），描述新款的車，能夠接受無限訊號，自動開到目的地。

103 年學測英文科試題修正意見

※ 103 年學測英文試題出得很嚴謹，只有三個地方建議修正：

題　　號	修　　正　　意　　見
第 45～48 題 第 4 行	I *don't* write a book about how great my family is. → I *didn't* write a book about how great my family is. * 敘述過去的事，應用過去式，句尾的 is 不改，因為是現在的事。
倒數第 3 行	Rahm *would* still be mayor of Chicago. → Rahm *will* still be mayor of Chicago. * Ari *will be* a superagent… Rahm *will* still *be*… I *will* probably *continue*… 說話、寫文章都應有一致性。
第 53 題 (C)	V2V is designed to decrease crashes by keeping *safety distance*. → …*a safety distance between cars*. * 為了句意清楚，須將 safety distance 改成 *a* safety distance *between cars*。

【103 年學測】綜合測驗：16-20 出題來源

—— http://www.hltmag.co.uk/sep02/ex.htm

The railway ticket
Aesop's fable

1. There were eight of us in the carriage, and seven tickets were soon found and punched.

2. A few hours later a mean-looking travell- er came down the road, and he too stopped and asked Aesop, 'Tell me, my friend, what are the people of Athens like?'

3. Aesop, the Greek writer of fables, was sitting by the road one day when a friend- ly traveller asked him, 'What sort of people live in Athens?'

4. 'All tickets, please!' said the railway inspector, appearing at the door of the carriage.

5. Frowning, the man replied, 'I'm from Argos and there the people are unfriend- ly, mean, deceitful and vicious. They're thieves and murderers, all of them.'

6. 'Funny thing, absence of mind,' said the helpful traveller when the inspector had gone. 'Absence of mind?' said the old man.

7. But the old man in the corner went on searching through his pockets, looking very unhappy.

8. Aesop replied, 'Tell me where you come from and what sort of people live there, and I'll tell you what sort of people you'll find in Athens.'

9. So he was, and the inspector looked anything but pleased as he hastily punched the mangled ticket.

10. Smiling, the man answered, 'I come from Argos, and the people there are all friendly, generous and warm- hearted. I love them all.'

11. Again Aesop replied, 'Tell me where you come from and what people are like there and I will tell you what the people are like in Athens.'

12. 'I was chewing off last week's date!'

13. 'You haven't lost your ticket,' said the man next to him, helpfully.
    You're holding it in your teeth!'

14. At this Aesop answered, 'I'm happy to tell you, my dear friend, that
    you'll find the people of Athens much the same.'

15. 'I'm afraid you'll find the people of Athens much the same,' was
    Aesop's reply.

【103 年學測】綜合測驗：21-25 出題來源

——http://www.redorbit.com/news/science/135907/global_warming_thaws_
mount_kilimanjaro/

Global Warming Thaws Mount Kilimanjaro

LONDON (AFP)— Mount Kilimanjaro, the highest mountain in Africa,
has been photographed stripped of its millennia-old snow and glacier peak
for the first time, in a move used by environmentalists to show the perils of
global warming.

The picture is the first time anyone has caught the Tanzanian
mountain's dramatic change, according to the Climate Change group
which led a project to document the effects of global warming across the
world.

The launch of the photo project NorthSouthEastWest coincides with a
meeting of environment and energy ministers from 20 countries at a
British-sponsored conference on climate change that opened on Tuesday in
London.

It also comes ahead of a further meeting of G8 ministers in Derbyshire,
central England, later in the week.

Mount Kilimanjaro's crowning snow and glaciers are melting and
likely to disappear completely by 2020, triggering major disruptions to
ecosystems on the dry African plains that spread out at its feet below,
scientists have warned.

The forests on Kilimanjaro's lower slopers absorb moisture from the cloud top hovering near the peak, and in turn nourish flora and fauna below.

"Rising temperatures threaten not only the ice-cap, but also this essential natural process," Climate Change warned.

The mountain, one of Africa's most stunning landscapes, was memorialized in Ernest Hemingway's 1938 short story "The Snows of Kilimanjaro". The story, and the 1952 film which followed, has brought tens of thousands of visitors to Tanzania for decades.

The loss of snows on the 19,330-foot (5,892-meter) peak, which have been there for about 11,700 years, could have disastrous effects on the Tanzanian economy, US researchers warned in a 2001 Science article warning about the melting.

The NorthSouthEastWest project also includes images from Magnum agency photographers of 10 "climate hotspots" including the Marshall Islands and Greenland, as well as Kilimanjaro, showing "the most dramatic examples of the impact of global warming", Climate Change's Denise Meredith told AFP Tuesday.

⋮

【103 年學測】綜合測驗：26-30 出題來源

——http://www.pbs.org/wgbh/aso/databank/entries/dh05te.html

Better Decision Making: From Who's Right to What's Right; A Computer-Aided Structured-Inquiry Method Offers a Better Way to Make Tough Decisions

⋮

The evidence for that way of making decisions and setting policies is not very reassuring. One only has to look at some of the more colossal failed decisions--the disastrous choice by American leaders to pursue the war in Vietnam, the pouring of billions of dollars of investment capital into

imaginary dot-com businesses, and any number of misguided corporate
mergers--to question the wisdom of decision making by advocacy.
We must ask, If the various advocates of the conflicting options are all
smart, experienced, and well-informed, why do they disagree so
completely? Wouldn't they all have thought the issue through carefully and
come to approximately the same--"best"--conclusion?

The answer to that crucial question lies in the structure of the human
brain and the way it processes information.

First We Decide, Then We Justify

Most human beings actually decide before they think. When any
human being--executive, specialized expert, or person in the
street—encounters a complex issue and forms an opinion, often within a
matter of seconds, how thoroughly has he or she explored the implications
of the various courses of action? Answer: not very thoroughly. Very few
people, no matter how intelligent or experienced, can take inventory of the
many branching possibilities, possible outcomes, side effects, and
undesired consequences of a policy or a course of action in a matter of
seconds. Yet, those who pride themselves on being decisive often try to do
just that. And once their brains lock onto an opinion, most of their thinking
thereafter consists of finding support for it.

⋮

【103 年學測】文意選填：31-40 出題來源
—http://answers.yahoo.com/question/index?qid=20080606000607AAdE5OS

How do you name your children?

The choice of first names for children can be prompted by many
factors: Nationality; Tradition ; Politics; Religion; Beliefs; Culture; Social
status; Fashion and trends; Fads; Popularity, to name but some.

One's ethnic origins come into play: people will in general choose for their children names that are comprehensible in their country or the society that they move in and that will not be a burden for them in life.

Certain people like to give a name that has been handed down the family either for sentimental reasons or as a tribute to a relative whom they love(d) or admire(d) (who may be alive or dead). Some families have a tradition of passing down the father's first name to the first born son. In certain families a surname is included in the selection of a child 's given names to keep an ancestral surname going. It may be the mother's maiden surname for instance.

Certain classes choose a certain kind of first name that is traditional to their class. There are names that are deemed to be aristocratic whilst others denote a working class origin.

For a long time religion had an important place and names were chosen from the Bible such as the names of apostles (John, Peter ,Thomas etc..) from the New Testament or those of characters from the Old Testament (David, Samuel, Josh, Rachel, Rebecca, Suzannah etc...). Saints names have always been popular, even amongst non believers, and tradition is a factor in the sense that though some names have been disputed as non genuine, they are still chosen (Saint Christopher's existence is now much in doubt for instance, yet the name "Christopher" is still very popular for to boys).

For a long time people liked to give their children names that embodied Christian qualities especially for girls: Faith, Charity, Patience, Sophie (wisdom) but which are constant in most religions or civilisations. Some people choose names from deities in antiquity (Juno, Venus), prophets, or beings with superhuman powers (Angel, Ariel, Gabriel, Michael).

　　Those that are not necessarily religious and are fond of nature pick names that evoke beautiful things: flowers or plants (Heather, Rosemary, Violet, Iris, Vinca etc..) or minerals (Amber, Opal, Pearl etc..) but this can run across social classes and even nationalities and simply reflect personal preferences.

⋮

【103 年學測】閱讀測驗：41-44 出題來源

——http://www.biography.com/people/toni-morrison-9415590

Toni Morrison: biography

Synopsis

　　Born on February 18, 1931, in Lorain, Ohio, Toni Morrison is a Nobel Prize- and Pulitzer Prize-winning American novelist, editor and professor. Her novels are known for their epic themes, vivid dialogue and richly detailed black characters. Among her best known novels are *The Bluest Eye*, *Song of Solomon* and *Beloved*. Morrison has won nearly every book prize possible. She has also been awarded honorary degrees.

Early Career

　　Born Chloe Anthony Wofford on February 18, 1931, in Lorain, Ohio, Toni Morrison was the second oldest of four children. Her father, George Wofford, worked primarily as a welder, but held several jobs at once to support the family. Her mother, Ramah, was a domestic worker. Morrison later credited her parents with instilling in her a love of reading, music, and folklore.

　　Living in an integrated neighborhood, Morrison did not become fully aware of racial divisions until she was in her teens. "When I was in first grade, nobody thought I was inferior. I was the only black in the class and the only child who could read," she later told a reporter from The New York Times. Dedicated to her studies, Morrison took Latin in school, and read many great works of European literature. She graduated from Lorain High School with honors in 1949.

At Howard University, Morrison continued to pursue her interest in literature. She majored in English, and chose the classics for her minor. After graduating from Howard in 1953, Morrison continued her education at Cornell University. She wrote her thesis on the works of Virginia Woolf and William Faulkner, and completed her master's degree in 1955. She then moved to Texas to teach English at Texas Southern University. In 1957, Morrison returned to Howard University to teach English. There she met Harold Morrison, an architect originally from Jamaica. The couple got married in 1958 and welcomed their first child, son Harold, in 1961. After the birth of her son, Morrison joined a writers group that met on campus. She began working on her first novel with the group, which started out as a short story.

Morrison decided to leave Howard in 1963. After spending the summer traveling with her family in Europe, she returned to the United States with her son. Her husband, however, had decided to move back to Jamaica. At the time, Morrison was pregnant with their second child. She moved back home to live with her family in Ohio before the birth of son Slade in 1964. The following year, she moved with her sons to Syracuse, New York, where she worked for a textbook publisher as a senior editor. Morrison later went to work for Random House, where she edited works for such authors as Toni Cade Bambara and Gayl Jones.

⋮

【103 年學測】閱讀測驗：45-48 出題來源

——http://content.time.com/time/magazine/article/0,9171,2139175,00.html

10 Questions for Zeke Emanuel

You're the older brother of Rahm, the mayor of Chicago, and Ari, an extremely successful talent agent. And you're a bioethicist and one of the architects of Obamacare. Isn't writing a book about how great your family is a bit unseemly?

I didn't write a book about how great my family is. There are lots of warts and idiocies and foolishness--a lot to make fun of in the book. I wrote Brothers Emanuel because I had begun jotting down stories for my kids. And then we began getting a lot of questions: What did Mom put in the cereal?

⋮

【103 年學測】閱讀測驗：49-52 出題來源

——http://faculty.washington.edu/chudler/ener.html

Massive open online course

A Massive Open Online Course (MOOC) is an online course aimed at unlimited participation and open access via the web. In addition to traditional course materials such as videos, readings, and problem sets, MOOCs provide interactive user forums that help build a community for students, professors, and teaching assistants (TAs). MOOCs are a recent development indistance education.

Although early MOOCs often emphasized open access features, such as connectivism and open licensing of content, structure, and learning goals, to promote the reuse and remixing of resources, some notable newer MOOCs use closed licenses for their course materials, while maintaining free access for students.

⋮

In the fall of 2011 Stanford University launched three courses. The first of those courses was Introduction Into AI, launched by Sebastian Thrun and Peter Norvig. Enrollment quickly reached 160,000 students. The announcement was followed within weeks by the launch of two more MOOCs, by Andrew Ng and Jennifer Widom. Following the publicity and high enrollment numbers of these courses, Thrun started a company he named

Udacity and Daphne Koller and Andrew Nglaunched Coursera. Coursera subsequently announced university partnerships with University of Pennsylvania, Princeton University,Stanford University and The University of Michigan.

Concerned about the commercialization of online education, MIT created the not-for-profit MITx. The inaugural course, 6.002x, launched in March 2012. Harvard joined the group, renamed edX, that spring, and University of California, Berkeley joined in the summer. The initiative then added the University of Texas System, Wellesley College and Georgetown University.

In November 2012, the University of Miami launched first high school MOOC as part of Global Academy, its online high school. The course became available for high school students preparing for the SAT Subject Test in biology.

⋮

【103 年學測】閱讀測驗：53-56 出題來源

——http://www.economist.com/news/leaders/21576384-cars-have-already-chang ed-way-we-live-they-are-likely-do-so-again-clean-safe-and-it

Clean, safe and it drives itself

SOME inventions, like some species, seem to make periodic leaps in progress. The car is one of them. Twenty-five years elapsed between Karl Benz beginning small-scale production of his original *Motorwagen* and the breakthrough, by Henry Ford and his engineers in 1913, that turned the car into the ubiquitous, mass-market item that has defined the modern urban landscape. By putting production of the Model T on moving assembly lines set into the floor of his factory in Detroit, Ford drastically cut the time needed to build it, and hence its cost. Thus began a revolution in personal mobility. Almost a billion cars now roll along the world's highways.

Today the car seems poised for another burst of evolution. One way in which it is changing relates to its emissions. As emerging markets grow richer, legions of new consumers are clamouring for their first set of wheels. For the whole world to catch up with American levels of car ownership, the global fleet would have to quadruple. Even a fraction of that growth would present fearsome challenges, from congestion and the price of fuel to pollution and global warming.

Yet, as our special report this week argues, stricter regulations and smarter technology are making cars cleaner, more fuel-efficient and safer than ever before. China, its cities choked in smog, is following Europe in imposing curbs on emissions of noxious nitrogen oxides and fine soot particles. Regulators in most big car markets are demanding deep cuts in the carbon dioxide emitted from car exhausts. And carmakers are being remarkably inventive in finding ways to comply.

Granted, battery-powered cars have disappointed. They remain expensive, lack range and are sometimes dirtier than they look—for example, if they run on electricity from coal-fired power stations. But car companies are investing heavily in other clean technologies. Future motorists will have a widening choice of super-efficient petrol and diesel cars, hybrids (which switch between batteries and an internal-combustion engine) and models that run on natural gas or hydrogen. As for the purely electric car, its time will doubtless come.

⋮

103年學測英文科非選擇題閱卷評分原則說明

閱卷召集人：劉慶剛（國立台北大學應用外語學系教授）

　　103 學年度學科能力測驗英文考科的非選擇題題型共有「中譯英」和「英文作文」兩大題。第一大題是「中譯英」，題型與過去幾年相同，考生需將兩個中文句子譯成正確、通順、達意的英文，兩題合計為 8 分。第二大題是「英文作文」，考生須從三幅連環圖片的內容，想像第四幅圖片可能的發展，再以至少 120個單詞寫出一個涵蓋連環圖片內容並有完整結局的故事。

　　閱卷之籌備工作，依循閱卷標準程序，於 1 月 20 日先召開評分標準訂定會議，由正、副召集人及協同主持人共 14 人，參閱了約 3,000 份來自不同地區的試卷，經過一整天的討論之後，訂定評分標準，選出合適的評分參考樣卷及試閱樣卷，並編製成閱卷參考手冊，以供閱卷委員共同參閱。

　　本年度共計聘請 166 位大學教授擔任閱卷委員，1 月 22 日上午 9:00 至 11:00 為試閱會議，首先由召集人提示評分標準並舉例說明；接著分組進行試閱，參與評分之教授須根據閱卷參考手冊的試閱樣卷分別評分，並討論評分準則，務求評分標準一致，以確保閱卷品質。為求慎重，試閱會議後，正、副召集人及協同主持人進行評分標準再確定會議，確認評分原則後才開始正式閱卷。

　　評分標準與歷年相同，在「中譯英」部分，每小題總分 4 分，原則上是每個錯誤扣0.5分。「英文作文」的評分標準是依據內容、組織、文法句構、詞彙拼字、體例五個項目給分，字數明顯不足的作文則扣總分 1 分。閱卷時，每份試卷皆會經過兩位委員分別評分，

最後成績以二位閱卷委員給分之平均成績為準。如果第一閱與第二閱分數差距超過差分標準,則由第三位委員(正、副召集人或協同主持人)評閱。

今年的「中譯英」與「年輕人返鄉種植有機蔬菜」的趨勢有關,評量的重點在於考生能否能運用常用的詞彙與基本句型將兩句中文翻譯成正確達意的英文句子,所測驗之句型為高中生熟悉的範圍,詞彙亦控制在大考中心詞彙表四級內之詞彙,中等程度以上的考生,如果能使用正確句型並注意用字、拼字,應能得理想的分數。例如:「辭掉都市裡的高薪工作」若譯成 (have) quit high-paying/well-paid job/jobs in the city 即可得分;「藉由決心與努力」則可翻譯為 through/with/because of determination and effort/efforts。在選取樣卷時,我們發現有不少考生對於英文詞彙的使用及英文拼字仍有加強的空間,如第一句的「返回家鄉」有考生翻譯為 backed to home,「成功了」有不少考生翻譯為 success 或 successed;在拼字方面,「更健康」healthier 有考生少寫了字母 "i",「蔬菜」vegetables 這個字拼錯的考生也不少,相當可惜。

今年的「英文作文」主題與考生日常生活經驗相關,重點在於說明青少年若過度使用 3C 電子產品,甚至在走路時還像圖片二裡的女生忙著滑手機或像圖片三裡的男生沉迷於耳機裡的音樂中,將會造成意外,嚴重時還可能危及性命。大部分的考生應能從不同的角度發揮想像力,寫出一個涵蓋連環圖片內容並有完整結局的故事。評分的考量重點為作文內容是否切題,組織是否具連貫性、句子結構及用字是否適切、以及拼字與標點符號的使用是否正確得當。

103年學測英文考科試題或答案之反映意見回覆

※ 題號：9

【題目】

9. Most young people in Taiwan are not satisfied with a high school _____ and continue to pursue further education in college.

(A) maturity　　　　　　　(B) diploma
(C) foundation　　　　　　(D) guarantee

【意見內容】

選項 (C) foundation 有「基礎」的意思，應爲合理選項。

【大考中心意見回覆】

本題測驗考生能否掌握詞彙 diploma 的語意及用法。作答線索爲題幹中 …not satisfied with a high school 與 pursue a further education in college 之語意關係。foundation 當可　名詞時，爲「機構」（基金會等，如 Pine High School Foundation）或「建築的基礎」（如：This lot has a sound foundation and good chimney built.）的意思，但並無 a high school foundation 的搭配用法。

※ 題號：12

【題目】

12. If student enrollment continues to drop, some programs at the university may be _____ to reduce the operation costs.

(A) relieved　　　　　　　(B) eliminated
(C) projected　　　　　　(D) accounted

【意見內容】

選項 (C) projected 作爲「提出某計畫」，應爲合理選項。

【大考中心意見回覆】

本題測驗考生能否掌握詞彙 eliminate 的語意及用法。題幹中 student enrollment continues to drop（學生報到率降低）與 to reduce the operation costs（降低營運成本）之間的語意關係為本題作答線索。若 project 一詞依考生之解讀作為「提出某計畫」的意思，但因是被動語態，為求語意連貫，則應該是 some plans（計畫）或 some measures（措施）作為主詞而「被提出來」（be projected）；若選項 (C) 與本題幹主詞 some programs at the university（大學某些系所）一起使用，則跟上下文 student enrollment continues to drop（學生報到率降低）與 to reduce the operation costs（降低營運成本）之間的前後語意不連貫（原本題意為學生報到率降低與大學某些系所被刪減以降低營運成本之間的因果語意關係），因此選項 (C) 非本題正答選項。

※ 題號：15

【題目】

12. The baby panda Yuan Zai at the Taipei Zoo was separated from her mother because of a minor injury that occurred during her birth. She was _____ by zookeepers for a while.
(A) departed
(B) jailed
(C) tended
(D) captured

【意見內容】

四個選項皆為合理選項，此題應送分。

【大考中心意見回覆】

本題主要測驗考生能否掌握詞彙 tend 的語意及用法。作答線索在於題幹中 ...separated from her mother because of a minor injury...（因為小傷被迫與媽媽隔離）及 ...by zookeepers...（由動物園的保育員……）之間的語意關係。除了 tended（照顧）外，其他選項與本句語意皆不符。

※ 題號：16

【題目】

第 16 至 20 題為題組

Aesop, the Greek writer of fables, was sitting by the roadside one day when a traveler asked him what sort of people lived in Athens. Aesop replied, "Tell me where you come from and what sort of people live there, and I'll tell you what sort of people you'll find in Athens."   16   , the man answered, "I come from Argos, and there the people are all friendly, generous, and warm-hearted. I love them."   17   this, Aesop answered, "I'm happy to tell you, my dear friend, that you'll find the people of Athens much the same."

A few hours later,   18   traveler came down the road. He too stopped and asked Aesop the same question.   19   , Aesop made the same request. But frowning, the man answered, "I'm from Argos and there the people are unfriendly,   20   , and vicious. They're thieves and murderers, all of them." "Well, I'm afraid you'll find the people of Athens much the same," replied Aesop.

16. (A) Amazing   (B) Smiling
     (C) Deciding   (D) Praying

【意見內容】

選項 (A) Amazing 應為合理選項。

【大考中心意見回覆】

Amazing（令人感到驚訝的）一詞通常用來修飾事物，若要修飾人應為amazed，例：John was amazed at the news.，因此選項 (A) 非本題正答。

※ 題號：17

【題目】

　　Aesop, the Greek writer of fables, was sitting by the roadside one day when a traveler asked him what sort of people lived in Athens. Aesop replied, "Tell me where you come from and what sort of people live there, and I'll tell you what sort of people you'll find in Athens." ___16___, the man answered, "I come from Argos, and there the people are all friendly, generous, and warm-hearted. I love them." ___17___ this, Aesop answered, "I'm happy to tell you, my dear friend, that you'll find the people of Athens much the same."

　　A few hours later, ___18___ traveler came down the road. He too stopped and asked Aesop the same question. ___19___, Aesop made the same request. But frowning, the man answered, "I'm from Argos and there the people are unfriendly, ___20___, and vicious. They're thieves and murderers, all of them." "Well, I'm afraid you'll find the people of Athens much the same," replied Aesop.

17. (A) At
　　(C) For
(B) By
(D) In

【意見內容】

1. 請說明選項 (B) 與 (C) 不妥之處。
2. at 與 for 皆有「因為、由於」的意義，因此選項 (C) 應為合理選項。

【大考中心意見回覆】

本題測驗考生能否掌握片語 at this 在篇章中的用法。At this 的語意為「Upon hearing this」（一聽到就回答……），故根據上下文意，選項 (A) 為本題正答；其餘選項語意皆不符（By 語意為「藉由……」；For 語意為「因為……」）。

※ 題號：20

【題目】

Aesop, the Greek writer of fables, was sitting by the roadside one day when a traveler asked him what sort of people lived in Athens. Aesop replied, "Tell me where you come from and what sort of people live there, and I'll tell you what sort of people you'll find in Athens." ___16___, the man answered, "I come from Argos, and there the people are all friendly, generous, and warm-hearted. I love them." ___17___ this, Aesop answered, "I'm happy to tell you, my dear friend, that you'll find the people of Athens much the same."

A few hours later, ___18___ traveler came down the road. He too stopped and asked Aesop the same question. ___19___, Aesop made the same request. But frowning, the man answered, "I'm from Argos and there the people are unfriendly, ___20___, and vicious. They're thieves and murderers, all of them." "Well, I'm afraid you'll find the people of Athens much the same," replied Aesop.

20. (A) brave   (B) lonely
    (C) mean   (D) skinny

【意見內容】

選項 (D) skinny 有「低劣的、吝嗇的」意思，應為合理選項。

【大考中心意見回覆】

本題測驗考生能否掌握詞彙 mean 之語意與能否掌握上下文意對比的關係：第一段內容中的 friendly、generous、warm-hearted 與第二段的 unfriendly、mean，以及 vicious。作答線索在於空格前後的 unfriendly 與 vicious，以及下一句 They're thieves and murderers, all of them.。此外，skinny 通常意指身體的瘦弱，考生所指 skinny

作爲「低劣、吝嗇」的語意並不常見，再者，根據本文全文文意，
「低劣、吝嗇」的語意亦不妥適。

※ 題號：43

【題目】

第 41 至 44 題爲題組

American writer Toni Morrison was born in 1931 in Ohio.
She was raised in an African American family filled with songs
and stories of Southern myths, which later shaped her prose. Her
happy family life led to her excellent performance in school,
despite the atmosphere of racial discrimination in the society.

After graduating from college, Morrison started to work as a
teacher and got married in 1958. Several years later, her marriage
began to fail. For a temporary escape, she joined a small writers'
group, in which each member was required to bring a story or
poem for discussion. She wrote a story based on the life of a girl
she knew in childhood who had prayed to God for blue eyes. The
story was well received by the group, but then she put it away,
thinking she was done with it.

In 1964, Morrison got divorced and devoted herself to writing.
One day, she dusted off the story she had written for the writers'
group and decided to make it into a novel. She drew on her
memories from childhood and expanded upon them using her
imagination so that the characters developed a life of their own.
The Bluest Eye was eventually published in 1970. From 1970 to
1992, Morrison published five more novels.

In her novels, Morrison brings in different elements of the African American past, their struggles, problems and cultural memory. In *Song of Solomon*, for example, Morrison tells the story of an African American man and his search for identity in his culture. The novels and other works won her several prizes. In 1993, Morrison received the Nobel Prize in Literature. She is the eighth woman and the first African American woman to win the honor.

43. According to the passage, what is one of the themes in Morrison's works?
    (A) A search for African American values.
    (B) Divorced black women in American society.
    (C) Songs and stories of African Americans in Ohio.
    (D) History of African Americans from the 1970s through the 1990s.

【意見內容】

選項 (C) 應為合理選項。

【大考中心意見回覆】

本題測驗考生能否掌握文章內容細節之間的關係。作答線索在於第三段 ...memories fromchildhood；第四段 ...different elements of the African American past, their struggles, problems andcultural memory, search for identity in black culture 等字詞的提示。選項 (C) Songs and stories of African Americans in Ohio. 與第一段第二句 She was raised in an African American family filled with songs and stories of Southern myths... 之語意並不相符，故非合理之選項。

※ 題號：45

【題目】

第 45 至 48 題為題組

Below is an excerpt from an interview with Zeke Emanuel, a health-policy expert, on his famous brothers.

> Interviewer: You're the older brother of Rahm, the mayor of Chicago, and Ari, an extremely successful talent agent. And you're a bioethicist and one of the architects of Obamacare. Isn't writing a book about how great your family is a bit odd?
>
> Zeke: I don't write a book about how great my family is. There are lots of idiocies and foolishness—a lot to make fun of in the book. I wrote *Brothers Emanuel* because I had begun jotting stories for my kids. And then we began getting a lot of questions: What did Mom put in the cereal? Three successful brothers, all different areas.
>
> I: To what do you attribute the Emanuel brothers' success?
>
> Z: I would put success in quotes. We strive. First, I think we got this striving from our mother to make the world a better place. A second important thing is you never rest on the last victory. There's always more to do. And maybe the third important thing is my father's admonition that offense is the best defense. We don't give up.
>
> I: Do you still not have a TV?
>
> Z: I don't own a TV. I don't own a car. I don't Facebook. I don't tweet.
>
> I: But you have four cell phones.
>
> Z: I'm down to two, thankfully.
>
> I: Your brothers are a national source of fascination. Where do you think they'll be in five years?

> Z: Ari will be a superagent running the same company. Rahm would still be mayor of Chicago. I will probably continue to be my academic self. The one thing I can guarantee is none of us will have taken a cruise, none of us will be sitting on a beach with a pina colada.

45. What does Zeke Emanuel have in mind when saying "What did Mom put in the cereal?"
    (A) The secret to bringing up successful kids.
    (B) The recipe for a breakfast food.
    (C) The difference among the brothers.
    (D) The questions from his kids.

【意見內容】

選項 (C) 應爲合理選項。

【大考中心意見回覆】

本題測驗考生能否根據上下文推測 What did Mom put in the cereal? 的句意。作答線　在於第一段對答中提及三兄弟成功處之各句文意，尤其是在回應的最後一句 Three successful brothers, all different areas.。而後文的內容都與三兄弟的成功相關，例如：下一個問題爲 To what do you attribute the Emanuel brothers' success?。全文並未提及三兄弟彼此間相異之處，且選項 (C) 的陳述未能表達成功的原因或秘訣，故選項 (C) 非合理選項。

※ 題號：50

【題目】

第 49 至 52 題爲題組

　　MOOC, a massive open online course, aims at providing large-scale interactive participation and open access via the web.

In addition to traditional course materials such as videos, readings, and problem sets, MOOCs provide interactive user forums that help build a community for the students, professors, and teaching assistants.

MOOCs first made waves in the fall of 2011, when Professor Sebastian Thrun from Stanford University opened his graduate-level artificial intelligence course up to any student anywhere, and 160,000 students in more than 190 countries signed up. This new breed of online classes is shaking up the higher education world in many ways. Since the courses can be taken by hundreds of thousands of students at the same time, the number of universities might decrease dramatically. Professor Thrun has even envisioned a future in which there will only need to be 10 universities in the world. Perhaps the most striking thing about MOOCs, many of which are being taught by professors at prestigious universities, is that they're free. This is certainly good news for **cash-strapped** students.

There is a lot of excitement and fear surrounding MOOCs. While some say free online courses are a great way to increase the enrollment of minority students, others have said they will leave many students behind. Some critics have said that MOOCs promote an unrealistic one-size-fits-all model of higher education and that there is no replacement for true dialogues between professors and their students. After all, a brain is not a computer. We are not blank hard drives waiting to be filled with data. People learn from people they love and remember the things that arouse emotion. Some critics worry that online students will miss out on the social aspects of college.

50. Which of the following is **NOT** one of the features of MOOCs?
    (A) It is free to take the courses.
    (B) Many courses are offered by famous universities.
    (C) Most courses address artificial intelligence.
    (D) Many students can take the course at the same time.

【意見內容】

選項 (B) 應為合理選項。

【大考中心意見回覆】

本題測驗考生能否掌握文章主旨與細節之間的關係。作答線索在於第
二段內容，尤其是第二句以後的 …the courses can be taken by
hundreds of thousands of students at the same time、being taught
by professors at prestigious universities、they're free 等字詞的提示，
選項 (A)、選項 (B) 與選項 (D) 都是 MOOCs 的特質（feature）。其中，
由第二段的內容 …many of which are being taught by professors at
prestigious universities（許多課程由知名大學的教授授課），得知
選項 (B) Many courses are offered by famous universities. 為特質之
一；而根據文章第二段第一句，MOOCs 最初雖是由 Professor Thrun
所開設的 artificial intelligence 課程造成後續風潮，但此並非 MOOCs
的特點，且選項 (C) 的敘述在文章中並未提及，與文意不符，因此選
項 (C) 為本題正答。

※ 題號：51

【題目】

　　MOOC, a massive open online course, aims at providing
large-scale interactive participation and open access via the web.
In addition to traditional course materials such as videos, readings,
and problem sets, MOOCs provide interactive user forums that
help build a community for the students, professors, and teaching
assistants.

MOOCs first made waves in the fall of 2011, when Professor Sebastian Thrun from Stanford University opened his graduate-level artificial intelligence course up to any student anywhere, and 160,000 students in more than 190 countries signed up. This new breed of online classes is shaking up the higher education world in many ways. Since the courses can be taken by hundreds of thousands of students at the same time, the number of universities might decrease dramatically. Professor Thrun has even envisioned a future in which there will only need to be 10 universities in the world. Perhaps the most striking thing about MOOCs, many of which are being taught by professors at prestigious universities, is that they're free. This is certainly good news for cash-strapped students.

There is a lot of excitement and fear surrounding MOOCs. While some say free online courses are a great way to increase the enrollment of minority students, others have said they will leave many students behind. Some critics have said that MOOCs promote an unrealistic one-size-fits-all model of higher education and that there is no replacement for true dialogues between professors and their students. After all, a brain is not a computer. We are not blank hard drives waiting to be filled with data. People learn from people they love and remember the things that arouse emotion. Some critics worry that online students will miss out on the social aspects of college.

51. What is the second paragraph mainly about?
   (A) The impact of MOOCs.
   (B) The goal of MOOCs.
   (C) The size of MOOC classes.
   (D) The cost of MOOC courses.

【意見內容】

根據字典，size 有「巨大」的意思，選項 (C) 應為合理選項。

【大考中心意見回覆】

本題測驗考生能否掌握段落大意。作答線索在於第二段全段文意，第二句 This new breed of online classes is shaking up the higher education world in many ways. （這類網路課程對於高等教育有震撼性的影響）爲本段主題句，接下來的內容皆爲支撐主題的細節，如：the number of universities might decrease（大學數量將大幅減少）。第二段內容雖然談及 Since the courses can be taken by hundreds of thousands of students at the same time…，但後半句 the number of universities might decrease dramatically 才是主要的重點，因此選項 (C) 並非本段大意。

※ 題號：56

【題目】

第 53 至 56 題爲題組

　　Today the car seems to make periodic leaps in progress. A variety of driver assistance technologies are appearing on new cars. A developing technology called Vehicle-to-Vehicle communication, or V2V, is being tested by automotive manufacturers as a way to help reduce the number of accidents. V2V works by using wireless signals to send information back and forth between cars about their location, speed and direction, so that they keep safe distances from each other. Another new technology being tested is Vehicle-to-Infrastructure communication, or V2I. V2I would allow vehicles to communicate with road signs or traffic signals and provide information to the vehicle about safety issues. V2I could also request traffic information from a traffic management system and access the best possible routes. Both V2V and V2I have the potential to reduce around 80 percent of vehicle crashes on the road.

　　More and more new cars can reverse-park, read traffic signs, maintain a safe distance in steady traffic and brake automatically to avoid crashes. Moreover, a number of firms are creating cars that drive themselves to a chosen destination without a human at the controls. It is predicted that driverless cars will be ready for sale within five years. If and when cars go completely driverless, the benefits will be enormous. Google, which already uses prototypes of such cars to ferry its staff along Californian freeways, once put a blind man in a prototype and filmed him being driven off to buy takeaway hamburgers. If this works, huge numbers of elderly and disabled people can regain their personal mobility. The young will not have to pay crippling motor insurance, because their reckless hands and feet will no longer touch the wheel or the accelerator. People who commute by car will gain hours each day to work, rest, or read a newspaper.

56. What can be inferred from the passage?
　(A) Cars will refuse to start if the driver is drunk.
　(B) The future may be a vehicle-accident-free era.
　(C) Everyone, including children, can afford a car.
　(D) The production of driverless cars is still far away.

【意見內容】

文章中第一段內容只提到新的科技只能將車禍率降低百分之八十，因此選項 (B) 敘述不夠嚴謹，與文章敘述相違，建議送分。

【大考中心意見回覆】

本題測驗考生能否做適當的推論（inference）與判斷。作答線索在於對全文內容的理解。第一段最後一句 Both V2V and V2I have the potential to reduce around 80 percent of vehicle crashes on the road. 的語意可能還有約 20% 的機率產生車禍，選項 (B) 中用了 may be 正確且適度地表達了這個語意，是四個選項中對未來發展最合理的推論。根據第二段第一句至第三句，選項 (A) 與選項 (D) 皆非正確答案，而文章內容都未提及「所有的人都可以買車」這個概念，因此選項 (C) 亦非正解，故維持選項 (B) 為唯一正答。

103年大學入學學科能力測驗試題
數學考科

第壹部分：選擇題（佔60分）

一、單選題（佔30分）

說明：第1題至第6題，每題有5個選項，其中只有一個是正確或最適當的
　　　選項，請畫記在答案卡之「選擇（填）題答案區」。各題答對者，
　　　得5分；答錯、未作答或畫記多於一個選項者，該題以零分計算。

1. 請問下列哪一個選項等於 $\log\left(2^{(3^5)}\right)$ ？
   - (1) $5\log\left(2^3\right)$
   - (2) $3 \times 5\log 2$
   - (3) $5\log 2 \times \log 3$
   - (4) $5(\log 2 + \log 3)$
   - (5) $3^5 \log 2$

2. 令 $A(5,0,12)$、$B(-5,0,12)$ 為坐標空間中之兩點，且令 P 為 xy 平面
   上滿足 $\overline{PA} = \overline{PB} = 13$ 的點。請問下列哪一個選項中的點可能為 P ？
   - (1) $(5,0,0)$
   - (2) $(5,5,0)$
   - (3) $(0,12,0)$
   - (4) $(0,0,0)$
   - (5) $(0,0,24)$

3. 在坐標平面上，以 $(1,1), (-1,1), (-1,-1)$ 及 $(1,-1)$ 等四個點為頂點的
   正方形，與圓 $x^2 + y^2 + 2x + 2y + 1 = 0$ 有幾個交點？
   - (1) 1 個
   - (2) 2 個
   - (3) 3 個
   - (4) 4 個
   - (5) 0 個

4. 請問滿足絕對值不等式 $|4x-12| \le 2x$ 的實數 x 所形成的區間，其
   長度為下列哪一個選項？
   - (1) 1
   - (2) 2
   - (3) 3
   - (4) 4
   - (5) 6

5. 設 $(1+\sqrt{2})^6 = a+b\sqrt{2}$，其中 a, b 為整數。請問 b 等於下列哪一個選項？

(1) $C_0^6 + 2C_2^6 + 2^2 C_4^6 + 2^3 C_6^6$

(2) $C_1^6 + 2C_3^6 + 2^2 C_5^6$

(3) $C_0^6 + 2C_1^6 + 2^2 C_2^6 + 2^3 C_3^6 + 2^4 C_4^6 + 2^5 C_5^6 + 2^6 C_6^6$

(4) $2C_1^6 + 2^2 C_3^6 + 2^3 C_5^6$

(5) $C_0^6 + 2^2 C_2^6 + 2^4 C_4^6 + 2^6 C_6^6$

6. 某疾病可分為兩種類型：第一類占 70%，可藉由藥物 A 治療，其每一次療程的成功率為 70%，且每一次療程的成功與否互相獨立；其餘為第二類，藥物 A 治療方式完全無效。在不知道患者所患此疾病的類型，且用藥物 A 第一次療程失敗的情況下，進行第二次療程成功的條件機率最接近下列哪一個選項？

(1) 0.25　　(2) 0.3　　(3) 0.35　　(4) 0.4　　(5) 0.45

二、多選題（佔 30 分）

說明：第 7 題至第 12 題，每題有 5 個選項，其中至少有一個是正確的選項，請將正確選項畫記在答案卡之「選擇（填）題答案區」。各題之選項獨立判定，所有選項均答對者，得 5 分；答錯 1 個選項者，得 3 分；答錯 2 個選項者，得 1 分；答錯多於 2 個選項或所有選項均未作答者，該題以零分計算。

7. 設坐標平面上，x 坐標與 y 坐標皆為整數的點稱為格子點。請選出圖形上有格子點的選項。

(1) $y = x^2$

(2) $3y = 9x + 1$

(3) $y^2 = -x - 2$

(4) $x^2 + y^2 = 3$

(5) $y = \log_9 x + \dfrac{1}{2}$

8. 關於下列不等式，請選出正確的選項。

(1) $\sqrt{13} > 3.5$

(2) $\sqrt{13} < 3.6$

(3) $\sqrt{13} - \sqrt{3} > \sqrt{10}$

(4) $\sqrt{13} + \sqrt{3} > \sqrt{16}$

(5) $\dfrac{1}{\sqrt{13} - \sqrt{3}} > 0.6$

9. 一物體由坐標平面中的點 $(-3,6)$ 出發，沿著向量 $\vec{v}$ 所指的方向持續前進，可以進入第一象限。請選出正確的選項。

(1) $\vec{v} = (1,-2)$

(2) $\vec{v} = (1,-1)$

(3) $\vec{v} = (0.001,0)$

(4) $\vec{v} = (0.001,1)$

(5) $\vec{v} = (-0.001,1)$

10. 設 $f(x)$ 為實係數二次多項式，且已知 $f(1) > 0$、$f(2) < 0$、$f(3) > 0$。令 $g(x) = f(x) + (x-2)(x-3)$，請選出正確的選項。

(1) $y = f(x)$ 的圖形是開口向下的拋物線

(2) $y = g(x)$ 的圖形是開口向下的拋物線

(3) $g(1) > f(1)$

(4) $g(x) = 0$ 在 1 與 2 之間恰有一個實根

(5) 若 α 為 $f(x) = 0$ 的最大實根，則 $g(\alpha) > 0$

11. 設 $a_1 = 1$ 且 $a_1, a_2, a_3, \ldots$ 為等差數列。請選出正確的選項。

(1) 若 $a_{100} > 0$，則 $a_{1000} > 0$

(2) 若 $a_{100} < 0$，則 $a_{1000} < 0$

(3) 若 $a_{1000} > 0$，則 $a_{100} > 0$

(4) 若 $a_{1000} < 0$，則 $a_{100} < 0$

(5) $a_{1000} - a_{10} = 10(a_{100} - a_1)$

12. 所謂某個年齡範圍的失業率，是指該年齡範圍的失業人數與勞動
    力人數之比，以百分數表達（進行統計分析時，所有年齡以整數
    表示）。下表為去年某國四個年齡範圍的失業率，**其中的年齡範**
    圍有所重疊。

年齡範圍	35～44 歲	35～39 歲	40～44 歲	45～49 歲
失 業 率	12.66(%)	9.80(%)	13.17(%)	7.08(%)

請根據上表選出正確的選項。

(1) 在上述四個年齡範圍中，以 40～44 歲的失業率為最高
(2) 40～44 歲勞動力人數多於 45～49 歲勞動力人數
(3) 40～49 歲的失業率等於 $\left(\dfrac{13.17+7.08}{2}\right)\%$
(4) 35～39 歲勞動力人數少於 40～44 歲勞動力人數
(5) 如果 40～44 歲的失業率降低，則 45～49 歲的失業率會升高

第貳部分：選填題（佔 40 分）

說明：1. 第 A 至 H 題，將答案畫記在答案卡之「選擇（填）題答案
      區」所標示的列號（13−36）。
    2. 每題完全答對給 5 分，答錯不倒扣，未完全答對不給分。

A. 設圓 O 之半徑為 24，$\overline{OC} = 26$，$\overline{OC}$ 交
   圓 O 於 A 點，$\overline{CD}$ 切圓 O 於 D 點，B 為
   A 點到 $\overline{OD}$ 的垂足，如右邊的示意圖。
   則 $\overline{AB} = \dfrac{⑬⑭⑮}{⑯⑰}$。（化為最簡分數）

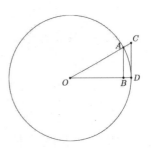

B. 坐標平面上，若直線 $y = ax + b$（其中 a, b 爲實數）與二次函數
$y = x^2$ 的圖形恰交於一點，亦與二次函數 $y = (x - 2)^2 + 12$ 的圖形
恰交於一點，則 $a =$ ⑱ ，$b =$ ⑲⑳ 。

C. 小鎭 A 距離一筆直道路 6 公里，並與道路上的小鎭 B 相距 12 公
里。今欲在此道路上蓋一家超級市場使其與 A，B 等距，則此超
級市場與 A 的距離須爲 ㉑√㉒ 公里。（化爲最簡根式）

D. 坐標空間中有四點 $A(2,0,0)$、$B(3,4,2)$、$C(-2,4,0)$ 與 $D(-1,3,1)$。若
點 P 在直線 CD 上變動，則內積 $\overrightarrow{PA} \cdot \overrightarrow{PB}$ 之最小可能值爲 $\dfrac{㉓}{㉔}$ 。
（化爲最簡分數）

E. 設 $\vec{u}, \vec{v}$ 爲兩個長度皆爲 1 的向量。若 $\vec{u} + \vec{v}$ 與 $\vec{u}$ 的夾角爲 75°，
則 $\vec{u}$ 與 $\vec{v}$ 的內積爲 $\dfrac{㉕\sqrt{㉖}}{㉗}$ 。（化爲最簡根式）

F. 一個房間的地面是由 12 個正方形所組成，
如右圖。今想用長方形瓷磚舖滿地面，已
知每一塊長方形瓷磚可以覆蓋兩個相鄰的

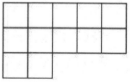

正方形，即  。則用 6 塊瓷磚舖滿房間地面的方
法有 ㉘㉙ 種。

G. 已知 $\begin{bmatrix} a & b \\ c & d \end{bmatrix}$ 是一個轉移矩陣，並且其行列式（值）為 $\dfrac{5}{8}$。

則 $a + b = \dfrac{\text{㉚㉛}}{\text{㉜}}$ 。（化爲最簡分數）

H. 如圖，正三角形 ABC 的邊長爲 1，並且 $\angle 1 = \angle 2 = \angle 3 = 15°$。已知 $\sin 15° = \dfrac{\sqrt{6} - \sqrt{2}}{4}$ ，則正三角形 DEF 的邊長爲 $\dfrac{\sqrt{\text{㉝}}}{\text{㉞}} - \dfrac{\sqrt{\text{㉟}}}{\text{㊱}}$ 。（化爲最簡根式）

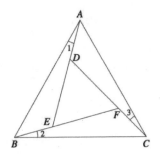

參考公式及可能用到的數值

1. 首項爲 a，公差爲 d 的等差數列前 n 項之和爲 $S = \dfrac{n(2a + (n-1)d)}{2}$

　首項爲 a，公比爲 r（$r \neq 1$）的等比數列前 n 項之和爲 $S_n = \dfrac{a(1 - r^n)}{1 - r}$，

2. 三角函數的和角公式：　$\sin(A + B) = \sin A \cos B + \cos A \sin B$

　　　　　　　　　　　　$\cos(A + B) = \cos A \cos B - \sin A \sin B$

　　　　　　　　　　　　$\tan(A + B) = \dfrac{\tan A + \tan B}{1 - \tan A \tan B}$

3. $\triangle ABC$ 的正弦定理：$\dfrac{a}{\sin A} = \dfrac{b}{\sin B} = \dfrac{c}{\sin C} = 2R$，

（R 爲 $\triangle ABC$ 的外接圓半徑）

$\triangle ABC$ 的餘弦定理：$c^2 = a^2 + b^2 - 2ab\cos C$

4. 一維數據 $X : x_1, x_2, \ldots, x_n$，

算術平均數：$\mu_X = \dfrac{1}{n}(x_1 + x_2 + \cdots + x_n) = \dfrac{1}{n}\sum\limits_{i=1}^{n} x_i$

標準差：$\sigma_X = \sqrt{\dfrac{1}{n}\sum\limits_{i=1}^{n}(x_i - \mu_X)^2} = \sqrt{\dfrac{1}{n}\left(\left(\sum\limits_{i=1}^{n} x_i^2\right) - n\mu_X^2\right)}$

5. 二維數據 $(X, Y) : (x_1, y_1), (x_2, y_2), \ldots, (x_n, y_n)$，

相關係數 $r_{X,Y} = \dfrac{\sum\limits_{i=1}^{n}(x_i - \mu_X)(y_i - \mu_Y)}{n\sigma_X \sigma_Y}$

迴歸直線（最適合直線）方程式 $y - \mu_Y = r_{X,Y} = \dfrac{\sigma_Y}{\sigma_X}(x - \mu_X)$

6. 參考數值：$\sqrt{2} \approx 1.414$，$\sqrt{3} \approx 1.732$，$\sqrt{5} \approx 2.236$，$\sqrt{6} \approx 2.449$，

$\pi \approx 3.142$

7. 對數值：$\log_{10} 2 \approx 0.3010$，$\log_{10} 3 \approx 0.4771$，$\log_{10} 5 \approx 0.6990$，

$\log_{10} 7 \approx 0.8451$

103年度學科能力測驗數學科試題詳解

第壹部分：選擇題

一、單選擇

1. 【答案】(5)

　　【解析】根據對數運算性質：$\log a^b = b \log a$ 可得 $\log\left(2^{(3)^5}\right) = (3)^5 \log 2$

　　　　　　故選 (5)

2. 【答案】(4)

　　【解析】設 $P(s,t,0)$，已知 $\overline{PA} = \overline{PB} = 13$，可得：

$$(s-5)^2 + (t-0)^2 + (12-0)^2 = 13^2 \cdots(1)$$
$$(s+5)^2 + (t-0)^2 + (12-0)^2 = 13^2 \cdots(2)$$

　　　　　　兩式相減得 $s=0$，代回(1)式得 $t=0$

　　　　　　可得 $P(0,0,0)$，故選 (4)

3. 【答案】(2)

　　【解析】已知圓：$x^2 + y^2 + 2x + 2y + 1 = 0$，

　　　　　　標準式：$(x+1)^2 + (y+1)^2 = 1$，

　　　　　　圓心 $(-1, -1)$，圓半徑 $r=1$，

　　　　　　可得圓圖形與正方形相交情

　　　　　　形如右圖，共有 2 個交點，

　　　　　　故選 (2)

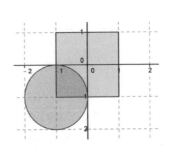

4. 【答案】 (4)

　　【解析】 $|4x-12| \leq 2x$，去絕對值不等式得：$\begin{cases} -2x \leq 4x-12 \\ 4x-12 \leq 2x \\ 2x \geq 0 \end{cases}$

$$\Rightarrow \begin{cases} 2 \leq x \\ x \leq 6 \\ x \geq 0 \end{cases}，取交集得：2 \leq x \leq 6$$

所以實數 x 的區間長度 $= 6-2 = 4$，故選 (4)

5. 【答案】 (2)

　　【解析】 $(1+\sqrt{2})^6 = C_0^6 1^6 \cdot (\sqrt{2})^0 + C_1^6 1^5 \cdot (\sqrt{2})^1 + C_2^6 1^4 \cdot (\sqrt{2})^2 + \cdots$

$$+ C_6^6 1^0 \cdot (\sqrt{2})^6$$

$$= (C_0^6 + C_2^6 \cdot 2 + C_4^6 \cdot 4 + C_6^6 \cdot 8) + (C_1^6 + C_3^6 \cdot 2 + C_5^6 \cdot 4)\sqrt{2} = a + b\sqrt{2}$$

比較係數得 $b = C_1^6 + C_3^6 \cdot 2 + C_5^6 \cdot 4 = C_1^6 + 2 \cdot C_3^6 + 2^2 \cdot C_5^6$，
故選 (2)

6. 【答案】 (2)

　　【解析】 依題意所求為條件機率：

$$P_{(第二次成功 | 第一次失敗)} = \frac{P_{(第二次成功且第一次失敗)}}{P_{(第一次失敗)}}$$

$$= \frac{0.7 \times 0.3}{0.7 \times 0.3 + 0.3 \times 1} \times 0.7 = \frac{49}{170} \approx 0.288$$

故選 (2)

二、多選題

7. 【答案】(1) (3) (5)

　　【解析】依選項逐一分析：

(1) ○：$y = x^2$ 為開口向上的拋物線，頂點 $V(0,0)$ 即為格子點

(2) ✕：$3y = 9x+1$ 為直線，移項整理得 $3(y-3x) = 1$，

若 (x,y) 為格子點代入：

$3(y-3x) = 3k$ (k 為整數)，為 3 的倍數，與條件不符

(3) ○：$y^2 = -x-2$，令 $y = 2$ 代入可得 $x = 6 \Rightarrow$ 格子點

$(x,y) = (6,2)$ 在 $y^2 = -x-2$ 上

(4) ✕：$x^2 + y^2 = 3$ 為圓心 $(0,0)$ 且半徑 $r = \sqrt{3}$ 的圓，

可得圓上無格子點

(5) ○：$y = \log_9 x + \dfrac{1}{2}$，令 $x = 3$ 代入可得 $y = 1 \Rightarrow$ 格子點

$(x,y) = (3,1)$ $y = \log_9 x + \dfrac{1}{2}$ 上

故選 (1)(3)(5)

8. 【答案】(1) (4)

　　【解析】依選項逐一分析：

(1) ○：$(\sqrt{13})^2 = 13 > (3.5)^2 = 12.25 \Rightarrow \sqrt{13} > 3.5$

(2) ✕：$(\sqrt{13})^2 = 13 > (3.6)^2 = 12.96 \Rightarrow \sqrt{13} > 3.6$

(3) ✕：考慮 $(\sqrt{10} + \sqrt{3})^2 = 13 + 2\sqrt{30} > 13 = (\sqrt{13})^2$

$\Rightarrow \sqrt{10} + \sqrt{3} > \sqrt{13}$，

移項得 $\sqrt{13} - \sqrt{3} < \sqrt{10}$

(4) ○：$(\sqrt{10}+\sqrt{6})^2 = 16 + 2\sqrt{60} > 16 = (\sqrt{16})^2$

$\Rightarrow \sqrt{10}+\sqrt{6} > \sqrt{16}$

(5) ×：$\dfrac{1}{\sqrt{13}-\sqrt{3}} = \dfrac{\sqrt{13}+\sqrt{3}}{10} < \dfrac{6}{10}$

$(\because \sqrt{13} < 4, \sqrt{3} < 2, \Rightarrow \sqrt{13}+\sqrt{3} < 6)$

故選 (1)(4)

9. 【答案】 (2) (3) (4)

　　【解析】 依題意，可利用求出過點$(-3,6)$的直線方程式加以判斷是否通過第一象限：

(1) ×：$\vec{v} = (1,-2)$，得斜率 $m = \dfrac{2}{-1} \Rightarrow$ 方程式 $2x+y=0$，不過第一象限

(2) ○：$\vec{v} = (1,-1)$，得斜率 $m = \dfrac{1}{-1} \Rightarrow$ 方程式 $x+y=3$，通過第一象限

(3) ○：$\vec{v} = (0.001,0)$，得斜率 $m = 0 \Rightarrow$ 方程式 $y=6$，為水平線，通過第一象限

(4) ○：$\vec{v} = (0.001,1)$，得斜率 $m = 1000$

$\Rightarrow$ 方程式 $1000x-y=-3006$，通過第一象限

(5) ×：$\vec{v} = (-0.001,1)$，得斜率 $m = \dfrac{1000}{-1}$

$\Rightarrow$ 方程式 $1000x+y=-2994$，不過第一象限

故選 (2)(3)(4)

10. 【答案】(3) (4)

　　【解析】已知實係數二次函數 $f(1)>0$，$f(2)<0$，$f(3)>0$，

　　　　　可知 $f(x)$ 為一開口向上的拋物線

　　　　　（如圖所示）

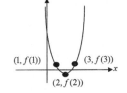

　　　　　$\Rightarrow g(x)=f(x)+(x-2)(x-3)$ 亦為一

　　　　　開口向上的拋物線

　　　　　$\Rightarrow$ 選項 (1) (2) 皆錯誤

　　　　　(3) ○：　$g(1)=f(1)+(1-2)(1-3)=f(1)+2>f(1)$

　　　　　(4) ○：　$g(1)=f(1)+(1-2)(1-3)=f(1)+2>0$，

　　　　　　　　$g(2)=f(2)+(2-2)(2-3)=f(2)<0$，

　　　　　　　　$g(3)=f(3)+(3-2)(3-3)=f(3)>0$

　　　　　　　　$\Rightarrow g(1)\cdot g(2)<0$ 且 $g(2)\cdot g(3)<0$

　　　　　　　　$\Rightarrow$ 根據勘根定理 $g(x)=0$ 在 $1<x<2$ 與 $2<x<3$

　　　　　　　　皆有實根

　　　　　　　　$\Rightarrow g(x)=0$ 在 $1<x<2$ 恰有一實根

　　　　　(5) ✕：若 α 為 $f(x)=0$ 的最大實根 $\Rightarrow f(\alpha)=0$ 且 $2<\alpha<3$

　　　　　　　　$\Rightarrow g(\alpha)=f(\alpha)+(\alpha-2)(\alpha-3)=(\alpha-2)(\alpha-3)<0$

　　　　故選 (3)(4)

11. 【答案】(2) (3) (5)

　　【解析】已知 $<a_n>$ 為等差數列，首項 $a_1=1$，假設公差為 d：

　　　　　(1) ✕：若 $a_{100}=a_1+99d>0 \Rightarrow d>-\dfrac{1}{99}$，

　　　　　　　取 $d=-\dfrac{1}{111}$，可得 $a_{1000}=a_1+999d=1+999\times(\dfrac{-1}{111})=-8<0$

　　　　　(2) ○：若 $a_{100}=a_1+99d<0 \Rightarrow d<-\dfrac{1}{99}$，

　　　　　　　$\Rightarrow a_{1000}=a_1+999d=a_{100}+900d<0$

(3) ○：若 $a_{1000} = a_1 + 999d > 0 \Rightarrow d > -\dfrac{1}{999}$ ，

可得 $a_{100} = a_1 + 99d > 1 + 99 \times (\dfrac{-1}{999}) = \dfrac{10}{11} > 0$

(4) ×： 若 $a_{1000} = a_1 + 999d < 0 \Rightarrow d < -\dfrac{1}{999}$ ，

取 $d = -\dfrac{1}{990}$ ，可得 $a_{100} = a_1 + 99d = 1 + 99 \times (\dfrac{-1}{990}) = \dfrac{9}{10} > 0$

(5) ○： $a_{1000} - a_{10} = 990d$ ， $a_{100} - a_1 = 99d$

$\Rightarrow a_{1000} - a_{10} = 10(a_{100} - a_1)$ 　　故選 (2)(3)(5)

12. 【答案】 (1) (4)

　　【解析】 依題意，假設各年齡範圍失業人數與勞動力人數如下表：

年齡範圍	35~44 歲	35~39 歲	40~44 歲	45~49 歲
失業率	12.66(%)	9.80(%)	13.17(%)	7.08(%)
失業人數	$a_1 + a_2$	a_1	a_2	a_3
勞動力人數	$b_1 + b_2$	b_1	b_2	b_3

(1) ○：表格中，40~44 歲失業率 13.17(%)最高

(2) ×：由失業率得： $\dfrac{a_2}{b_2} > \dfrac{a_3}{b_3}$ ，但無法判斷勞動力人

數 b_2 與 b_3 的大小關係

(3) ×：40~49 歲的失業率應為 $\dfrac{a_2 + a_3}{b_2 + b_3} = (\dfrac{13.17b_2 + 7.08b_3}{b_2 + b_3})\%$

(4) ○：由表格得 $\dfrac{a_1}{b_1} = 9.80\%$ ， $\dfrac{a_2}{b_2} = 13.17\%$ ， $\dfrac{a_1 + a_2}{b_1 + b_2} = 12.66\%$

$\Rightarrow a_1 = 0.098b_1$ ， $a_2 = 0.1317b_2$ 代入 $\dfrac{a_1 + a_2}{b_1 + b_2}$

可得 $\dfrac{0.098b_1 + 0.1317b_2}{b_1 + b_2} = 0.1266$

$\Rightarrow 2.86b_1 = 0.51b_2 \Rightarrow b_1 < b_2$

(5) ×：由表格資料無法判定 40～44 歲失業率 ($\dfrac{a_2}{b_2}$) 與

45～49 歲失業率 ($\dfrac{a_3}{b_3}$) 有負相關

故選 (1)(4)

第貳部份：選填題

A. 【答案】 $\dfrac{120}{13}$

　　【解析】 依題意條件得 $\Delta OCD \cong \Delta OAB$，且皆為直角三角形，

又已知 $\overline{OC} = 26$，$\overline{OD} = 24$，

得 $\overline{CD} = \sqrt{26^2 - 24^2} = 10$，

設 $\overline{AB} = x \Rightarrow \dfrac{\overline{OA}}{\overline{AB}} = \dfrac{\overline{OC}}{\overline{CD}}$

$\Rightarrow \dfrac{24}{x} = \dfrac{26}{10}$，得 $x = \overline{AB} = \dfrac{120}{13}$

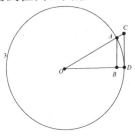

B. 【答案】 6，–9

　　【解析】 $\because y = ax + b$ 與 $y = x^2$ 圖形恰一個交點，

$\Rightarrow y = ax + b$ 代入 $y = x^2$ 整理得方程式：

$x^2 - ax - b = 0$ 恰一解（重根）

$\Rightarrow$ 即判別式 $\Delta_1 = (-a)^2 - 4 \cdot 1 \cdot (-b) = a^2 + 4b = 0 \cdots (1)$

同理，$y = ax + b$ 與 $y = (x - 2)^2 + 12$ 圖形恰一個交點，

$\Rightarrow y = ax + b$ 代入 $y = (x - 2)^2 + 12$

整理得方程式：$x^2 - (a + 4)x + 16 - b = 0$ 恰一解（重根）

⇒即判別式

$$\Delta_2 = (a+4)^2 - 4 \cdot 1 \cdot (16-b) = a^2 + 8a + 4b - 48 = 0 \cdots (2)$$

(1) (2)兩式相減：$8a = 48$，得 $a = 6$，$b = -\dfrac{a^2}{4} = -9$

C. 【答案】 $4\sqrt{3}$

【解析】 依題意可得市場 A 與小鎮 B 以及超級
市場 M 的相對位置如右圖所示：

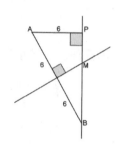

⇒ $\triangle ABP$ 為直角三角形，且 $\angle B = 30^\circ$，

⇒所求 $\overline{AM} = \overline{BM} = \dfrac{6}{\cos B} = 6 \times \dfrac{2}{\sqrt{3}} = 4\sqrt{3}$

D. 【答案】 $\dfrac{5}{4}$

【解析】 已知 $C(-2,4,0)$，$D(-1,3,1)$ 且 P 為直線 $\overline{CD}$ 上的動點，

取方向向量 $\overrightarrow{CD} = (1,-1,1)$，可假設參數式 $P(-2+t, 4-t, t)$

又已知 $A(2,0,0)$，$B(3,4,2)$ ⇒ $\overrightarrow{PA} = (4-t, -4+t, -t)$，

$\overrightarrow{PB} = (5-t, t, 2-t)$，

$\overrightarrow{PA} \cdot \overrightarrow{PB} = (4-t)(5-t) + (-4+t)(t) + (-t)(2-t)$

$\qquad\qquad = 3t^2 - 15t + 20 = 3(t - \dfrac{5}{2})^2 + \dfrac{5}{4}$

當 $t = \dfrac{5}{2}$ 時，$\overrightarrow{PA} \cdot \overrightarrow{PB}$ 有最小值 $\dfrac{5}{4}$

E. 【答案】 $\dfrac{-\sqrt{3}}{2}$

【解析】 依題意可得 $\overrightarrow{u}$，$\overrightarrow{v}$ 如
右圖所示，

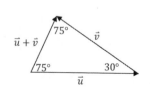

$$\Rightarrow \text{向量} \overrightarrow{u} \text{ 與 } \overrightarrow{v} \text{ 夾角} \theta = 180^\circ - 30^\circ = 150^\circ,$$

$$\Rightarrow \overrightarrow{u} \cdot \overrightarrow{v} = |\overrightarrow{u}||\overrightarrow{v}|\cos\theta = 1 \cdot 1 \cdot (-\frac{\sqrt{3}}{2}) = -\frac{\sqrt{3}}{2}$$

F. 【答案】 11

　　【解析】 依題意條件討論：（觀察可知橫矩形必須為奇數個
　　　　　　　才有解）

　　　情況(1)，使用 1 個橫矩形，5 個長矩形：

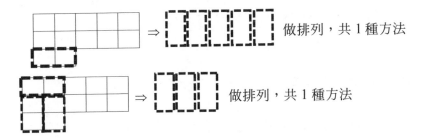

　　　情況(2)，使用 3 個橫矩形，3 個長矩形：

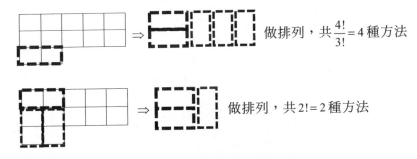

　　　情況(3)，使用 5 個橫矩形，1 個長矩形：

　　⇒由(1),(2),(3)討論可得總共有11種方法

G. 【答案】 $\dfrac{13}{8}$

　　【解析】 已知 $A=\begin{bmatrix} a & b \\ c & d \end{bmatrix}$ 為一轉移矩陣 $\Rightarrow a+c=1$ 且 $b+d=1$，

　　　　　　又 $\det(A)=\begin{vmatrix} a & b \\ c & d \end{vmatrix}=ad-bc=\dfrac{5}{8}$，

　　　　　　將 $c=1-a$，$b=1-d$ 代入得：$ad-(1-d)(1-a)=\dfrac{5}{8}$

　　　　　　$\Rightarrow ad-(1-d-a+ad)=\dfrac{5}{8}$　$\Rightarrow a+d=\dfrac{5}{8}+1=\dfrac{13}{8}$

H. 【答案】 $\dfrac{\sqrt{6}}{2}-\dfrac{\sqrt{2}}{2}$

　　【解析】 依題意條件，設 $\overline{AD}=\overline{BE}=\overline{CF}=x$，

　　　　　　$\overline{DE}=\overline{EF}=\overline{FD}=y$，如右圖所示，

　　　　　　根據正弦定理：

　　　　　　$\triangle ABE$ 中，$\dfrac{1}{\sin 120^\circ}=\dfrac{x}{\sin 15^\circ}=\dfrac{x+y}{\sin 45^\circ}$

　　　　　　$\Rightarrow x=\dfrac{\sin 15^\circ}{\sin 120^\circ}=\dfrac{\sqrt{6}-\sqrt{2}}{4}\times\dfrac{2}{\sqrt{3}}=\dfrac{3\sqrt{2}-\sqrt{6}}{6}$，

　　　　　　$x+y=\dfrac{\sin 45^\circ}{\sin 120^\circ}$

　　　　　　$\Rightarrow y=\dfrac{\sin 45^\circ}{\sin 120^\circ}-x=\dfrac{\sqrt{2}}{2}\times\dfrac{2}{\sqrt{3}}-\dfrac{3\sqrt{2}-\sqrt{6}}{6}=\dfrac{\sqrt{6}}{2}-\dfrac{\sqrt{2}}{2}$

103 年大學入學學科能力測驗試題
社會考科

單選題（佔 144 分）

說明：第 1 題至第 72 題皆計分。每題有 4 個選項，其中只有一個是最
正確或最適當的選項，請畫記在答案卡之「選擇題答案區」。
各題答對者，得 2 分；答錯、未作答或畫記多於一個選項者，
該題以零分計算。

1. 大明代表學校參加棒球比賽，卻因不慎漏接導致球隊以一分飲恨，
賽後檢討時，教練批評指責其反應太慢，他因此認為自己很笨、
能力不好，不適合打棒球。下列哪個概念最符合大明的處境？
(A) 米德（George H. Mead）：概化他人（the generalized others）
(B) 顧里（Charles H. Cooley）：鏡中自我（looking-glass self）
(C) 佛洛依德（Sigmund Freud）：超我（super ego）
(D) 艾瑞克森（Erik Erikson）：自我混淆（self-confusion）

2. 在現實社會中，不同文化常因誤會或偏見，產生彼此有高低的區
分，形成文化位階與歧視的現象，衍生出不平等問題。以臺灣社
會為例，下列哪個現象涉及文化歧視與不平等？
(A) 教育部在大學入學考試中，為原住民身分考生設有增額錄取
的制度
(B) 地方政府特別為東南亞外籍配偶舉辦國語文及臺灣風俗民情
的課程
(C) 政府規定大陸籍配偶取得國民身分證的時間，要比其他外籍
配偶多幾年
(D) 政府在組織上增設客家事務委員會，並在多所大學裡成立客
家文化學院

3. 由於刻板印象而產生性別迷思的狀況常可見，近來性別平等教育
融入課程已成為校園的重要課題。下列何者可反映出校園內的性
別刻板印象？
(A) 訓導主任大力呼籲學生們不要霸凌弱小同學
(B) 性別平等委員會是為保障女性教職員生而成立
(C) 體育老師徵求班上男女各十位同學參加拔河比賽
(D) 開學第一天導師請班上力氣大的同學幫忙搬新課本

4. 根據聯合國定義，非政府組織是在地方、國家或國際上成立的非
營利性自願公民團體，不屬於政府、也非由政府所設立。下列哪
個組織最符合上述定義的非政府組織？
(A) 世界展望會
(B) 世界衛生大會
(C) 世界貿易組織
(D) 經濟合作暨發展組織

5. 2011 年北韓領導人金正日過世，北韓新聞主播穿著韓國喪服播報
這項消息；某國有位新聞主播當天也故意穿著韓服，並戲謔地夾
雜韓語播報。從媒體識讀的角度，某國這則報導是否符合媒體的
表現？
(A) 符合，憲法保障媒體言論自由
(B) 符合，媒體追求創意勇於突破
(C) 不符合，媒體罔顧新聞倫理及專業
(D) 不符合，媒體不應以創意沖淡哀傷新聞

6. 有學者提出「全球在地化」（glocalization）的概念，指涉企業考
量世界各地的特殊情況，將商品或服務進行適當地調整，以符應
當地文化和社會特性及需求，並藉以增加銷售業績。下列何者屬
於全球在地化現象？

(A) 德國麵包、香腸與豬腳深受臺灣民眾喜愛，德式餐廳數量大增

(B) 全球咖啡連鎖店結合臺灣當地素材，推出獨特的烏龍茶口味咖啡

(C) 客家桐花季吸引了大量民眾的參與，有助於客家聚落文化傳承與產業振興

(D) 全球電腦大廠推出新型平板電腦，因款式新穎，引起本地消費者搶購熱潮

7-8 為題組

某內閣制國家共有 10 個行政區，各行政區的國會議員選舉投票結果如表 1 所示。如果該國國會總共有 20 個席次，政黨代表與地方選區席次各半，並且各自計算；其中，選民可投二票，一票投給政黨，一票投給選區候選人。

表 1

行政區	甲黨得票率	乙黨得票率	丙黨得票率	丁黨得票率
1	38%	50%	5%	7%
2	35%	34%	21%	10%
3	10%	11%	59%	20%
4	50%	10%	5%	35%
5	30%	20%	15%	35%
6	15%	10%	65%	10%
7	45%	30%	5%	20%
8	30%	50%	10%	10%
9	50%	30%	10%	10%
10	25%	65%	5%	5%
政黨得票率	30%	50%	10%	10%

7. 針對前述條件，此次選舉後國會最大黨應該為何？

(A) 甲黨　　　(B) 乙黨　　　(C) 丙黨　　　(D) 丁黨

8. 根據該國國會選舉結果，其後可能的政治發展，下列敘述何者最為正確？
   (A) 甲黨可以與任一政黨結盟，都能組成過半多數政府
   (B) 乙黨擁有穩定過半的多數支持，可以單獨組成政府
   (C) 丙黨可在甲乙政黨間，扮演關鍵角色爭取組閣利益
   (D) 丁黨是國會中席次最少的政黨，沒有機會加入內閣

9. 有學者主張，兩岸關係從對立走向和緩，其實與臺灣政治民主化發展有密切的關連。請問下列何項歷史事實及其影響最能印證上述的看法？
   (A) 1979 年臺灣用「三民主義統一中國」來取代原有的「反攻大陸」
   (B) 1991 年臺灣透過修憲程序終止動員戡亂，承認兩岸分治的現實
   (C) 1991 年先後成立行政院陸委會與海基會，展開兩岸事務性對話
   (D) 1993 年海基會、海協會於新加坡首次會談，創兩岸交流的先河

10. 我國自 1991 年展開七次憲法增修，下列何者<u>不是</u>這幾次修憲的成果？
   (A) 總統直選、實施雙首長體制，強化我國民主深化的基礎
   (B) 單一國會、席次減半、任期四年，確立代議政治的內涵
   (C) 明定大法官會議為釋憲機制，維繫我國憲政運作的穩定
   (D) 修憲案交由公民複決、落實公投之法源，實踐人民主權

11. 基於權力制衡，我國行政與立法機關各有權力制衡彼此。有關這些權力運作的敘述，何者並<u>不正確</u>？

(A) 立法院對政府施政不滿，可以發動委員連署提出倒閣案

(B) 行政院針對立法院不妥之決議事項，可移請立法院覆議

(C) 立法委員基於施政弊案，發動調查權糾舉彈劾失職官員

(D) 國會因政府施政不當，拒絕行政首長上台進行施政報告

12. 近年來，許多先進民主國家政府信任度持續下滑，有學者指出傳統代議民主國家強調依法行政的形式「合法性」（legality），而忽略人民實際感受與回應的實質「正當性」（legitimacy）。下列敘述何者乃是強調「正當性」更高於「合法性」的現象？

(A) 張三違規右轉被罰而心生不滿，欲聯合相同經驗民眾上街遊行

(B) 夜市居民網路舉發少數攤販違規營業，獲得眾多網友按讚支持

(C) 現任首長要求檢調單位監聽敵對陣營候選人，以利其競選連任

(D) 市長因鄰縣受災時未搶救而造成嚴重傷亡，引爆民怨提前下台

13. 立法院通過會計法修正案時因漏字問題引發巨大爭議，引起各界對立法品質的關注。假設法律生效施行後，如發現法律條文有重大疏漏，該進行何種程序修正？

(A) 立法院依立法程序將修正案通過後，送請總統公布

(B) 由大法官會議宣告該法律違憲後，立法院進行修改

(C) 先由總統召集五院院長會商後，交由立法院修改

(D) 行政院長經總統核可後，向立法院提出覆議案要求修改

14. 2010 年底，一位突尼西亞青年因抗議政府而自焚，此消息藉由手機及網路等迅速傳開，引起許多對高失業率及高糧價不滿的群眾上街示威抗議，導致執政多年的總統下台。下列對於人民基本權利保障的敘述，何者正確？

(A) 糧價飆高，許多人沒錢購買食物，顯示政府並未充分保障人民之財產權

(B) 許多年輕人找不到工作，此高失業率表示國家未充分保障人民之工作權

(C) 人民以網路及手機等傳遞相關訊息，是人民行使憲法上結社自由的表現

(D) 能讓長期執政的總統迅速下台，是因為人民行使創制權與複決權的結果

15. 請以現代法治國家的觀點，判斷以下對於人民上街示威遊行的敘述何者正確？

(A) 人民示威抗議的行為屬於憲法集會自由的保障範圍，其行為當屬合法

(B) 人民對政府施政不滿就應提起訴願及訴訟，故示威抗議違反法律程序

(C) 示威抗議的行為必須要先得到主管機關的許可，否則示威抗議即違法

(D) 為防止妨礙他人自由或增進公共利益，法律可合理限制示威抗議活動

16. 某記者連線報導內容為：「為您插播最新消息，涉及重大貪瀆案的被告小明今天下午終於到案，檢察官開庭偵訊後，決定將他收押，預料案情還會有進一步的發展。」此報導主要發生下列哪一項法律爭議？

(A) 違反偵查不公開原則　　　(B) 侵犯被告的隱私權

(C) 違背無罪推定原則　　　　(D) 誤解檢察官的職權

17. 大華與小英結婚後，育有一女佩佩。佩佩五歲時，兩人因故離婚，但對佩佩之監護權發生爭執。下列關於佩佩監護權的敘述何者正確？

(A) 若小英取得對佩佩之監護權，她可決定是否讓大華探視佩佩

(B) 若大華取得對佩佩之監護權，小英對佩佩依法即不須再負扶養之義務

(C) 若對佩佩之監護權歸屬有爭議時，大華與小英亦可約定由雙方共同行使

(D) 若大華取得對佩佩監護權，但未盡監護義務，小英即取得對佩佩之監護權

18. 過去有「戡亂時期預防匪諜再犯管教辦法」，其中規定人民因匪諜罪判處徒刑或受感化教育執行期滿後，如其思想行狀未改善，認有再犯之虞者，得令入勞動教育場所，強制工作嚴加管訓。此規定後遭司法院大法官宣告違憲。你認為下列哪一選項的說法正確？

(A) 過去這個辦法只屬行政命令而已，如果是以法律規定，就沒有違憲疑慮

(B) 再犯之虞定義太過模糊，違反明確性要求，如果語意明確，此規定就沒有違憲疑慮

(C) 此規定等於讓國家對人民進行思想考核，在任何情況都違反人性尊嚴保障

(D) 課以強制工作及嚴加管訓的處罰效果太強烈，如果較輕微，此規定就不違憲

19. 黃色小鴨旋風席捲全臺，造成民眾對小鴨玩具的需求大增，加上廠商無法立刻提高產能，即使以原有價格的兩倍購買，也無法解決小鴨玩具供不應求的問題。請問以下有關小鴨玩具價格措施以及對經濟效率或福祉影響的敘述何者正確？

(A) 提高玩具價格可降低需求數量、提升整體經濟效率

(B) 提高玩具價格可提高供給數量，但會損害生產者剩餘

    (C) 管制玩具價格在原價兩倍之下可保障民眾權益，避免降低經
        濟效率

    (D) 限制玩具維持原有價格，可讓經濟效率的損失達到最低

20. 不少企業將客戶服務委外經營，以美國企業為例，便將電話客戶
    服務委由印度、菲律賓等同是英語國家的公司經營。下列有關企
    業業務委外並透過跨國方式經營的敘述，何者正確？

    (A) 印度、菲律賓等國勞工可因此直接受雇於美國企業，提高當
        地人民所得

    (B) 美國勞工可因此輕易移動至外國獲得就業機會，降低美國失
        業問題

    (C) 企業基於機會成本的考量，選擇有利的經營方式以降低成本
        提高獲利

    (D) 企業考慮貧窮問題，藉此援助開發中國家，改善其與已開發
        國家的差距

21. 表 2 為 X 國生產蘋果、香蕉兩種商品的生產可能組合。該表顯示，
    生產第一、第二、第三以及第四單位蘋果的機會成本，分別為一
    單位、二單位、三單位以及四單位的香蕉。請問有關該生產可能
    組合的敘述，何者正確？

    (A) 生產第十單位香蕉的機會
        成本高於生產其他單位香
        蕉之水準

    (B) 組合乙的香蕉與蘋果總量
        大於組合丁，故 X 國不會
        以組合丁進行生產

    (C) 組合甲的香蕉與蘋果總量
        大於組合戊的水準，故組合甲的效率高於組合戊

表 2

組合	香蕉	蘋果
甲	10	0
乙	9	1
丙	7	2
丁	4	3
戊	0	4

(D) 生產第十單位香蕉的機會成本與生產第一至第四單位香蕉的
水準相同，顯示機會成本不變

22. 為避免市場買賣器官之非法行為，主管機關除立法規範器官捐贈
與移植的醫療行為外，也會依據某些原則決定受贈者的優先順
序。若不考慮其他條件，僅以極大化社會福利原則決定受贈者的
順位，請問下列何者最適合作為決策的依據？
(A) 受贈者受贈時的所得水準，因所得愈高者受贈後的存活率
愈高
(B) 受贈者願意付的價格水準，因願付愈高價者對社會的貢獻
愈大
(C) 受贈者受贈後的存活時間，如此才能讓器官捐贈發揮最大
效益
(D) 受贈者等待器官移植時間長短，等待愈短者愈先獲得適度
回饋

23. 無償住在父母提供房屋的小明，早上洗完衣服、整理完家中環境
後，便搭乘公車上班。途中經過開立發票的便利商店購買咖啡，
也在不開立發票的路邊攤購買三明治。根據以上內容，請問下列
敘述何者正確？
(A) 洗衣等家務活動雖未經市場交易，但仍可以估算的方式計入
GDP
(B) 住在父母提供之房屋，因未繳交房租，該住宅提供的勞務未
計入 GDP
(C) 在不開發票的路邊攤消費，由於也經過市場交易，所以可計
入 GDP
(D) 向開立發票的便利商店買咖啡消費，因經過市場交易，所以
計入 GDP

24. 政府可透過改變公共政策之收入與支出的方式，達到調節景氣，促進經濟發展，進而穩定整體經濟社會的目標。請問以下有關政府收入與支出的敘述，何者正確？
   (A) 政府在制訂支出政策、分配資源時，道德與公平為其權衡取捨的依據
   (B) 民間利益團體透過管道影響政府公共政策，為造成市場失靈的原因
   (C) 民眾繳納交通違規罰金、戶籍謄本工本費等，屬於政府收入項目之列
   (D) 政府增加敬老津貼支出，可達到照顧年長者與提高國內生產毛額之目標

25. 某一時期中，一位政治人物表示：臺灣經濟仍以農業為主，農民占人口總數 60% 以上，而佃農戶約占總農戶總額的 68.8%。如想要社會安定，經濟發展，必須實施此項新政策。此項新政策應是：
   (A) 三七五減租　(B) 漲價歸公　　(C) 土地國有　　(D) 肥料換穀

26. 一份民間刊物針對臺灣當時的政治現況提出幾點呼籲，包括：政府應依據憲法行政、總統不可擴權、總統不應連選連任；政府應保障基本人權，反對國民黨一黨專政，要求政府應當准許成立其他政黨；以及軍隊國家化。這份刊物最可能是：
   (A) 1910 年代的《新青年》　　(B) 1920 年代的《臺灣青年》
   (C) 1920 年代的《臺灣民報》　(D) 1950 年代的《自由中國》

27. 某一時期中，臺灣某地曾經發生官民衝突，事件平定後，政府不僅嚴屬處分參與者，也連帶處罰其左鄰右舍，科以相當於一個工人半年工資的高額罰款。這種情形最可能發生於：
   (A) 荷蘭統治時期，因漢人人數較多，荷蘭人欲以連坐法威嚇

(B) 清朝統治時期，因財政短缺，欲以高額罰款彌補軍費不足

(C) 日本統治時期，為壓制臺民反抗政府，乃採行保甲連坐制

(D) 政府遷臺之後，為阻止共黨勢力蔓延，乃實施保甲連坐制

28. 幾位同學考察「臺灣考古遺址分布圖」時，發現臺灣西部海岸很少有新石器時代遺址，各人紛紛推測造成這個現象的原因，下列哪個說法最合理？

(A) 西部人口稠密，開發過速，遺址遭破壞殆盡

(B) 二次大戰時，美軍轟炸臺灣，遺址遭到破壞

(C) 西部海岸河口沙洲發達，史前人類活動困難

(D) 因斷層經過，地震頻繁，史前人類無法定居

29. 某人參訪都城後，認為首都氣象萬千、地理形勢佳，唯須仰賴東南的糧食。他說：前朝雖重修大運河，但糧米主要以海路運輸；本朝重新疏通運河，以利南方米糧北運。這是何時的首都？

(A) 東漢洛陽　　(B) 唐代長安　　(C) 宋代汴京　　(D) 明代北京

30. 日本統治臺灣初期，總督府認為男性留辮、女性纏足都為陋習，企圖禁止，但成效不彰。然而一段時間後，臺灣人民卻開始剪辮、放足，成為風潮。殖民官員檢討，認為這股風潮並非總督府的政策收效，而是受到其他因素影響。這位官員所指的因素最可能是：

(A) 辛亥革命推翻滿清政權　　(B) 威爾遜提倡的民族自決

(C) 蔣中正推動新生活運動　　(D) 七七事變引發中日戰爭

31. 瑞芳的金瓜石曾有座戰俘營，關押了一千多名來自英、美、加拿大等國的戰俘，被迫採掘銅礦。因為生活與工作條件都差，醫藥又不足，不少戰俘命喪於此。這些戰俘的來源應是：

(A) 1860 年英法聯軍之役中被俘虜的官兵

(B) 1914 年日本與德國開戰時俘虜的戰俘
(C) 1942 年日本在東南亞戰區俘虜的戰俘
(D) 1972 年越戰期間臺灣收容的各國戰俘

32. 中共史家對臺灣歷史上的重要人物施琅有頗多研究。1980 年以前，這些史家稱施琅為「背叛明朝，投降滿清的漢奸」；1980 年以後，改稱施琅「事親至孝，接受儒家薰陶」，是一位正面人物。他們對施琅評價轉變的最合理解釋是：
(A) 學者依當局政策，調整歷史解釋立場
(B) 引用西方觀點，拋棄道德史觀的框架
(C) 發現新史料，得以重新評估施琅功過
(D) 學術交流後，認同臺灣學者觀察角度

33. 某一時期，朝廷給予官員合法占田的特權，官位越大，土地越多。同時，許多大族家中動輒擁有千百名奴僕，依法均不需負擔稅役。這最可能是哪一時期的現象？
(A) 戰國時期，戰爭頻仍，藉以爭取大族合作
(B) 晉朝，世家大族基礎雄厚，皇帝亦需妥協
(C) 南宋，為對抗北方金人，以特權換取支持
(D) 清初，南方未統一，以優厚條件吸引歸順

34. 一位外國軍官在家書中提到：我們如果能攻下這座城市，將可以就近補充煤炭。但該城的砲臺頗為堅固，據說是德國工程師設計的，而且中國指揮官帶來自己一手訓練的部隊，地方士紳也組織民兵投入戰場，戰爭可能不會太順利。這位外國軍官所參加的戰爭是：
(A) 1840 年鴉片戰爭　　　　　(B) 1860 年英法聯軍
(C) 1874 年牡丹社事件　　　　(D) 1884 年中法戰爭

35. 老師在課堂中介紹西歐某一時期時提到：當時君主積極發展工商業，力求增加稅收；並改革法律制度，興辦教育事業，以提高行政效率及國民素質。這堂課的主題應是：
(A) 中古時期的莊園經濟活動　　(B) 十二世紀的東西文化交流
(C) 十六世紀西歐的重商主義　　(D) 十八世紀的開明專制理念

36. 某地位於歐洲通往中國的航路上，早在 1819 年，英國商船便在此建立交易據點，逐漸發展成繁榮港口。二次世界大戰期間，日軍曾攻占此地，控制三年多。1945 年，日本投降，該地重歸英國管轄，但當地人民爭取自主，先脫離英國統治，進而獨立建國。這個國家是：
(A) 泰國　　　　(B) 新加坡　　　(C) 越南　　　　(D) 印度

37. 1792 年，英國派遣馬戛爾尼出使中國，使團於 9 月底乘船自英國出發，1793 年 8 月 5 日才抵達天津。1878 年，中國派遣曾紀澤為駐英國、法國欽差大臣，於 11 月 22 日自上海乘船赴任，1879 年 1 月 1 日便抵達法國馬賽港。這期間，哪一項重大變化縮短了航行的時間？
(A) 美國發明航空器　　　　(B) 蘇伊士運河通航
(C) 海圖製作更精良　　　　(D) 公海航行較安全

38. 某次戰爭之後，戰勝國要求：挑起戰事者要割地、賠款。有人呼籲：如果賠償金額遠超出發動戰爭者所能承擔，一定會造成經濟困境，引發民怨，無論任何一方都難逃捲入的命運，甚至引發下一場戰爭。不幸言中，不久之後，各國又捲入衝突之中。此人最可能是：
(A) 1815 年維也納會議中的奧地利首相梅特涅
(B) 1871 年德法戰爭後德意志帝國首相俾斯麥

(C) 1919 年巴黎和會召開時的英國代表凱因斯

(D) 1945 年二次大戰結束後的美國總統杜魯門

39. 西方學術傳到中國時，引起許多人的學習興趣。某位皇帝對數學非常有興趣，儘管國事紛擾，南方還有重臣叛變，他仍與幾位數學家一起研究科學，計算各種幾何問題。這位皇帝最可能是：

(A) 向馬可波羅學習西方科學的元朝皇帝

(B) 在宮廷討論歐基里德數學的明朝皇帝

(C) 向耶穌會傳教士學習數學的清初皇帝

(D) 在同文館學習數學、幾何的清末皇帝

40. 十八世紀中，閩南移民來臺後，多聚族而居；同姓之人，常共同興建祠堂，以強化關係。這種現象足以說明清代臺灣漢人社會的哪一項特色？

(A) 移墾社會重視地緣關係　　(B) 傳統宗族強調血緣連結

(C) 弱勢移民強調團結合作　　(D) 原鄉信仰深入移民社會

41. 圖 1 是近代新式學堂教科書的課文及插圖，從課文的敘述與插圖的呈現，其內容最可能反映了哪一種時代思潮？

(A) 尊君思想，以維護皇室地位

(B) 強化團練，以防止內亂再起

(C) 排滿思潮，以推翻滿清政權

(D) 保國強種，以對抗列強侵略

圖 1

42. 某地原為希臘人活動區域，後來才有其他民族移入，包括羅馬尼亞人、土耳其人、克羅埃西亞人、波士尼亞人、斯洛維尼亞人與

馬其頓人。居民分別信奉基督教與伊斯蘭教；基督教信仰又以希臘正教為主。當地曾經建立聯邦制國家，卻爆發內戰，民族紛爭至今不斷。這個地區是：

(A) 伊比利半島

(B) 巴爾幹半島

(C) 克里米亞半島

(D) 安那托利亞高原

43. 表 3 是一場戰爭之中各國人口損失的統計：

表 3

國家	百分比 (%)	國家	百分比 (%)
波蘭	20	德國	6.6
南斯拉夫	12.5	法國	1.3
希臘	7	英國	0.8
蘇聯	9		

這場戰爭是：

(A) 三十年戰爭

(B) 克里米亞戰爭

(C) 第一次世界大戰

(D) 第二次世界大戰

44. 一位外籍人士評論：「中國人與歐洲人並無衝突，並不憎惡他們，中國人只是憎惡歐洲資本家和唯資本家之命是從的歐洲各國政府。這些人到中國只是欺騙、掠奪和鎮壓中國人；為了販賣鴉片的權利，對中國作戰；用傳教的鬼話來掩蓋掠奪政策，以便自己大發橫財；中國人難道能不痛恨他們嗎？」這位人士最可能是：

(A) 希望來華通商的英國商務監督義律

(B) 宣揚共產主義的蘇聯革命領袖列寧

(C) 主張門戶開放的美國國務卿海約翰

(D) 提倡東亞共榮的日本首相近衛文麿

45. 老師在黑板上懸掛一幅地圖（如
圖 2），圖中將日本領域分別以
黑色及灰色標示。這幅地圖最可
能是反映哪一時期的東亞情勢？

    (A) 1871 年
    (B) 1905 年
    (C) 1935 年
    (D) 1971 年

圖 2

46. 某一時期中，英國議員知道普魯士已經實施強迫入學的政策，而
英國許多兒童仍然沒有受過任何教育。於是通過法案，設置教育
部，並提出「初等教育法」，撥款興學，同時要求父母督促 5 到
12 歲的兒童上學。這是何時的情況？
    (A) 十七世紀後期　　　　　(B) 十八世紀中期
    (C) 十九世紀後期　　　　　(D) 二十世紀中期

47. 旅行社推出城市觀光行程，訴求：「大唐遺風」，說明此行可以
參訪當地的唐式建築，體驗茶道，參拜佛寺，也可以參觀法律文
書的收藏，領略中國唐朝的風情。這個行程最可能是：
    (A) 京都物語　　　　　　　(B) 首爾采風
    (C) 河內漫遊　　　　　　　(D) 上海驚艷

48. 一個民族在中國建立政權後，國君諮詢學者，以了解統治中國之
術。一位漢人建議：「為政應以原本法令為主，並參酌中國制度」。
這種說法引起該民族的王公大臣反對，認為中國僅是帝國的一部
分，不必重視，而統治者也不需採用亡國者的制度。這個統治民
族是：
    (A) 女真　　　　(B) 鮮卑　　　　(C) 契丹　　　　(D) 蒙古

49. 一位同學想在暑假期間去海外遊學，他希望能利用這機會學習英語、認識當地的原住民文化，並體驗獨特的冰河地形和活火山景觀。下列哪個地區是該同學的最佳選擇？
    (A) 夏威夷　　　(B) 菲律賓　　　(C) 紐西蘭　　　(D) 愛爾蘭

50. 2013 年年初，瑞典財政官員在訪問南非後，認為非洲對於瑞典經濟發展具有相當大的助益，因此促成了以紡織業為主的經貿團，至衣索比亞、坦尚尼亞進行投資環境的考察。對於瑞典紡織業而言，非洲具有下列哪些區位優勢？
    甲、棉花原料來源供應充足；乙、可以避開亞洲企業競爭；
    丙、與瑞典本地時間差異大；丁、工廠勞力薪資便宜低廉。
    (A) 甲乙　　　(B) 甲丁　　　(C) 乙丙　　　(D) 丙丁

51. 以下是關於某個國家氣候與傳統農業活動的描述：「三到五月間因土地過於乾硬而無法種植水稻。六月雨季開始後，農民必須趕緊播種，才能在十月雨季結束後收割。」該國最可能是下列何國？
    (A) 日本　　　(B) 臺灣　　　(C) 印度　　　(D) 印尼

52. 圖 3 為中國某地區的風景油畫作品。該作品的取景地區具有下列哪項特色？

圖 3

    (A) 曾受冰河的侵蝕作用，山脊間成為交通要道
    (B) 土壤聚鐵鋁化作用旺盛，耕地養分含量有限
    (C) 農業生產以麥作為主，當地居民以麵為主食
    (D) 盛行風向多屬偏西風，夏冬降雨無明顯差異

53. 照片 1 是美國某種氣象災害的景觀，圖 4 的甲、乙、丙、丁代表
    美國的四個地區。該種氣象災害最可能出現在哪區？
    (A) 甲
    (B) 乙
    (C) 丙
    (D) 丁

照片 1　　　　　　　　　　　圖 4

54. 1998 年，捷克、波蘭、匈牙利、斯洛維尼亞、愛沙尼亞等國開始
    與歐盟展開入會談判。2000 年，保加利亞、拉脫維亞、羅馬尼亞、
    斯洛伐克、立陶宛等國也陸續與歐盟展開入會談判。至 2007 年，
    這些國家都順利加入歐盟。下列哪種現象最有可能在這些國家加
    入歐盟後發生？
    (A) 歐盟每年必須增加預算，以供作縮小區域差距的基金
    (B) 歐洲議會有更大的發言權，可增進歐盟的民主正當性
    (C) 西歐產業結構得以快速轉型，各國之間貧富差距縮短
    (D) 歐洲法院可更有效的審理和裁決會員國之間各種爭執

55. 圖 5 是全球不同緯度地區雪線、氣溫和降水量的關係圖。根據此
    圖，可獲得下列哪些結論？
    甲、南半球地區平均降水量多寡和平均氣溫高低成正比；
    乙、北半球地區平均降水量多寡和平均氣溫高低成反比；
    丙、緯度 45 度以上地區，平均氣溫高低和雪線高低成正比；
    丁、緯度 30 度以下地區，平均降水量多寡和雪線高低成反比。

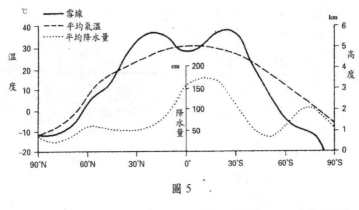

圖 5

(A) 甲乙　　　　(B) 甲丁　　　　(C) 乙丙　　　　(D) 丙丁

56. 照片 2 是某人正午時間，站在赤道正上方，面向西方，從上向下拍攝的照片。該照片的拍攝日期和下列哪個節氣最接近？

照片 2

(A) 立春（2 月 4 日或 5 日）
(B) 芒種（6 月 6 日或 7 日）
(C) 寒露（10 月 8 日或 9 日）
(D) 冬至（12 月 22 日或 23 日）

57. 近年來，全球電視購物及網路電子商務等無店鋪消費額比重增加，逐漸在零售業中占有一席之地。無店鋪販賣的興起與下列哪兩個社會經濟環境變遷的關係最密切？
甲、傳統產業外移嚴重；乙、交通革新快速發展；
丙、城鄉差距日益擴大；丁、物流產業迅速興起。
(A) 甲丙　　　　(B) 甲丁　　　　(C) 乙丙　　　　(D) 乙丁

58. 圖6爲某國2013年的人口
金字塔圖。該國人口中，
有40%的穆斯林，31%的
東正教徒，15%的天主教徒。
該國具有下列何種特色？

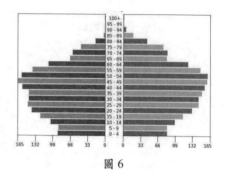

圖6

(A) 外國移入人口衆多

(B) 經濟呈現高度發展

(C) 地處於政治緩衝帶

(D) 種姓制度根深蒂固

59. 2013年9月29日，上海自由貿易區正式掛牌成立。自由貿易區
的企圖之一是：希望鼓勵跨國公司來此建立亞太地區總部，籌辦
可整合貿易、物流、結算等功能的營運中心，拓展專用帳戶的服
務貿易、跨境收付和融資功能，使之成爲國際貿易結算中心。上
海自由貿易區的成立，對下列哪個都市的經濟發展影響最大？

(A) 大阪　　　　(B) 天津　　　　(C) 香港　　　　(D) 新加坡

60-61爲題組

◎ 圖7是某半島經過處理後的衛星影
像。請問：

60. 圖7所示的地區，其位置具有下
列哪項特性？

(A) 位處板塊接觸地帶

(B) 土壤以草原黑土和栗鈣土爲主

(C) 海洋性氣候和季風氣候過渡區

(D) 墨西哥灣流和拉布拉多寒流交會區

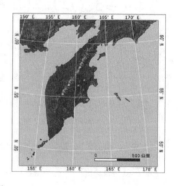

圖7

61. 該半島所屬的國家，是下列哪個國際組織的成員？
    (A) 歐洲聯盟（EU）
    (B) 北美自由貿易區（NAFTA）
    (C) 石油輸出國家組織（OPEC）
    (D) 亞洲太平洋經濟合作會議（APEC）

62-63 為題組

◎ 新疆地區民族多元，居民的宗教信仰和生活方式頗有差異，經常
　發生社會騷動。中國政府為了維持新疆地區社會秩序，於 2011年
　3 月起在烏魯木齊、北京等地，透過手機基地台獲得手機用戶的
　即時位置，以了解當地民眾聚散的即時情況。請問：

62. 新疆地區除漢族以外的居民，其宗教信仰和生活方式，和下列哪
    個文化區的居民最相似？
    (A) 西方文化區
    (B) 南亞文化區
    (C) 東南亞文化區
    (D) 西亞—北非文化區

63. 下列哪項技術最適用於分析新疆地區手機用戶的位置資料，以了
    解其聚集情況？
    (A) 地理資訊系統
    (B) 地圖投影判讀
    (C) 航照判釋分析
    (D) 遙感探測技術

64-65 為題組

◎ 照片 3 是世界四個地區的傳統民宅建築。請問：

照片 3

64. 從地基設計和屋頂形式的角度思考，照片 3 中傳統民宅建築形式的地區差異，和下列哪個因素的關係最密切？
(A) 日照時數　　(B) 宗教信仰　　(C) 降水多寡　　(D) 人口疏密

65. 從自然景觀帶的角度來看，哪種傳統民宅分布區，單位面積生物量大，環境破壞後則生態系不易回復？
(A) 甲　　　　(B) 乙　　　　(C) 丙　　　　(D) 丁

66-67 為題組

◎ 甲企業生產顯示器、液晶電視與筆記型電腦用面板，位於臺灣南部科學工業園區的總部，負責設計、研發與行銷；成品組裝基地設於浙江寧波和廣東佛山。該企業所需零組件包括韓國的彩色濾光片，美國的素玻璃，日本的驅動 IC 和偏光片以及臺灣的背光模組。近兩年來，半數的背光模組重要零組件「增亮膜」由臺灣的乙廠商供應，但乙廠商不以此為滿足，決定再投資 20 億美元，研發新產品。請問：

66. 甲企業位於臺灣南部科學工業園區的總部負責設計、研發與行銷，
　　不涉足生產製造的部分，這樣的型態最能反映下列工業發展的哪
　　項特性？
　　(A) 進口替代　　(B) 知識經濟　　(C) 三角貿易　　(D) 聚集經濟

67. 乙廠商生產的「增亮膜」，雖占有近半的市場，但決策者仍不以
　　此為滿足，而進一步投資研發新產品。乙廠商的營運策略，和下
　　列高科技產業的哪項特性有關？
　　(A) 空間分工鏈緊密　　　　　(B) 即時生產需求強
　　(C) 產品生命週期短　　　　　(D) 市場資金流動快

68-70 為題組

◎ 圖 8 是臺灣某地區的地圖，圖中數字為地形等高線的數值，單位
　　為公尺。照片 4 是在圖上某處拍攝的一幢民居。請問：

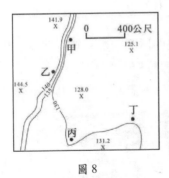

　　　　　圖 8　　　　　　　　　　　　　照片 4

68. 涵蓋圖 8 的整體範圍最可能屬於下列何種地形？
　　(A) 平原　　　　(B) 台地　　　　(C) 盆地　　　　(D) 沖積扇

69. 圖 8 中甲、乙、丙、丁是三合院所在地點，子、丑、寅、卯是拍
　　攝照片的地點。照片 4 的拍攝方向最可能是下列何者？

(A) 從丑向甲拍攝　　　　　　(B) 從子向乙拍攝

(C) 從卯向丙拍攝　　　　　　(D) 從寅向丁拍攝

70. 假設圖 8 中子、丑、寅、卯代表四處農地坵塊。在日治時代早期，這四處的土地利用，有三處為水田，一處為茶園。根據圖中等高線分布的資訊，從天然灌溉水源的角度思考，其中哪塊農地最可能是茶園？

(A) 子　　　　　(B) 丑　　　　　(C) 寅　　　　　(D) 卯

71-72 為題組

◎ 照片 5 為臺灣四個火車站的舊式站牌。請問：

71. 1919 年，日人為興建日月潭水力發電廠，曾鋪設一條鐵路，以搬運工程所需機具與建材。照片 5 的四個車站中，哪個車站位於該條鐵路路線上？

(A) 新城　　　　(B) 龍泉　　　　(C) 豐富　　　　(D) 六塊厝

72. 這四個車站皆與長度超過 50 公里的溪流相鄰。其中哪個車站旁的溪流，其河口堆積物質的平均顆粒最大？

(A) 新城　　　　(B) 龍泉　　　　(C) 豐富　　　　(D) 六塊厝

照片 5

103年度學科能力測驗社會科試題詳解

單選題

1. **B**
   【解析】 顧里「鏡中自我」，是指個人自我概念的形成，是在生活
   中與人不斷互動而來，經由他人當借鏡反映出自己，或從
   別人的回饋中，統合出自我的形象。因此依題意「教練批
   評指責其反應太慢，他因此認為自己很笨、能力不好」，
   大明因教練的批評而否定自己的能力，即屬「鏡中自我」。

2. **C**
   【解析】 平等原則的精神在於「相同事務，相同對待；不同事務，
   不同對待」，因此
   (C) 同為外籍配偶，但政府對於大陸籍配偶的規範，卻
   　　 與其他外籍配偶不同，恐違反「平等原則」。
   (A) 為合理的差別待遇
   (B) (D) 則都是促進文化交流或保護。

3. **B**
   【解析】 性別刻板印象，指社會將男人或女人的性格特質過度簡
   化的看法。
   (B) 而性別平等委員會，應是為保障性別平等而設，因
   　　 並非只有「女性」才會受到性別歧視等不平等對待。
   (A) 並未涉及性別議題
   (C) (D) 皆未違反性別平等精神。

4. **A**
   【解析】 (B) 世界衛生大會，為聯合國轄下的政府間組織
   (C) (D) 則為政府間的經貿組織。

5. **C**

【解析】 媒體從業人員應本著新聞專業及遵守新聞倫理,避免流於戲謔及新聞娛樂化的情況。

6. **B**

【解析】 (A) (D) 屬全球化

(B) 全球咖啡連鎖店,考量臺灣人對於茶飲的喜好 (即為題意中所指,當地文化和社會特性及需求當地素材)

(C) 無關全球化。

7-8 為題組

7. **B**

【解析】 先依題意「該國國會總共有 20 個席次, 政黨代表與地方選區席次各半,並且各自計算」,可知該國採「並立制」,因此各黨當選情況如下:

行政區	當選人所屬政黨　(得票最高者當選)			
	甲	乙	丙	丁
1		乙		
2	甲			
3			丙	
4	甲			
5				丁
6			丙	
7	甲			
8		乙		
9	甲			
10		乙		
政黨得票率(政黨代表應分配席次)	30%x10 席 = 3 席	50%x10 席 = 5 席	10%x10 席 = 1 席	10%x10 席 = 1 席
各黨總計	7 席	8 席	3 席	2 席

因此最大黨為 (B) 乙黨。

8. **C**

【解析】 (A) 甲黨（7 席），因此只能與丙黨結盟，才都能組成過半多數政府

(B) 乙黨（8 席），並未過半

(C) 丙黨（3 席）與若與甲、乙政黨結盟，皆可過半，因此可扮演關鍵角色

(D) 丁黨（2 席），雖是國會中席次最少的政黨，但仍可能與乙黨合作。

9. **B**

【解析】 1991 年，我國宣布終止動員戡亂時期，一反過去的緊張對立的主張，不再視中共政權為叛亂團體。符合題意「兩岸關係從對立走向和緩」。

10. **C**

【解析】 我國歷經七次修憲，在憲政上有許多變革，但題意題問「何者不是這幾次修憲的成果」，(C) 明定大法官會議為釋憲機制……，此為「憲法本文」明定的分權制衡機制，並非藉由修憲而確立。

11. **C**

【解析】 我國採「五權分立」的體制，其中調查權（彈劾權）歸屬於監察院，因此

(C) 立法委員，無權發動調查權糾舉彈劾失職官員。

(D) 國會本職為監督行政機關，因此可於法令許可範圍內監督施政。

12. **D**

【解析】 (A) 人民依法上街遊行，但述求內容不具「正當性」

(B) 符合「正當性」及「合法性」

(C) 違法監聽，且違反民主精神，不符合「正當性」及「合法性」

(D) 「鄰縣受災時未搶救」並非市長的法定職權（符合「合法性」），但因民眾觀感不佳，而下台(屬「正當性」)。

13. **A**

【解析】 (A) 「假設法律生效『施行後』」請注意，題目是問『施行後』，換言之，若要修改只能由立法院（委員）或提案機關（如行政院）提出修正草案，再由立院依立法程序修法，若通過後再呈請總統公布。至於「(D)行政院長經總統核可後，向立法院提出覆議案要求修改」，是在立院三讀後，總統尚未公布前（法律尚未生效），政院可依法提出覆議。

14. **B**

【解析】 (A) 沒錢購買食物，屬「生存權」

(C) 以網路及手機等傳遞訊息，屬言論自由及秘密通訊自由

(D) 透過抗爭使總統負起政治責任下台，屬人民的反抗權或罷免權（不確定，因題目並未具體說明總統下台，是否經人民投票罷免）。

15. **D**

【解析】 (A) 雖憲法保障人民集會自由，但亦不得濫用自由，因此其行為不一定完全合法，

(D) 國家為防止妨礙他人自由或增進公共利益，法律可合理限制示威抗議活動

(B) 人民示威抗議，為憲法保障的自由權

(C) 雖我國現行「集會遊行法」規定遊行採「許可制」，但該制度長久以來為人詬病，反對者以為該制度恐使行政機關，可藉核准與否的權限，限制人民的集會遊行自由。因此 (D) 相較於 (C) 更為適合。

16. **D**
　【解析】　依題意「檢察官開庭偵訊後，決定將他收押」，我國羈押
　　　　　　權已回歸法院，應由檢察官依法向法院聲請羈押，並由
　　　　　　法院核准。

17. **C**
　【解析】　民法修正後，對於子女監護權的歸屬，改採以「兒童最
　　　　　　佳利益」為考量，同學可依此觀念為基礎，作為判斷參
　　　　　　考，
　　　　　　(A) (B) 雖小英取得對佩佩之監護權，但大華仍為佩佩的
　　　　　　　　　父親（仍應負扶養之義務），因此是否給予探視權應
　　　　　　　　　由法院決定
　　　　　　(D) 因現行民法以「兒童最佳利益」為考量，因此法院決
　　　　　　　　定監護權歸屬時，並非只會考量父或母，因此若大華
　　　　　　　　取得對佩佩監護權，但未盡監護義務，小英「不一
　　　　　　　　定」即取得對佩佩之監護權。

18. **C**
　【解析】　依題意「戡亂時期預防匪諜再犯管教辦法」以人民的
　　　　　　「思想行狀」改善與否作為考量，顯然在進行人民思想
　　　　　　的控制，恐有違反憲法對於言論自由的保障，因此
　　　　　　(A) 縱使改以法律規定，仍有違憲疑慮
　　　　　　(B) (D) 關鍵在於「思想控制」即屬違憲，與語意是否明
　　　　　　　　　確或處罰方式之寬嚴，並無關係。

19. **A**
　【解析】　(A) 提高玩具價格，將使供給增加，需求數量下降，並出
　　　　　　　　現「供不應求」的情況，因此需求價格將上升，效益
　　　　　　　　上升，有助提升整體經濟效率
　　　　　　(B) 提高玩具價格可提高供給數量，並使生產者剩餘增加
　　　　　　(C) 政府管制價格，將造成「絕對損失」，會減損經濟
　　　　　　　　效率

(D) 在需求大增前提下，若限制玩具維持原有價格，將使「供不應求」的情況更嚴重，反減損經濟效率。

20. **C**

【解析】 (A) (D) 跨國企業尋求廉價勞動力以降低成本，因此印度、菲律賓等國勞工，未必能因此獲得較高收入，甚至可能出現剝削的情況

(B) 跨國企業透過網際網路等資訊設備，進行跨國外包，因此美國勞工並不會移動到國外就業，相反的美國本土的工作機會會流失的更為嚴重。

21. **A**

【解析】 依題意表 2「X 國生產蘋果、香蕉兩種商品的生產可能組合」，因此蘋果及香蕉兩產品分別位在生產可能曲線上，由表中可得知，生產第一～四單位香蕉（4 單位），機會成本為 1 單位蘋果；生產第五～七

表 2

組合	香蕉	蘋果
甲	10	0
乙	9	1
丙	7	2
丁	4	3
戊	0	4

單位香蕉（3 單位），機會成本為 1 單位蘋果；生產第八～九單位香蕉（1 單位），機會成本為 1 單位蘋果；生產第十單位香蕉（1 單位），機會成本為 1 單位蘋果；因此可知生產越多香蕉，所需付出的機會成本越高（機會成本遞增）。

(A) (D) 第十單位香蕉的機會成本與高於前面香蕉的生產

(B) (C) 組合甲、乙皆位在生產可能曲線上，因此皆為資源充分運用的生產情況，X 國都可採用。

22. **C**

【解析】 依題意「以極大化社會福利原則」決定受贈者的順位，依此推斷此贈與行為主要的效益在於延長受贈者的生命，因此應以受贈者受贈後的存活時間作為決策依據為最適合。

23. **D**

【解析】 (A) (C) 家務活動及不開發票的路邊攤，其生產雖有價值，
但因估計困難因此不計入GDP

(B) 為避免低估GDP，因此自有房屋必須「設算租金」，
住在父母提供之房屋，仍應「設算租金」應計入
GDP。

24. **C**（送分）

【解析】 (A) 政府應以成本與效益作為其權衡取捨的依據

(B) 民間利益團體透過管道影響政府公共政策，非但政
策無法充分發揮作用，甚至引發更大的問題，稱為
政府失靈

(C) 交通違規屬行政罰，因此應為罰鍰，而非「罰金」

(D) 敬老津貼支出，屬「移轉性支出」，不計入國內生產
毛額。

25. **A**

【解析】 (A) 民國 38 年，臺灣實行「三七五減租」，規定地租不
可超過佃農收穫總量 37.5%，改善佃農的生活，有
助社會安定，經濟發展；

(B) (C) 是孫文民生主義的理想，在台灣根本未實施；

(D) 中華民國遷台後，早期「農業培養工業」，採行肥
料換穀措施，政府獲取利潤，農民損失不少收益，
民怨四起，未助社會安定。

26. **D**

【解析】 (D) 1950 年代雷震、殷海光等人借《自由中國》雜誌，
提倡民主、自由；主張「政府應依據憲法行政、總
統不可擴權、總統不應連選連任；政府應保障基本
人權，反對國民黨一黨專政，要求政府應當准許成
立其他政黨；以及軍隊國家化」，甚至提出「反攻大
陸無望論」，建設台灣為一個獨立的國家，後來發生
「雷震事件」(民國49年)；

    (A) 1910 年代的《新青年》是民初新文化運動時期的雜誌，主張全盤西化，打倒孔家店等，與題意無關；

    (B) 1920 年代的《臺灣青年》

    (C) 1920 年代的《臺灣民報》皆為日本統治時期臺灣人創辦的報刊雜誌，不可能出現「總統不可擴權、總統不應連選連任」、「反對國民黨一黨專政」等內容，故題幹不合。

27. **C**

【解析】(C) 日本統治台灣時期，透過總督統治臺灣，並藉警察與保甲制度（定十戶為甲，十甲為保，設甲長、保正；實行連保連坐責任），進行嚴密的社會控制；

    (A) 荷蘭在臺灣未實施連坐法；

    (B) 清領時期曾在台灣推行聯庄制度，用來教化遊民、管理地方治安，非以高額罰款彌補軍費不足；

    (D) 政府遷臺後，為阻止共黨勢力蔓延，嚴懲匪諜及知匪不報者，且課以刑責。

28. **A**

【解析】(A) 臺灣西部海岸很少有新石器時代遺址主因是台灣發展由南而北，由西而東，「西部人口稠密，開發過速，遺址遭破壞殆盡」；

    (B) 二次大戰時，美軍轟炸臺灣時，西部未遭到全面的破壞，不可能使臺灣西部海岸很少有新石器時代遺址；

    (C) 西部海岸河口沙洲發達，史前人類活動困難，也可能被颱風等破壞，但不至於影響新石器時代遺址的形成；

    (D) 臺灣地震雖然頻繁，東部不少於西部，且臺灣西部影響人類無法定居的大地震次數不多。

29. **D**

【解析】(D) 由題幹「前朝雖重修大運河，但糧米主要以海路運輸；本朝重新疏通運河」可知是明代北京，因隋朝

雖開鑿五條運河，使唐朝時華北政治軍事的穩定有賴於南方經濟支援，但元代時隋朝開鑿的運河已阻塞，忽必烈重修聯繫南北的大運河，明成祖在位時重新疏通運河，以利南方米糧北運。

30. **A**

【解析】(A) 日本統治臺灣初期，總督府認為台灣「三大惡習」－吸鴉片、辮髮、纏足，臺灣解纏、斷髮運動發端於 1900 年至 1914 年，如 1900 年黃玉階等在臺北成立「天然足會」及「斷髮不改裝會」等，至 1915 年日本政府將剪辮、放足納入保甲規約中，又受到辛亥革命推翻滿清政權影響，中國人已剪掉辮子，台灣人才減少辮髮纏足習俗；

(B) 美國總統威爾遜提倡「民族自決」是在第一次世界大戰後提倡，強調各民族在政治等的自決，與剪辮、放足運動屬於社會習俗改良性質不同；

(C) 蔣中正推動新生活運動是在北伐後的 1934 年；

(D) 七七事變引發中日戰爭於 1937 年，這兩項的時間與臺灣剪辮、放足的時間不符。

31. **C**

【解析】(C) 此題關鍵處在「金瓜石曾有座戰俘營，關押了一千多名來自英、美、加拿大等國的戰俘」，第二次大戰期間日本攻佔中國之外，又佔領香港、東南亞等地，俘虜不少各國戰俘；其他戰役不可能俘虜這多國戰俘。

32. **A**

【解析】(A) 1980 年以前，中共史家稱施琅為「背叛明朝，投降滿清的漢奸」；1980 年以後，改稱施琅「事親至孝，接受儒家薰陶」，是一位正面人物，1980 年起中共對施琅歷史地位重新評估，是和他們對台的政策改變－鼓吹兩岸統一有關，施琅率兵「收復」臺灣一事成了中共對台政策的歷史根據；另一方面鄭成功

歷史地位的提昇，也和「民族主義意識的被強調」以及「政治宣傳」有關，國民黨推崇鄭成功的「反清復明」，因為這符合反攻復國的宣傳，而中共強調鄭成功驅除荷人一事，可用來強化中共解放台灣的口號。

33. **B**

【解析】 (B) 由題幹「朝廷給予官員合法占田的特權」、「許多大族家中動輒擁有千百名奴僕，依法均不需負擔稅役」可知是 (B) 晉朝，世家大族基礎雄厚，皇帝亦需妥協；

(A) 世家大族興起於漢代後，戰國時期沒有；

(C) 士族沒落於唐代黃巢亂後，宋朝士族政治結束，南宋不需要以特權換取支持；

(D) 清朝沒有施行占田制度來吸引歸順者。

34. **D**

【解析】 (D) 由題幹「我們如果能攻下這座城市，將可以就近補充煤炭」，指的是台灣基隆，中法戰爭時法軍曾攻到此處，清廷派劉銘傳來臺，劉銘傳帶來自己一手訓練的部隊－淮軍士兵，地方士紳也組織民兵投入戰場－臺中霧峰林朝棟率臺勇協防；

(A) 1840 年鴉片戰爭時中國仍是天朝上國的心態，對「船堅炮利」所知有限，不可能「砲臺頗為堅固，據說是德國工程師設計的」；

(B) 1860 年英法聯軍戰火未波及台灣，且戰敗後才開始「船堅炮利」的自強運動；

(C) 1874 年牡丹社事件發生在屏東恆春，事後沈葆楨才在台灣築砲台。

35. **D**

【解析】 (D) 十八世紀歐洲君主受到啟蒙運動思想影響，表現開明形象，俄國女皇凱薩琳二世與普魯士腓特烈大帝等實行開明專制；當時君主積極發展工商業，力求增加稅收；並改革法律制度，興辦教育事業，以提高行政效率及國民素質；

(A) 中古時期的莊園經濟活動屬於自給自足的農業經濟，工商業不發達；

(B) 十二世紀的東西文化交流，應指「十字軍東征」，促使城市商業復興，中等（產）階級興起，但未改革法律制度，興辦教育事業；

(C) 十六世紀西歐的重商主義，**各國政府想盡辦法來提升本國貨品的競爭力，陷入激烈的商業競爭，甚至演變成武力衝突**，未改革法律制度，興辦教育事業。

36. **B**

【解析】 (B) 新加坡位於歐洲通往中國的航路上，早期英國商船便在此建立交易據點，逐漸 發展成繁榮港口，二次世界大戰期間，日軍曾攻占此地，1945 年日本投降，該地重歸英國管轄，1963 年新加坡連同當時的馬來亞聯合邦、砂拉越以及北婆羅洲（現沙巴）共組成立馬來西亞聯邦，脫離英國統治，後來新加坡脫離馬來西亞獨立建國；

　　　　 (A) 泰國在十九世紀及二十世紀初，西方列強入侵亞洲時，未受西方列強統治；

　　　　 (C) 越南在十九世紀時爲法國殖民地；

　　　　 (D) 印度十八世紀淪爲英國殖民地，但日本在二次大戰時未占領印度。

37. **B**

【解析】 (B) 蘇伊士運河（Suez Canal）通航於 1869 年，處於埃及西奈半島西側，爲溝通地中海與紅海的交通要道，是連結歐洲與亞洲間的南北雙向水運，不必繞過非洲南端的好望角，可縮短約一半的航程；

　　　　 (A) 美國萊特兄弟（Wright brothers）於二十世紀初（1903年）發明能夠飛行的航空器，時間與題幹不符；

　　　　 (C) 「海圖」又稱「航海圖」，是精確測繪海洋水域和沿岸地物的專門地圖，最早的航海圖爲盛行於 14 世紀

的波特蘭型海圖（portolan chart），航行者藉助這些
海圖，確保在海洋上之方向，後來海圖製作更精良，
但時間與題幹不符；

(D) 十七世紀荷蘭格勞秀斯（Hugo Grotius）曾發表《海
洋自由論》，主張「一切國家都擁有自由出入公海的
權利」，公海航行較安全，**這種「公海自由」的法學
觀念不只合乎新與海權國家荷蘭的利益，且象徵著
「民族國家」及「商業資本主義」已成為主力**，但
與題幹無關。

38. **C**

【解析】(C) 第一次世界戰後的巴黎和會，戰勝國對德國簽訂
《凡爾賽和約》，要求割地、巨額賠款等，造成德
國後來發生嚴重的通貨膨脹，經濟瀕於破產，社會
秩序混亂，希特勒的納粹黨以撕毀《凡爾賽和約》，
爭取人民支持，迅速擴展勢力取得政權，引發下一
場戰爭－第二次世界大戰；

(A) 1815 年維也納會議是為解決拿破崙帝國瓦解後的歐
洲政局，由梅特涅操縱會議，挑起戰爭者－法國未遭
到戰勝國報復，會中未要求法國割地賠款，而是協助
波旁王朝復辟，與題意不合；

(B) 挑起戰事的德國是戰勝國，不可能被要求割地、賠款；

(D) 二次大戰結束後戰勝國對對發動戰爭者（戰敗國）
－軸心國處置立場不一致，並沒有採取嚴厲作為，如
報復性賠款等，與題意不合。

39. **C**

【解析】(C) 明末清初耶穌會傳教士到中國，將西方科技介紹給國
人，清聖祖因愛西算，曾據西士所編的講義撰『數理
精蘊』一書，題幹中「某位皇帝對數學非常有興趣，
儘管國事紛擾，南方還有重臣叛變，他仍與幾位數學
家一起研究科學，計算各種幾何問題」，最可能是清
初康熙皇帝；國事紛擾指臺灣鄭氏反清復明等，南方

重臣叛變指的是三藩之亂；

(A) 十三世紀時義大利商人馬可波羅東來中國經商，受元世祖忽必烈欣賞，但馬可波羅並未向元朝皇帝傳授西方學術；

(B) 明末西學多在士大夫階層進行；

(D) 清末在英法聯軍後，推動船堅砲利的自強運動，需要熟悉外國語文的人才，清廷於同治元年在北京設立同文館，以培植交涉翻譯人才，北京同文館是中國最早自辦新式學堂，入學學生資格要求頗高，但非皇帝。

40. **B**

【解析】 (B) 清領前期，中國移民透過血緣關係，形成各宗族組織；先是「唐山祖」型，係指選擇大陸原鄉較顯赫的同姓祖先為祭祀對象，參加成員不一定有血緣關係，目的只在凝聚同姓情誼，以求互助團結；後是「開臺祖」型，以來臺第一代祖先或其後裔為祭祀對象，其成員率皆開臺祖後代，彼此間有清楚的系譜關係，題幹中有「同姓之人，常共同興建祠堂，以強化關係」，可知傳統宗族不管「唐山祖」或「開臺祖」皆強調血緣連結；

(C) 與是否弱勢移民無關；

(D) 清朝閩南移民來臺後，多聚族而居，繼續供奉原鄉信仰神明，如保生大帝（大道公）、清水祖師、開漳聖王等，與題幹「同姓之人，常共同興建祠堂」不符。

41. **D**

【解析】 (D) 清末屢受外力衝擊，「師夷長技以制夷」模仿西法的運動勃興，自強運動和戊戌變法時曾設新式學堂，但零星而分散，「庚子後新政」（慈禧變法）後興辦各級新式學堂，此一新式學堂教科書的內容展現了軍人英勇的形象，反映「保國強種，以對抗列強侵略」的時代思潮；

(A) 新式學堂內容以學習西方事物為主，未強調尊君思想；

(B) 團練為中國傳統地方武力，此圖是新式軍隊，不是「強化團練，以防止內亂再起」；

(C) 這張插圖僅是顯現新式軍隊軍容，沒有排滿思潮。

42. B

【解析】 (B) 巴爾幹半島原為古希臘人主要活動地區，又稱希臘半島，故可先刪除 (A) 地中海西側的伊比利半島、(C) 黑海北岸的克里米亞半島兩項；東羅馬（拜占庭）帝國曾統治此地，故巴爾幹半島信仰原以希臘正教為主，後巴爾幹半島成為鄂圖曼土耳其帝國領土，伊斯蘭教徒移入，故居民分別信奉希臘正教與伊斯蘭教；巴爾幹半島因位於歐亞大陸交界，種族及宗教複雜，衝突不斷，素有「歐洲火藥庫」之稱，民族紛爭至今不斷；

(D) 安那托利亞（Anatolia），又名小亞細亞（Asia Minor）是亞洲西南部的一個半島，位於黑海和地中海之間，屬於土耳其。

43. D

【解析】 (D) 由題目中出現「蘇聯」可知為 (D) 第二次世界大戰，因為 1917 年十月革命後俄國發生內戰，布爾什維克黨取得政權後，1922 年定國名為「蘇維埃社會主義共和國聯邦」（The Union of Soviet Socialist Republics），簡稱「蘇聯」，又稱「蘇俄」，其他答案時「蘇聯」未成立；

(A) 三十年戰爭（1618－1648 年）；

(B) 克里米亞戰爭（1853－1856 年）；

(C) 第一次世界大戰（1914－1918 年）。

44. B

【解析】 (B) 從題幹「中國人只是憎惡歐洲資本家和唯資本家之命是從的歐洲各國政府」可知最可能出自敵視資本主義、主張共產主義的列寧；

(A) 英國商務監督義律主張中英自由貿易，尤其是鴉片販
　　賣，不會批判「爲了販賣鴉片的權利，對中國作戰」；
(C) 主張門戶開放的美國國務卿海約翰是爲維護各國在華
　　貿易利益均等，不會認爲中國人「憎惡歐洲資本家」；
(D) 日本「東亞共榮圈」是強調日本、滿洲國和中國合作，
　　建立政治、經濟等各方面同盟關係，無敵視歐洲資本
　　主義。

45. **C**
　　【解析】(C) 日本領域圖中黑色區域包含日本、朝鮮（1910 年簽
　　　　　　訂《日韓併合條約》後，成爲日本殖民地）及臺灣
　　　　　　（1895 年《馬關條約》簽訂後割讓給日本），灰色區
　　　　　　域爲九一八事變後 1932 年日本在中國東北扶植成立
　　　　　　的滿洲國，最可能的時間應爲 (C) 1935 年。

46. **C**
　　【解析】(C) 十八世紀初期（1717 年）普魯士推動小學義務教育，
　　　　　　是世界上最早建立義務教育制度的國家；1870 年英
　　　　　　國福斯特提出「初等教育法」獲得通過，該法案亦
　　　　　　稱《福斯特教育法》，法令規定兒童 5－12 歲入學，
　　　　　　1871 年要求實施某種程度的強迫入學制度，1891 年
　　　　　　完全實行初等免費教育。

47. **A**
　　【解析】(A) 隋唐時日本常派遣留學生、學問僧等遣唐使來中國學
　　　　　　習禮儀和佛法，西元七世紀中葉，日本孝德天皇推動
　　　　　　「大化革新」，大量模仿唐朝制度、律令、生活、文
　　　　　　字、佛法等，八世紀建的平安京（今日之京都）仿長
　　　　　　安城，日本茶道、花道、書道及節令可看出受唐文化
　　　　　　影響至深，「京都物語」最能領略「大唐遺風」；
　　　　　　(B) 東漢至隋唐朝鮮分裂爲高麗、百濟、新羅三國，三國
　　　　　　皆引入中國文化，新羅傾慕中國文化至深，仿唐衣冠

年曆、製漢字，號稱「君子國」，但歷經戰爭和朝鮮
去中國化影響，韓國首都首爾不如「京都」能領略
「大唐遺風」；

(C) 越南從秦漢開始受中國統治，受中國影響深，不是
只有「大唐遺風」，尤其近代受法國及共產黨統治，
更難領略「大唐遺風」；

(D) 上海於清末鴉片戰後開港通商後崛起，曾為各國租
界，不可能充滿「大唐遺風」。

48. **D**

【解析】 (D) 由題幹「中國僅是帝國的一部分」可知為 (D) 蒙古，
因蒙古帝國，除中國外，尚包括蒙古西征後建立的
欽察、察合臺、窩闊臺、伊兒等汗國，版圖橫跨歐
亞兩洲，且元朝滅南宋後，採「蒙古至上主義」的
統治方式，歧視漢人，故該民族的王公大臣說「統
治者也不需採用亡國者的制度」；

(A) 女真（金）對漢文化接受度高；

(C) 契丹（遼）也能漢化，且與其對立的北宋、南宋尚
未亡國；

(B) 鮮卑族漢化程度高，如北魏孝文帝的漢化政策。

49. **C**

【解析】 1. 由題中「英語」、「原住民文化」、「冰河」、「活
火山」等關鍵條件，判知為紐西蘭。紐西蘭：昔為英
國殖民地，英語是官方語言；有原住民毛利人文化，
並有「活的地形教室」之稱，南島有冰河地形，北島
有活火山地形。

2. (A) 夏威夷、(B) 菲律賓只有活火山，無冰河地形。
(D) 愛爾蘭無活火山景觀。

50. **B**

【解析】 1. 對於瑞典紡織業而言，非洲具有下列區位優勢：

甲、 非洲爲世界重要棉花產地，氣候條件比高緯度的
　　　瑞典適合種植棉花，棉花原料豐富。
丁、 紡織業爲勞力密集型產業，非洲具有「工廠勞力
　　　薪資便宜低廉」的優勢，工資比瑞典低廉。
2. 乙、 工業區位的全球化，無法避開亞洲企業競爭，亞
　　　洲企業也可到非洲投資設廠。
丙、 與瑞典本地時間差異大，對資訊產業較具區位優
　　　勢，對紡織業區位優勢影響較小。

51. C

【解析】 1. 三到五月爲乾季、六到十月爲雨季，全年乾濕季分
　　　　　明，可判斷爲熱帶季風氣候的 (C) 印度。
　　　　2. (A) 日本爲溫帶季風氣候。
　　　　　(B) 臺灣爲熱帶和副熱帶季風氣候。
　　　　　(D) 印尼爲熱帶雨林氣候，全年有雨。

52. B

【解析】 1. 油畫作品爲岩溶地形中的峰林，是石灰岩地形的錐丘
　　　　　或殘丘期景觀，主要分布於中國廣西、雲南一帶。因
　　　　　氣候溼熱，淋溶作用旺盛，鈣、鉀、鈉等礦物質易流失，
　　　　　聚鐵鋁化作用亦旺盛，鐵、鋁氧化物因無法淋溶，殘
　　　　　留在土壤表層，土壤貧瘠，偏酸性，故選 (B)。
　　　　2. (A) 爲冰蝕地形U型谷。
　　　　　(C) 麥作主要分布於中國秦嶺、淮河以北地區。
　　　　　(D) 分布於大陸西側的西風帶。

53. C

【解析】 照片 1 的柱狀氣流可判斷爲龍捲風，易出現於 (C) 美國
　　　　中部大平原。龍捲風常發生在冷空氣穿過暖空氣時，暖
　　　　空氣急速抬升，產生直立管狀的氣流，並同氣旋般的快
　　　　速旋轉，主要發生於春、夏之交，常造成嚴重的風災。

54. **A**

【解析】 1. 1998年歐盟東擴，加入的會員國相較於西歐國家，多
　　　　　為經濟發展程度相對落後的東歐國家，大多是人均
　　　　　GDP不到歐盟平均75%的地區，所以符合結構基金
　　　　　的補貼範圍。

　　　　2. 歐盟為縮小內部的貧富差距，成立結構基金，透過專
　　　　　案補助、邊界合作區等方式，以縮小區域差距；故歐
　　　　　盟須增加資金，補貼區域平衡發展。

55. **D**

【解析】 判讀圖中三條曲線趨勢，研判選項是否正確：
　　　　甲、 南半球地區平均降水量多寡和平均氣溫高低成正比
　　　　　　（×）【不成正比】
　　　　　　讀圖：南半球平均氣溫線隨緯度增高而下降，但降
　　　　　　水量曲線則有高低起伏變化。
　　　　乙、 北半球地區平均降水量多寡和平均氣溫高低成反
　　　　　　比（×）【不成正比】
　　　　　　讀圖：北半球平均氣溫線隨緯度增高而下降，但降
　　　　　　水量曲線則有高低起伏變化。
　　　　丙、 緯度45度以上地區：平均氣溫高→雪線高、平均
　　　　　　氣溫低→雪線低，故平均氣溫高低和雪線高低成
　　　　　　正比。
　　　　丁、 緯度30度以下地區：平均降水量多→雪線低、平
　　　　　　均降水量少→雪線高，故平均降水量多寡和雪線高
　　　　　　低成反比。

　　　　如下圖：

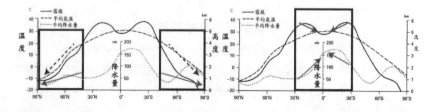

56. **B**

【解析】 1. 由某人正午站在赤道正上方，
面向西方，從上向下拍攝的照
片，可判知照片上方為西，右
為北，下方為東，左為南。因
為影子偏南，表示太陽直射地

區位於赤道以北，此時為北半球的夏季。可判斷此時
為接近夏至（6/22）前後的 (B) 芒種。

2. 正午時間：春、秋分時，太陽直射赤道；而夏至則直
射北回歸線，冬至則直射南回歸線。

57. **D**

【解析】 無店舖零售業能快速崛起，除了網路電子商務平臺與電
視媒體的普遍，物流端（商品配送）更為重要。

乙、 關鍵因素就是交通革新（包括運輸革新使旅運時程
縮短、資訊革新使無店舖零售業興起）。

丁、 物流業興起，商品的傳遞有賴物流產業提供服務，
使送貨流程效率更快，消費者不用到實體店面，也
可享受到購物的便利。

58. **C**

【解析】 由該國的宗教（40％ 的穆斯林，31％ 的東正教徒，15％
的天主教徒）判斷，最可能位於政治宗教緩衝帶的東歐，
其宗教人口比例最可能是波士尼亞國，所以選 (C)。

59. **C**

【解析】 香港為外資進入中國的金融轉運中心，是全球第一個人
民幣離岸中心，全球 80％ 的人民幣交易結算在此進行。
若「上海自由貿易區」成立，使之成為國際貿易結算中
心，對香港的離岸人民幣流動造成較大的影響。

60-61 為題組

60. **A**

【解析】 半島的經緯度，位東經 155～170 度、北緯 50～60 度，
判斷為俄羅斯的「堪察加半島」，位於北美板塊與太平洋
板塊交界處，屬環太平洋火環帶，堪察加火山群名列世
界遺產，故選 (A) 板塊接觸地帶。
(B) 土壤以冰沼土或灰化土為主。
(C) 為副極地氣候和苔原氣候過渡區。
(D) 有親潮流經。

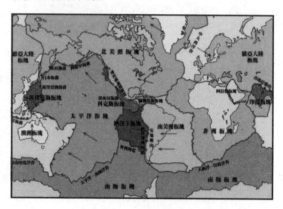

61. **D**

【解析】 堪察加半島為俄羅斯的領土，屬獨立國家國協，是 (D) 亞
洲太平洋經濟合作會議會員國。

62-63 為題組

62. **D**

【解析】 新疆地區鄰近中亞地帶，新疆的維吾爾族人主要信仰伊斯
蘭教，生活方式與宗教信仰最接近 D) 亞—北非文化區。
(A) 西方文化區: 主要宗教為基督教與天主教。
(B) 亞文化區: 主要宗教信仰為印度教、佛教、伊斯蘭教。
(C) 南亞文化區: 宗教多元，有佛教、道教、薩滿信仰、
伊斯蘭教、天主教等。

63. **A**

【解析】 1. 透過基地臺，將手機用戶發信端位置回傳至電腦後，可結合 (A) 地理資訊系統（GIS），將手機用戶位置的地理座標點標示於電子地圖，可監測手機用戶位置以了解其聚集情況。

2. (B) 地圖投影判讀
(C) 航照判釋分析
(D) 遙感探測技術：均無法了解手機用戶的聚集情況。

64-65 為題組

64. **C**

【解析】 照片：甲 高架屋；乙 斜頂屋；丙 窰洞；丁－平頂屋。
四種建築形式差異的因素在 (C) 降水多寡。

1. 地基設計：降水多的地區，植被繁盛，建築材料多為竹木，房屋地基高架。
降水少的地區，植被稀疏，建材多用土石。

2. 屋頂形式：高架屋、斜頂屋：降雨和降雪量大的地區，屋頂斜度大，以加快排水和減少屋頂積雪。
窰洞、平頂屋：降雨少的地區，屋頂斜度小，屋頂較平。

65. **A**

【解析】 1. 甲、高架屋：為適應高溫潮濕的傳統民宅建築，分布於熱帶雨林氣候區，單位面積生物量最大，因為物種多樣性高，環境遭受破壞後，可能產生食物鏈失衡，生態系不易回復。

2. 照片乙：為歐式建築，主要分布在溫帶濕潤區。
丙：為中國黃土高原窰洞，分布於溫帶季風區。
丁：為伊斯蘭式建築，從白色牆面推測，分布在溫帶地中海區。

66-67 為題組

66. **B**

【解析】 1. 甲企業總部負責設計、研發、行銷，不涉足生產製造，以知識創造產出，屬於知識經濟。

2. 「知識經濟」：據經濟合作與發展組織（OECD）定義，指以知識資源的擁有、配置、產生和使用，為最重要生產因素的經濟型態，主要表現在「人力資源」和「科技」方面。

67. **C**

【解析】 因高科技產業的 (C) 產品生命週期短，產品推陳出新速度快。

當新功能新技術出現，新產品上市後，前代產品便易滯銷，所以須增加投資研發速度，否 則將會快速被淘汰。

68-70 為題組

68. **B**

【解析】 圖中甲、乙兩點之間有三條較密集的等高線（為陡崖地形）；圖中其餘地區等高線約 100 多公尺，且間距不大，等高線稀疏，因此判斷為地形平坦的 (B) 台地。

69. **A**

【解析】 1. 圖中左側為高度 140 公尺以上的高地（子地區），照片中三合院後方為高地、且位陡崖前方、面向低平的原面，甲三合院符合此條件；所以只有 (A) 由丑拍向甲，後方才會出現高地。

2. (B) (C) (D) 皆是由高處往低處拍攝。

70. **A**

【解析】 1. 根據圖中的等高線分布判讀出 (A) 子區的高度最高，以
灌溉水源（水性就下）判斷，地勢較高較不易灌溉，
且地表水順地勢而下，排水良好，最可能是茶園。

2. 其餘 (B) 丑、(C) 寅、(D) 卯三處農地，地勢較低，利於
灌溉，適合水田。

71-72 為題組

71. **B**

【解析】 1. 日月潭水力發電廠位南投縣，水源來自濁水溪上游補
注，所以選經過 (B) 龍泉車站及濁水→集集的鐵路。
集集支線為臺鐵最長的鐵路支線，也是南投縣唯一營
運的鐵路，最初為運輸發電機組進入而興建，今日成
為旅遊路線。

2. (A) 新城：位於花蓮。

(B) 龍泉：位於南投；

(C) 豐富：位於苗栗；

(D) 六塊厝：位於屏東。

72. **A**

【解析】 1. 車站的鄰近河流：(A) 新城：立霧溪；(B) 龍泉：濁水
溪；(C) 豐富：後龍溪；(D) 六塊厝：高屏溪。
僅 (A) 立霧溪為臺灣東部河川，坡度相對西部河川陡，
故河口堆積物粒徑較大。

2. 新城車站位太魯閣地區，立霧溪切穿中央山脈後奔騰
入海，河流坡度大，搬運力強，河口堆積物質粒徑最
大。

103 年大學入學學科能力測驗試題
自然考科

第壹部分（佔 80 分）

一、單選題（佔 46 分）

說明：第 1 題至第 23 題，每題均計分。每題有 n 個選項，其中只有
一個是正確或最適當的選項，請畫記在答案卡之「選擇題答案
區」。各題答對者，得 2 分；答錯、未作答或畫記多於一個選
項者，該題以零分計算。

1. 甲、乙、丙、丁四種不同坡度的海岸地形，在相同的潮差下，哪
一種地形的潮間帶最大？

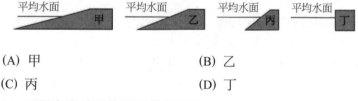

    (A) 甲   (B) 乙
    (C) 丙   (D) 丁
    (E) 四種海岸地形的潮間帶都相同

2. 地球歷史上氣候變遷是因為全球能量收支或分配的情況改變所造
成，下列何者<u>不是</u>直接造成氣候變遷的主要因素？
    (A) 地表海陸分布情況改變
    (B) 大型的火山噴發
    (C) 地球磁場反轉
    (D) 溫鹽環流改變
    (E) 地球繞日軌道的改變

3. 火山由地下深處的岩漿伴隨
著氣體、碎屑從地表噴出而
形成，多數與板塊的運動有
關。圖1何處為現今有火山
分布的地區？

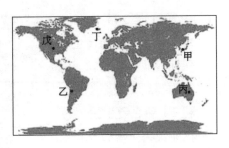

圖 1

(A) 甲乙丙

(B) 乙丙丁

(C) 丙丁戊

(D) 甲乙丁

(E) 乙丙戊

4. 氣壓可以代表單位面積上方空氣柱的重量，某一氣象站的海拔高
度大約是 3000 公尺，平均氣壓大約是 700 百帕，在 3000 公尺高
度以下的大氣層，約佔整個大氣層空氣重量的多少百分比？

(A) 10 　　　　　　(B) 20 　　　　　　(C) 30

(D) 40 　　　　　　(E) 50

5. 一般認為銀河系中心有一個超大質量的黑洞。有些天文學家估計
這黑洞的質量大約是太陽的四百萬倍，太陽離此超大質量黑洞的
距離約為 28,000 光年。如果太陽、該超大質量黑洞與地球排成一
直線，且二者對地球的主要影響只有萬有引力，則這個超大質量
黑洞和地球之間的萬有引力，大約是地球和太陽之間萬有引力的
多少倍？（28,000 光年大約是 1.8×10^9 天文單位）

(A) 1.2×10^{-12} 　　　(B) 2.5×10^{-7} 　　　(C) 2.2×10^{-3}

(D) 4×10^6 　　　　　(E) 8.1×10^{11}

6. 在 2011 年 3 月 11 日，日本東北部外海發生強烈地震並引發海嘯。臨海的福島核電廠（見圖 2）隨之發生嚴重的核能災害，導致含輻射的廢水意外地洩漏到海洋中。由於日本東北部外海有親潮自北方沿岸向南流，到日本東部外海（約北緯 35°）碰到

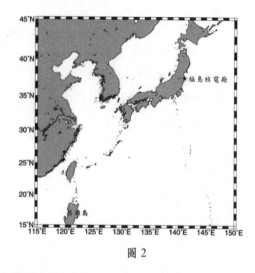

圖 2

黑潮，因此長時間後，在表層的輻射廢水最可能的漂流去向為何？

(A) 先向南流，之後順著黑潮向西南流到臺灣附近

(B) 先向南流，遇到黑潮後轉向東流向中太平洋

(C) 先向南流，碰到黑潮後湧升到表層並滯留在日本東南部海域

(D) 往北流到北海道海域再轉入日本海

(E) 先向南流，碰到黑潮後下沉到深層並滯留在日本東南部海域

7. 孟德爾曾利用試交來鑑定顯性性狀個體的基因型，下列有關試交實驗的敘述，何者正確？

(A) 是指雜交後所產生之第一子代（F1）間互相交配

(B) 是一個 F1 個體與一個顯性同型合子（AA）個體的交配

(C) 對 F1 個體進行試交實驗，可用以判定其親代（P）之基因型

(D) 是一個不明基因型個體與一個隱性同型合子（aa）個體的交配

(E) 是一個顯性同型合子個體與一個隱性同型合子個體的交配

8-9 為題組

　　藥廠的科學家研發出一種可藉由抑制動物細胞中某個構造內一種酵素之功能，進而降低體內膽固醇的新藥物。為檢測該藥物可能的副作用而進行人體實驗，其中一位受試者於服藥前後進行尿液檢查，其部分結果如下表所示：

檢測項目	正常範圍值	檢測單位	服藥前檢測值	服藥後檢測值
酸鹼值	4.5～8.0	pH 值	5.5	5.8
葡萄糖	≦220	mg/100 mL	320	330
蛋白質	≦10	mg/100 mL	8	12
鈉	2.7～28.7	mEq/100 mL	20.7	26.7
鉀	2.6～12.3	mEq/100 mL	8.3	10.6

8. 該藥物造成細胞的膽固醇製造減少，則下列何者最可能是其所作用的細胞構造？
　(A) 核糖體　　　　　(B) 內質網　　　　　(C) 高基氏體
　(D) 細胞核　　　　　(E) 粒線體

9. 研究人員根據上表數據，推論該藥物會對腎臟功能造成影響。下列哪一腎臟組織最可能受此藥物的破壞？
　(A) 絲球體　　　　　(B) 入球小動脈　　　(C) 腎小管
　(D) 腎動脈　　　　　(E) 集尿管

10. 下列哪一項人類的活動，最可能會增加該地區的生物多樣性？
　(A) 自然林改為人造林
　(B) 水泥地改建為生態池
　(C) 野生池塘改建為吳郭魚飼養場
　(D) 濕地海岸填海以增加農地面積
　(E) 原始河岸以混凝土槽化

11. 生物的演化過程相當漫長，不易直接觀察，常藉由各種證據方能
    推論其演變的歷程。下列有關各種演化證據的敘述，何者錯誤？
    (A) 根據化石及其所在地層，可推測古生物外形及其生活的環境
    (B) 根據鯨的鰭與麻雀翅膀的骨骼構造，可推測兩構造為同源器
        官（同源構造）
    (C) 根據昆蟲與爬蟲類的胚胎發育過程，可推測兩者在綱的階層
        上具有共同祖先
    (D) 根據化石的地理分布，可推測當時大陸板塊的位置與現今是
        否相同
    (E) 根據物種之 DNA 分子核苷酸序列的相似性，可推測物種間
        的親緣關係之遠近

12. 銀有兩種同位素，其原子質量為 107 amu 和 109 amu，而其天然
    含量分別為 51.35% 及 48.65%，故銀的平均原子量為 107.9 amu。
    試問任一銀原子，其原子質量為 107.9 amu 的機率（%）為何？
    (A) 0   (B) 2.70   (C) 48.65   (D) 51.35   (E) 100

13. 王同學在不同的溫度分別進行鹽類
    化合物甲（□）與乙（◆）在水中
    的溶解度實驗，得到的結果如圖 3。
    已知溶解度定義為每 100 克的水所
    溶解的化合物質量（克），則下列
    敘述，哪一項正確？

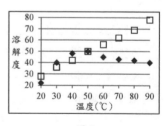

圖 3

    (A) 甲的溶解度總是比乙大
    (B) 在攝氏 80 度時，甲的溶解度是乙的兩倍
    (C) 當溶液溫度上升，甲與乙溶解度皆變大
    (D) 在攝氏 50 度時，甲與乙溶解度幾乎相同
    (E) 於攝氏 80 度時，將 20 克的乙溶於 50 克的水中，將此溶液溫
        度緩慢降低至攝氏 50 度，溶液中會出現化合物乙結晶

14. 在常溫常壓，未知體積之氧氣與 40 公升的一氧化碳，在催化劑的存在下進行反應。反應後氣體之組成為二氧化碳與氧氣，總體積為 70 公升。若反應後，溫度與壓力維持不變，則氧氣在反應前、反應後的體積分別是多少公升？

(A) 60、20　　　　　(B) 50、30　　　　　(C) 40、40

(D) 30、50　　　　　(E) 20、60

15. 已知 25℃ 時，甲瓶水溶液的 pH 值為 2，乙瓶水溶液的 OH^- 濃度為 10^{-3} M，則甲瓶的 H^+ 濃度為乙瓶 H^+ 濃度的多少倍？

(A) 10^{-9}　　(B) 10^{-5}　　(C) $\dfrac{2}{3}$　　(D) 10^5　　(E) 10^9

16. 下列哪一項為氧化還原反應？

(A) $NH_{3(g)} + HCl_{(g)} \longrightarrow NH_4Cl_{(s)}$

(B) $BaCl_{2(aq)} + Na_2SO_{4(aq)} \longrightarrow BaSO_{4(s)} + 2NaCl_{(aq)}$

(C) $CaCO_{3(s)} \xrightarrow{\Delta} CaO_{(s)} + CO_{2(g)}$

(D) $^{235}_{92}U + ^{1}_{0}n \longrightarrow ^{141}_{56}Ba + ^{92}_{36}Kr + 3^{1}_{0}n$

(E) $Zn_{(s)} + CuSO_{4(aq)} \longrightarrow ZnSO_{4(aq)} + Cu_{(s)}$

17. 太空載具常以氫氧化鋰吸收太空人所呼出的二氧化碳，其反應式如下：

$$2LiOH_{(s)} + CO_{2(g)} \longrightarrow Li_2CO_{3(s)} + H_2O_{(l)}$$

假設太空人平均每天所消耗的能量為 3000 大卡，而能量主要由氧化體內葡萄糖所提供，其反應式如下：

$$C_6H_{12}O_{6(s)} + 6O_{2(g)} \longrightarrow 6CO_{2(g)} + 6H_2O_{(l)} \qquad \Delta H = -2800 \text{ kJ}$$

則一位太空人執行任務 5 天所釋出的二氧化碳，至少需以多少公斤的氫氧化鋰，始能清除完畢？（已知 1 大卡相當於 4.2 kJ）

(A) 0.108　　(B) 0.538　　(C) 3.20　　(D) 6.50　　(E) 32.0

18. 下列有關物理或生物之相對尺度大小的比較，何者正確？
    (A) 夸克＜原子核＜紅血球＜原子
    (B) 夸克＜原子核＜細胞核＜原子
    (C) 木星＜地球＜太陽＜星系團＜銀河系
    (D) 地球＜太陽＜太陽系＜星系團＜銀河系
    (E) 地球＜太陽＜太陽系＜銀河系＜星系團

19. 克卜勒分析第谷的行星觀測資料發現
    等面積定律，即一個行星與太陽的連
    線，在等長的時間內，於行星軌道所
    掃過的面積必相等，如圖4中的五個
    灰色區域所示。已知太陽在右邊焦點
    上，則此行星在甲、乙、丙、丁、戊
    五點上，哪一點的動能最大？

    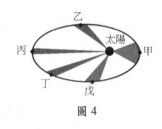
    圖4

    (A) 甲　　　(B) 乙　　　(C) 丙　　　(D) 丁　　　(E) 戊

20. 下列哪一個實驗可以最精確的判斷某一混合氣體中是否有氦氣存
    在？
    (A) 觀察氣體的光譜
    (B) 觀察氣體壓力隨溫度的變化
    (C) 用肉眼辨識氣體的顏色
    (D) 測量常溫常壓下氣體的密度
    (E) 測量常溫常壓下氣體的折射率

21. 太陽內部核融合的反應速率相當穩定，足以持續提供地球100億
    年的能源需求。根據研究，影響核融合反應速率的主要作用力，
    與中子衰變成質子、電子和另一個稱為反微中子的電中性粒子的
    過程，屬於同一種基本交互作用。由此可知下列何者為影響核融
    合反應速率的主要作用力？

(A) 靜電力　　　　　　　(B) 強力　　　　　　　(C) 弱力

(D) 重力（萬有引力）　　(E) 電力與磁力

22. 下列有關都卜勒效應的敘述，何者正確？

(A) 只適用於縱波

(B) 只適用於需要靠介質傳播的波動

(C) 適用於不同波長的聲波與電磁波

(D) 適用於無線電波及可見光，但對於 X 光及波長更短之電磁波則不適用

(E) 適用於超聲波及人耳可以聽到的聲波，但不適用於波長更長的次聲波

23. 棒球賽一名投手以水平速度 108 公里/小時，擲出質量約為 0.15 公斤的棒球。如果投手對原靜止棒球的加速時間約為 0.15 秒，則投手對棒球的平均施力約為多少牛頓？

(A) 16　　　　(B) 30　　　　(C) 45　　　　(D) 108　　　　(E) 200

二、多選題（佔 26 分）

說明：第 24 題至第 36 題，每題均計分。每題有 n 個選項，其中至少有一個是正確的選項，請將正確選項畫記在答案卡之「選擇題答案區」。各題之選項獨立判定，所有選項均答對者，得 2 分；答錯 k 個選項者，得該題 n-2k/n 的分數；但得分低於零分或所有選項均未作答者，該題以零分計算。

24. 外海形成的海嘯也是波浪的一種，當它傳遞接近岸邊時，下列哪些現象的敘述正確？（應選 2 項）

(A) 波速變快　　　　　(B) 波速不變　　　　　(C) 波速變慢

(D) 波高變高　　　　　(E) 波高不變　　　　　(F) 波高變小

25. 颱風是臺灣常見的天然災害之一，下列有關颱風的敘述，哪些正確？（應選 2 項）
    (A) 颱風中心的氣壓最低　　(B) 颱風眼牆的氣壓最高
    (C) 颱風眼牆的風速最小　　(D) 一般在颱風眼牆的降雨最大
    (E) 颱風眼的空氣上升運動最強

26. 地球是人類賴以生存的環境，地球系統中各部分的互動與平衡都可能會對生物的生存產生關鍵性的影響，下列有關地球系統的敘述，哪些正確？（應選 2 項）
    (A) 地球系統包括岩石圈、水圈、大氣圈與外太空四個系統
    (B) 透過地球系統中各部分的巧妙互動，有些物質會循環不已
    (C) 生態系統會受到地球環境變遷的影響，但是生態系統發生改變時不會影響地球系統的平衡
    (D) 相較於海水及大氣，板塊發生改變的時間尺度比較長，因此是系統中比較不重要的部分
    (E) 太陽是地球系統的主要能量來源

27. 下列哪些生物科技的成果，現階段運用到「重組 DNA」的技術？（應選 2 項）
    (A) 試管嬰兒　　　　　　　(B) 複製羊桃莉
    (C) 利用酵母菌生產胰島素
    (D) 具有抗蟲基因的轉殖玉米
    (E) 利用放射線誘發突變的植物種子

28. 下列有關生物進行無氧呼吸之敘述，哪些正確？（應選 3 項）
    (A) 會產生 CO_2　　　　　　(B) 會產生 ATP
    (C) 種子淹水過久，會由有氧呼吸轉變為無氧呼吸
    (D) 葡萄經由酵母菌的無氧呼吸作用可釀成葡萄酒
    (E) 人體劇烈運動後，肌肉缺氧時會產生酒精堆積

29. 下列有關人類活動對生物及環境影響的敘述，哪些正確？
（應選 3 項）
(A) 透過人為復育貓熊，可有效提高其族群之遺傳多樣性（基因多樣性）
(B) 將冷媒氟氯碳化物逸散於空氣中，是引起大氣臭氧層破洞擴大的原因之一
(C) 將硫化物過量排放於大氣，會影響水生棲地及水源的酸鹼值
(D) 大氣中二氧化碳濃度的增加，會造成紫外線到達地表量增加
(E) 殺蟲劑 DDT 釋入生態系後，會因食物鏈的傳遞而造成生物放大效應（生物累積）

30. 下列有關真核細胞遺傳物質表現的敘述，哪些正確？
（應選 2 項）
(A) 轉錄作用在核糖體上進行
(B) 轉譯作用在細胞質內進行
(C) 將 DNA 上的遺傳訊息抄錄至 RNA 上的過程稱為轉譯作用
(D) 利用 DNA 聚合酶，將 DNA 上遺傳訊息抄錄至 RNA 上
(E) 當基因表現時，DNA 的兩股會先分開，僅以其中一股的核苷酸序列為模版，合成一股 RNA

31. 已知氮氣與氧氣反應生成二氧化氮的平衡反應式如下：
$$N_{2(g)} + 2O_{2(g)} \longrightarrow 2NO_{2(g)} \qquad \Delta H = 68 \text{ kJ}$$
下列有關此一反應的敘述，哪些正確？（應選 2 項）
(A) 此反應為一放熱反應
(B) 二氧化氮的莫耳生成熱為 68 kJ
(C) 此反應式符合質量守恆定律
(D) 此反應中氮氣扮演氧化劑的角色
(E) 二氧化氮溶於水後，可使藍色石蕊試紙變成紅色

32. 將 100.0mL、0.40M 的 HCl 溶液加於 4.24g 的 Na_2CO_3 固體，會產生氣泡。下列關於此反應的敘述，哪些正確？（應選 2 項）

    (A) 此反應的平衡反應式為：

    $$Na_2CO_3 + HCl \longrightarrow 2NaCl + H_2O + CO_2$$

    (B) 若反應完全，則可產生 0.88 克的 CO_2

    (C) 反應後會剩餘 0.01 莫耳的 Na_2CO_3

    (D) 此反應的限量試劑為 HCl

    (E) 此反應為沉澱反應

33. 將下列反應式平衡後，若平衡係數皆取最簡單整數，則哪些反應式左邊的平衡係數總和比右邊的平衡係數總和少 2？

    （應選 3 項）

    (A) $NH_{3(g)} \xrightarrow{催化分解} N_{2(g)} + H_{2(g)}$

    (B) $Fe_2O_{3(s)} + CO_{(g)} \longrightarrow Fe_{(s)} + CO_{2(g)}$

    (C) $C_6H_4(OH)_{2(aq)} + H_2O_{2(aq)} \longrightarrow C_6H_4O_{2(aq)} + H_2O_{(l)}$

    (D) $Ca(HCO_3)_{2(s)} + HCl_{(aq)} \longrightarrow CaCl_{2(aq)} + CO_{2(g)} + H_2O_{(l)}$

    (E) $HC \equiv CH_{(g)} + Ag(NH_3)_2NO_{3(aq)} \longrightarrow AgC \equiv CAg_{(s)} + NH_4NO_{3(aq)}$
    $+ NH_{3(g)}$

34. 下列關於馬克士威在電磁學上貢獻的敘述，哪些正確？

    （應選 2 項）

    (A) 是第一位發現電磁感應者

    (B) 是第一位發現電流可產生磁場者

    (C) 是第一位預測電磁波存在者

    (D) 是第一位實驗證實電磁波存在者

    (E) 是第一位理論導出電磁波傳播速率者

35. 在十七世紀時,牛頓提出光的微粒說,認為光是由極輕的微小粒子所構成,由此可以解釋光線直進、反射等現象,但下列哪些光學現象,<u>無法</u>用牛頓的微粒說解釋?(應選 2 項)
(A) 針孔成像實驗,其像上下顛倒、左右相反
(B) 肥皂泡在空中飄浮時,呈現絢麗的色彩
(C) 物體在燈光照射下,其背光處有明顯的影子
(D) 在道路轉彎處豎立凸面鏡,可以擴大駕駛人的視野
(E) 光從空氣入射至玻璃中,其速率變慢,且行進路徑偏向法線

36. 十九世紀末,實驗發現將光照射在某些金屬表面,會導致電子自表面逸出,稱為光電效應,逸出的電子稱為光電子。下列關於光電效應的敘述,哪些正確?(應選 3 項)
(A) 光電效應實驗結果顯示光具有粒子的性質
(B) 愛因斯坦因首先發現光電效應的現象而獲得諾貝爾物理獎
(C) 光照射在金屬板上,每秒躍出的光電子數目與光照射的時間成正比
(D) 光照射在金屬板上,當頻率低於某特定頻率(底限頻率或低限頻率)時,無論光有多強,均不會有光電子躍出
(E) 光照射在金屬板上,當頻率高於某特定頻率(底限頻率或低限頻率)時,即便光度很弱,仍會有光電子躍出

三、綜合題(佔 8 分)

說明:第 37 題至第 40 題,每題 2 分,每題均計分,請將正確選項畫記在答案卡之「選擇題答案區」。單選題答錯、未作答或畫記多於一個選項者,該題以零分計算:多選題每題有 n 個選項,答錯 k 個選項者,得該題 $\dfrac{n-2k}{n}$ 的分數;但得分低於零分或所有選項均未作答者,該題以零分計算。

37-40 為題組

　　雷雨是因大氣強烈對流所產生的現象，也與氮的循環有關。發生時往往伴隨著閃電、狂風、暴雨，甚至冰雹、龍捲風等劇烈天氣。產生雷雨的積雨雲形成發展時，大氣環境一般具備下列三個條件：大氣處於不穩定狀態、有充沛的水汽和足夠的舉升力。

　　地球上的生物能生生不息，世代相傳，這不能不歸功於大氣的存在。事實上，自然界有天然的循環作用，使空氣的成分保持不變。俗話說「一場雷、一場肥」，空中的雷電可使氮與氧化合，遇雨水降落地面經細菌轉化成為植物的肥料。氮的固定係由空氣中取氮，將其轉化為氮化合物，例如製造氨、而氨是製造硝酸、尿素、硫酸銨肥料的中間物。

　　氮循環為自然界中氮和含氮化合物在生態系統中轉換的過程，其中將空氣中的氮氣轉化為氮化合物的固氮作用，對生物的生長息息相關。生物中僅有固氮細菌可進行固氮，因其具固氮酶可將氮氣形成銨鹽，再經由亞硝化細菌與硝化細菌轉化為硝酸鹽，以利植物根部吸收，而部分植物則可藉由與藍綠菌、根瘤菌等固氮細菌共生而獲取氮。

37. 雷雨一般較<u>不容易</u>發生在甚麼樣的天氣系統或條件中？
（應選 2 項）
(A) 極地大陸氣團中心　　　(B) 春天的鋒面系統
(C) 梅雨季的西南氣流　　　(D) 夏日午後旺盛的對流
(E) 太平洋高壓中心

38. 下列有關雷雨與肥料的化學反應敘述，哪些正確？（應選 3 項）
(A) 雷雨可能造成氮氣與氧氣作用，其反應式如右：$N_2 + O_2$
$\xrightarrow{\text{雷雨}} 2NO$
(B) 硝化細菌可進行的反應如右：$NO_2^- \xrightarrow{\text{硝化細菌}} NO_3^-$

(C) 硫酸銨是一種氮肥，其化學式為 NH_4SO_4

(D) 植物吸收銨鹽和硝酸鹽，合成蛋白質和核酸等含氮化合物

(E) 在實驗室常溫常壓即可由氮氣與氫氣合成氨，進一步可製造尿酸

39. 氮的獲取與生物生長息息相關，下列敘述，哪些正確？
（應選 3 項）

(A) 原核生物均可行固氮作用

(B) 真核生物均無法自行固氮作用

(C) 植物直接吸收一氧化氮而獲取氮素

(D) 若水稻田中有共生的藍綠菌，可減少氮肥的施加

(E) 若植物與根瘤菌共生，可藉由固氮作用而獲取氮源

40. 在雷雨天收聽廣播節目時，一道強烈閃電畫破天際，收音機隨之發出一陣雜訊，說明劇烈放電可產生電磁波。下列關於電磁波性質的敘述，哪些正確？（應選 2 項）

(A) 電磁波不需要介質即可傳播

(B) 電磁波的電場振盪方向與傳播方向相互垂直

(C) 電磁波的磁場振盪方向與傳播方向相互平行

(D) 電磁波的介質振動方向與傳播方向相互垂直

(E) 電磁波的介質振動方向與傳播方向相互平行

第貳部分（佔 48 分）

說明：第 41 題至第 68 題，每題 2 分。單選題答錯、未作答或畫記多於一個選項者，該題以零分計算；多選題每題有 n 個選項，答錯 k 個選項者，得該題 n-2k/n 的分數；但得分低於零分或所有選項均未作答者，該題以零分計算。此部分得分超過 48 分以上，以滿分 48 分計。

41. 天文學家觀測星系在天球的分布時，發現星系大致均勻分布，但部分天區的星系數量相當少，而這些區域圍繞天球一圈，呈現大圓之分布。下列哪一敘述為其原因？
    (A) 因為該天區的星系數量真的很少
    (B) 由於仙女座大星系遮掩了遠方的星系
    (C) 由於大、小麥哲倫星系遮掩了遠方的星系
    (D) 由於我們本身的銀河系遮掩了遠方的星系
    (E) 由於宇宙物質的分布呈現兩大部分

42. 河川攜帶泥砂至海岸時，不同粒徑的泥砂會沉積在出海口附近的不同地點。某地的地層由老到新的沉積順序依序為地層甲、乙、丙。圖 5 中的甲、乙、丙為各地層樣本的近照圖，各圖下方比例尺的單位為公分。若只單純考慮海進或海退所造成的影響，不考慮如河川季節流量變化及沿岸流等因素，則下列哪一種海水相對於陸地的變動，較可能造成此地由地層甲至地層丙的沉積環境變化？

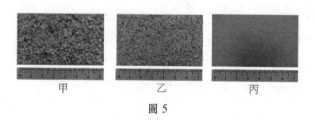

圖 5

    (A) 海退　　　　　(B) 海進　　　　　(C) 先海退、後海進
    (D) 先海進、後海退　　(E) 海水面保持不變動

43. 假設某地區發生地震時，P 波的傳遞速度為 6 公里/秒，S 波的傳遞速度為 4 公里/秒，則當該地區發生地震時，這兩種地震波到達甲測站的時間差為 10 秒，到達乙測站的時間差為 30 秒，如果

甲測站在上午 9:25:30（9 點 25 分 30 秒）測到初達 P 波，則乙測
站應在何時測到初達 P 波？

(A) 9:25:40 　　　　(B) 9:25:50 　　　　(C) 9:26:00

(D) 9:26:10 　　　　(E) 9:26:20

44. 科學家利用地震波探測地球內部的分層結構，經模式計算得到全
球各地的地殼厚度分布如圖 6。圖上等厚度線上的數值（單位為
公里）為各地地殼之厚度。下列有關此圖的敘述，哪一項錯誤？

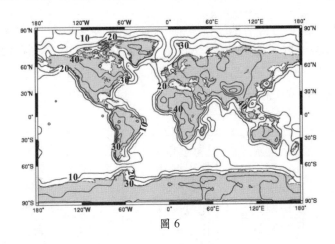

圖 6

(A) 海洋地殼的厚度大都比大陸地殼薄

(B) 地殼厚度大都小於 45 公里

(C) 地勢高的區域，地殼大多較厚

(D) 因為各地的地殼厚度不同，故莫氏不連續面的深度也不一樣

(E) 若要鑽探取得上部地函物質，以北緯 10 度、東經 15 度之地
　　點為最佳

45. 科學家已經了解光源與光譜的關係，所以藉由觀測遙遠天體的光
譜，可以獲得其訊息。下列有關光譜的敘述，哪些正確？

（應選 2 項）

(A) 白熾燈泡發出的光譜為連續光譜
(B) 如果在白熾燈泡四周有一團低溫的氣體，氣體會吸收能量而產生發光的明線
(C) 只有少數幾種原子才可能有發射光譜或吸收光譜
(D) 太陽的可見光光譜為發射光譜
(E) 如果氣體中的電子吸收了能量之後，電子躍遷至高能量狀態，當電跳回低能量狀態，便會發出特定波長的明線，稱為發射光譜

46. 如圖 7 所示，目前地球自轉軸指向為圖中 x，與繞日公轉軸交角約為 23.5 度。如果地球自轉軸的指向偏轉為圖中 y，但交角仍為 23.5 度。僅就天文的角度來看，則地球北半球的夏天與冬天，與實況（現況）相比為何？

選項	夏天	冬天
(A)	與現況差不多	與現況差不多
(B)	比現況冷	比現況熱
(C)	比現況冷	比現況冷
(D)	比現況熱	比現況熱
(E)	比現況熱	比現況冷

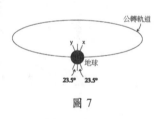

圖 7

47. 氣象觀測包括傳統氣象觀測與遙測，氣象局綜合了各種觀測資料，輸入氣象模式中，便可做數值天氣預報。以下關於傳統地面氣象站觀測氣溫、氣壓、濕度、露點、風及雲等項目的敘述，哪些正確？（應選 2 項）
(A) 北風指的是向北吹的風
(B) 乾濕球溫度計溫差越大時，相對濕度越小
(C) 露點的大小可以直接用來判斷相對濕度的高低
(D) 氣壓不受溫度影響，所以氣壓計可直接置於陽光下
(E) 各觀測項目中，雲量及雲狀目前仍以人工目視觀測

48-49 為題組

下表為四種脊椎動物的平均體重及平均腦重量資料：

動物名稱	平均體重（公克）	平均腦重量（公克）
小鼠	24	0.5
大象	2,550,000	5,000
黑猩猩	42,000	400
羊	40,000	100

48. 根據上表的資料，若 BB 值代表「平均腦重量」占「平均體重」的百分比，則 BB 值最大與最小的兩種動物，依序分別為何？
　(A) 小鼠，大象　　　(B) 大象，黑猩猩　　　(C) 黑猩猩，羊
　(D) 羊，小鼠　　　　(E) 黑猩猩，小鼠

49. 根據上表資料，下列何者是最合理的推論？
　(A) 靈長類的 BB 值最高
　(B) 個體越小則 BB 值越小
　(C) 體重越大則 BB 值越大
　(D) 雜食性動物的 BB 值較草食性的為高
　(E) 具社會行為的生物其 BB 值較沒有社會行為的為高

50. 李同學想了解生長素對某種植物組織培養苗各部位生長率的影響，於各培養基添加不同濃度的生長素，經過一段時間後，分別測量其根、芽及莖生長的長度變化，再與對照組相互比較後，得出如圖 8 的相對生長率。依據此圖，下列敘述哪些正確？（應選 2 項）

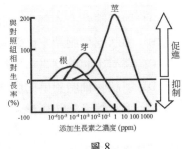

圖 8

(A) 莖對低濃度的生長素最為敏感

(B) 1 ppm 生長素可使莖有最大的生長效果

(C) 10^{-1} ppm 之生長素可使芽停止生長

(D) 10^{-2} ppm 之生長素可使根的長度縮短

(E) 10^{-3} ppm 之生長素可同時促進根、芽及莖生長

51-52 為題組

甲狀腺細胞生成甲狀腺素的過程中,利用碘幫浦蛋白將碘離子吸收至細胞內,過程中會消耗 ATP,最後甲狀腺球蛋白中的酪胺酸與碘離子結合,形成甲狀腺素。甲狀腺素進入標的細胞後,會與其位於細胞核中的受體結合,藉此活化與代謝作用相關的基因表現。

日本於 2011 年 3 月 11 日發生大地震,導致福島核電廠輻射外洩,為了降低輻射傷害,當地民眾會依醫生指示每日服用碘片一次。服用碘片的作用是讓甲狀腺細胞內的碘含量飽和,使放射性碘不易成為合成甲狀腺素的原料。一般而言,碘片服用約 30 分鐘後即可發揮效用,而自環境中接觸到的放射性碘,則需約 10～12 小時才會進到人體的甲狀腺。

51. 下列有關「甲狀腺」與「甲狀腺素」的敘述,哪些正確?
    (應選 3 項)

    (A) 甲狀腺共有 4 個,包埋在副甲狀腺的組織內

    (B) 甲狀腺細胞藉主動運輸將碘輸入細胞

    (C) 需有甲狀腺球蛋白才能合成甲狀腺素

    (D) 甲狀腺細胞對碘的吸收具有飽和現象

    (E) 甲狀腺素為胺類激素,其受體位在細胞膜上

52. 若某地區在 3 月 21 日早上 8 點遭受放射性碘污染,則該地區民眾在下列哪一個時間開始服用碘片的預防效用最低?

(A) 3 月 21 日早上 8 點　　　　(B) 3 月 21 日早上 9 點

(C) 3 月 21 日中午 12 點　　　　(D) 3 月 21 日傍晚 6 點

(E) 3 月 21 日晚上 10 點

53-54 為題組

　　棉花是錦葵科（Malvaceae）棉屬（*Gossypium*），為亞洲與非洲之重要的經濟作物，其種子之種皮毛細胞形成的纖維是紡織原料，種仁則含有豐富的蛋白質與脂質，但是卻同時具有多酚類化合物「棉酚」，只有反芻動物才能無毒消化，對人類則具有相當毒性而不能直接作為食物的來源。棉花的葉、莖與花也含有棉酚，其可保護植株避免受到病蟲害的侵襲。植物學家曾利用雜交培育出不含棉酚的品種，但卻因極易受到蟲害而大幅減產。美國科學家已成功利用基因轉殖技術（核糖核酸干擾技術或稱基因沉默技術），僅減弱種子內之棉酚基因的表現，但在其他器官則不受影響，植株仍能保有抵禦蟲害的能力。雖然研究人員已證實這種轉基因棉花的可遺傳性，但尚未能確定其基因穩定性的維持。

53. 下列有關棉花的敘述，哪些正確？（應選 3 項）

(A) 學名為 Malvaceae *gossypium*

(B) 纖維由種皮的毛細胞形成

(C) 種仁內含有豐富的蛋白質與脂質

(D) 種子可作為牛或羊的飼料

(E) 棉酚對昆蟲不具毒性，但對人類則具有毒性

54. 下列有關棉酚的相關敘述，哪些正確？（應選 2 項）

(A) 野生種的棉花植株，僅繁殖器官具有棉酚相關基因

(B) 雜交後不含棉酚的棉花品種，易受到蟲害而大幅減產

(C) 種子不含棉酚的棉花植株，均不具有抵禦蟲害的能力

(D) 去除棉酚毒性之基改棉花種子的可遺傳性與基因穩定性均已被確定

(E) 現階段基因轉殖後的棉花，其葉、莖、花與種子的細胞仍含有棉酚相關基因

55. 林同學在藥品櫃發現一瓶標示不明的有機藥品，由殘餘標籤得知其分子式爲 C_6H_{12}，該化合物可能爲下列哪幾類化合物？（應選 2 項）

(A) 直鏈烷烴   (B) 環烷烴   (C) 烯烴

(D) 環烯烴   (E) 炔烴

56. 下列有關醣類化合物的敘述，哪些正確？（應選 3 項）

(A) 平常食用的紅糖、白砂糖，其主要成分都是蔗糖

(B) 纖維素經水解可產生葡萄糖，可用於製造酒精

(C) 醣類化合物中的澱粉，可用碘酒驗出

(D) 蔗糖屬於雙醣類化合物，經水解可得兩分子的葡萄糖

(E) 醣類物質屬於碳水化合物，其化學成分通式均可寫爲 $(CH_2O)_n$

57. 透明質酸，又稱玻尿酸，最近常被應用在醫藥及美容上，其化學結構如下：

試問此多醣聚合物具有哪些官能基？（應選 3 項）

(A) 羧基   (B) 鹵基   (C) 酯基

(D) 羥基   (E) 醯胺基

58-59 為題組

　　元素週期表之前三週期的最後元素分別為氦、氖、氬，而其對應原子序為 2、10、18，已知甲、乙、丙是週期表上相鄰的三種元素，甲與乙是同週期的元素，乙與丙是同主族的元素。

58. 該三種元素的原子序之和為 27，則甲、乙、丙在週期表中的相對位置，最多有幾種可能？

(A) 1　　　　(B) 2　　　　(C) 3　　　　(D) 4　　　　(E) 5

59. 承上題，若此三種元素均為金屬，則甲、乙、丙在週期表中的相對位置，最多有幾種可能？

(A) 1　　　　(B) 2　　　　(C) 3　　　　(D) 4　　　　(E) 5

60. 王同學翻到一本舊書，看到一張記載一些早期元素分析結果的表格，其中甲、乙、丙、丁代表四種不同的元素。

	甲	乙	丙	丁
甲	甲元素很柔軟			
乙	甲與乙可形成化合物（甲$_2$乙）			
丙	甲與丙可形成離子化合物（甲丙）		丙分子具有顏色	
丁		乙與丁可形成離子化合物（乙丁）		丁元素在常溫常壓下為固體

註：表格中括號內的元素組合，分別代表該物質化學式之示意式

依甲、乙、丙、丁的順序,試問下列哪些元素組合,可符合上述的結果?(應選 2 項)

(A) 鉀、氧、氯、鎂 　　(B) 鈹、氯、氧、鐵

(C) 鈉、氧、溴、鈣 　　(D) 鈣、氧、溴、鈉

(E) 鉀、氯、氟、鈣

61. 圖 9 的分子模型,僅含碳氫氧氮四種元素,圖中一短線連結代表單鍵,=短線連結代表雙鍵。有關此分子模型的敘述,哪些正確?(應選 2 項)

(A) 碳與氫的原子個數總和為 21

(B) 碳與氧的原子個數總和為 11

(C) 氮與氧的原子個數總和為 4

(D) 氮與氫的原子個數總和為 14

(E) 碳與氮的原子個數總和為 9

圖 9

62. 三個點電荷 X、Y、Z 位於等腰直角三角形的三個頂點如圖 10 所示,Z 所受 X、Y 的庫侖靜電力之合力為 F。若 X 與 Y 的位置互換,而 Z 的位置不變,則下列何者為 Z 所受 X、Y 的庫侖靜電力之合力方向?

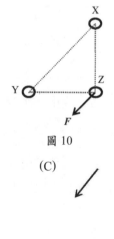

圖 10

(A) 　　　　　(B) 　　　　　(C)

(D) 　　　　　(E)

63-64 為題組

　　某生搭電梯由五樓直接下降到一樓，行進的距離為 12 公尺，取重力加速度為 10 公尺/秒^2。電梯的速率 v 隨時間 t 而變，如圖 11 所示。當電梯由靜止啟動後可分為三個階段：最初的 2.0 秒加速行進；接著有 t_0 秒以 2.0 公尺/秒等速行進；最後 4.0 秒減速直到停止。

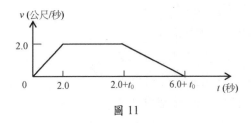

圖 11

63. 下列何者為圖 11 中的 t_0 值？
　(A) 2.5　　　　(B) 3.0　　　　(C) 3.5
　(D) 4.0　　　　(E) 4.5

64. 若該生的質量為 50 公斤，考慮在下降過程的三個階段中，電梯地板對該生在各階段的平均施力，三者中最大的量值為多少牛頓？
　(A) 25　　　　(B) 50　　　　(C) 500
　(D) 525　　　　(E) 550

65. 在光滑的水平面上有一靜止且質量為 M 的木塊，一質量為 m 的子彈以速度 v 向右水平射入該木塊。在陷入木塊的過程中，子彈受摩擦力而減速。子彈最後停留在木塊中，兩者以相同的速度運動。下列敘述哪些正確？（應選 3 項）
　(A) 當射入的子彈減速時，摩擦力對木塊作正功

(B) 子彈與木塊互施摩擦力，且兩力量值相同方向相反

(C) 當子彈減速停留在木塊後，木塊的末速為 mv/M

(D) 在子彈陷入木塊後，當兩者的速度相等時，摩擦力消失

(E) 由於沒有外力作用於子彈與木塊的系統，故系統的動能守恆

66. 一金屬球以質量可忽略的細線靜
止懸掛於天花板，如圖 12 所示。
此系統相關的受力情況如下：
W_1 為金屬球所受的重力，W_2 為
金屬球對地球的引力，T_1 為懸線
施於金屬球的力，T_2 為懸線施於
天花板的力，T_3 為金屬球施於懸
線的力。下列敘述哪些正確？（應選 3 項）

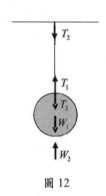

圖 12

(A) T_1 與 T_2 互為作用力與反作用力

(B) W_1 與 W_2 互為作用力與反作用力

(C) T_1 與 T_3 互為作用力與反作用力

(D) T_1 與 W_1 互為作用力與反作用力

(E) T_1、T_2、T_3、W_1 與 W_2 的量值均相等

67-68 為題組

科學家為了研究人類步伐與姿勢以了解肢體如何隨著感官以及
週遭環境而調適。使用如圖 13 的簡化模型，假設人體質量集中於
O 處，下肢為一長度為 L 的彈性體，踏下台階時腳底對著地面施
力，下肢受到地面之鉛直反作用力 F，所以長度會有所改變，設其
絕對值為 ΔL，則 F 與 ΔL 的比值 $S = \dfrac{F}{\Delta L}$，可用以代表人腳垂直踩
踏較低地面時下肢的僵硬程度，S 愈大代表踩踏時下肢愈僵硬。

圖 14 為甲受測者踏下固定落差的台階時，所受之 *F* 與對應之 Δ*L* 的實驗數據。當人在踏下不同落差的台階，或是在視力模糊的情況下，下肢的僵硬程度都會有所調適，實驗的結果彙整如圖 15。依據以上所述，回答第 67～68 題。

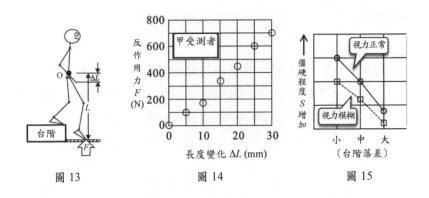

圖 13　　　　　圖 14　　　　　圖 15

67. 從圖 14 的實驗數據研判，甲受測者垂直踩踏台階時的「僵硬程度 *S*」約是多少 N/m？
    (A) 4.0×10^{-5}　　　(B) 6.5×10^{-1}　　　(C) 6.5×10^{2}
    (D) 1.0×10^{3}　　　(E) 2.4×10^{4}

68. 從圖 15 踏下台階的研究資料，可以推論出下列哪些結論？
    （應選 2 項）
    (A) 視力正常時，下肢較視力模糊時為柔軟
    (D) 視力正常時，下肢較視力模糊時為僵硬
    (C) 視力模糊與否，不影響下肢的柔軟或僵硬
    (D) 台階落差大時，下肢較落差小時為柔軟
    (E) 台階落差大時，下肢較落差小時為僵硬
    (F) 台階落差大小，不影響下肢的柔軟或僵硬

103年度學科能力測驗自然科試題詳解

第壹部分

一、單選題

1. **A**

   【解析】 潮間帶指位於高低潮線間的土地範圍；題幹敘述假設
   在相同潮差下，表高低潮間的垂直高度相同，故坡度
   越平緩者表涵蓋在相同高度範圍內面積越大。
   如圖所示

2. **C**

   【解析】 (A) 地表海陸比熱性質差異影響到熱量的吸收狀況；陸
   地的大小影響地表的逕流、水資源的多寡，進而影
   響水氣的蒸發散與氣溫狀況。

   (B) 大型火山噴發造成的火山灰與火山礫會吸收地表長
   波輻射與反射太陽輻射，影響氣候。火山噴發短期
   而言，會造成全球增溫；長期而言會造成降溫。

   (C) 地球的磁場會影響太陽帶電粒子的入射；若磁場的
   強度改變，可能會造成氣候變遷，但題目只敘述反
   轉，若磁場強度不變，只有磁力線方向相反，對氣
   候影響較小。根據科學家的研判，只有在反轉的過
   程，磁場強度由強減弱，此時較可能影響氣候。但
   此題並不是敘述反轉的過程，只是強調反轉，所以
   影響較小。

(D) 海水與大氣進行熱量的交換，若現今來自深層的溫
鹽環流被阻斷，將使得表層低緯的海水無法流至高
緯度地區，將熱量傳至大氣中；進而使得中高緯度
地區的大氣溫度比現今低。

(E) 由於地球自轉軸進動使得陽光直射的地區產生改
變，加上公轉的偏心率改變，使得地球與太陽間
的距離改變，均會造成地球氣候產生變遷。

3. **D**

【解析】由題幹判斷此題欲了解的是五地中何處位於板塊交
界。甲為日本，乙為安地斯山脈，丁為冰島；甲乙
均為聚合式板塊交界地；丁為中洋脊。

4. **C**

【解析】地表接近一大氣壓，約為 1013 百帕；
高度 3000 公尺的氣壓為 700hpa；
表 3000 以下的氣壓量為 1013 – 700 = 313 hpa；
所以 3000 公尺以下的大氣重量應占的比例為：
313/1013 = 0.3。

5. **A**

【解析】$F = \dfrac{GMm_{地}}{r^2} \propto \dfrac{M}{r^2} \Rightarrow \dfrac{4\times10^6}{(1.8\times10^9)^2} = \dfrac{4\times10^6}{3.24\times10^{18}} \approx 1.2\times10^{-12}$

6. **B**

【解析】此題考的是世界洋流，親潮往南走遇到黑潮後，受西
風吹拂往太平洋東側流動，形成北太平洋暖流。

7. **D**

【解析】試交是指用隱性的個體和不明基因型的個體交配，可

以從所產生的子代表現型來推論不明基因型親代的基因型。

(A) 第一子代（F1）間互相交配稱為「自交」不為試交。

(B) 第一子代（F1）和一顯性同型合子（AA）個體交配，沒有特殊的專有名詞。

(C) 對 F1 個體進行試交實驗，可以從 F2 的表現型推論 F1 的基因型，但無法推論 F1 之親代基因型。

(D) 選項之敘述為試交的正確敘述。

(E) 選項之敘述不正確。

8-9 為題組

8. **B**

【解析】 在真核細胞胞器中，平滑型內質網可以合成磷脂質、中性脂和膽固醇，故本題選內質網。而在基礎生物課本中並無特別提及平滑型內質網可以合成磷脂質、中性脂和膽固醇的功能敘述，在選修生物課本才有提及，因此本題有超出範圍的疑慮。

(A) 核糖體由蛋白質和 rRNA 組成，其中一條 rRNA 可以做為肽鍵合成酶，形成胺基酸之間的肽鍵，將胺基酸連結成多肽鏈。

(C) 高基氏體在細胞中的功能為：

① 接收來自粗糙型內質網的運輸小泡。

② 植物細胞中可以製造果膠質，和中膠層及細胞壁的形成有關。

③ 完成分泌性蛋白的修飾作用，故又稱為「細胞的分泌中心」。

④ 完成內共生胞器所需酵素的修飾作用。

(D) 細胞核為細胞的生命中樞，內含遺傳物質 DNA。

(E) 粒線體爲半自主胞器，含有 DNA、RNA 和核糖體，在細胞中參與有氧呼吸，產生能量供細胞使用，爲「細胞的發電廠」。

【註】此題完整概念在選修生物才會提及。

9. **A**

【解析】　由尿液的組成可以發現，在服藥前只有葡萄糖的濃度不在正常範圍，而服藥後發現除了葡萄糖濃度以外，蛋白質濃度也變成不正常。由此可推得：

1. 服藥前：

此受試者原本就患有糖尿病，因爲血糖濃度過高，腎小管對葡萄糖再吸收作用已達上限，所以多出來的血糖會從尿液排除。而從其他物質的濃度，可以判定腎小管和絲球體機能皆是正常的。

2. 服藥後：

尿液中的蛋白質濃度上升、其他物質濃度並無異常，表示腎小管再吸收功能仍正常。而因爲服藥後絲球體被破壞，所以使濾液中含有過高濃度的蛋白質，經腎小管再吸收作用後仍有部分留在尿液中。

因此答案選的是絲球體而非腎小管。

【註】本題爲本年度的難題，同學不易作答。此外，依照 99 課綱出題標準，本題範圍是基礎生物第五章，應該出在試題的第貳部分。所以本題對於非三類組同學而言會是一項重大的考驗。

10. **B**

【解析】　將水泥地改爲生態林，可以增加該地區生物可以利用的資源，因此可以使得生物多樣性增加。

(A) 若將自然林改爲人造林會造成植物種類單一化，使生物多樣性下降。

(C) 野生池塘改建爲吳郭魚飼養場，會造成魚類物種類單一化，使生物多樣性下降。

(D) 濕地塡海會破壞當地生態環境，造成生物多樣性下降。

(E) 原始河岸以混凝土槽化會破壞當地原始生態環境，也會造成生物多樣性下降。

11. **C**

【解析】 昆蟲爲節肢動物門昆蟲綱，爬蟲類爲脊索動物門爬蟲綱。在兩者的胚胎發育過程不相同，無法藉由胚胎學的證據推測兩者具有共同祖先。

(A) 化石的證據可以推測當時生物的外型、特徵，以及當時生物的生存環境。

(B) 鯨和麻雀都爲脊椎動物，從解剖學的證據上可以發現鯨的鰭與麻雀翅膀有相似的骨骼構造及排列方式，因此這兩個器官可以視爲胚胎發生來源相同的同源器官。

(D) 可將發現相同化石出現的不同地點來推測過去大陸板塊的關係。

(E) 透過分子生物學的技術，可以分析 DNA 序列和蛋白質中胺基酸序列來判斷物種的親緣關係，除了作爲演化上的證據，這項技術更應用在親緣關係樹的重建、刑事鑑定及預防醫學等。

12. **A**

【解析】 $107 \times 51.35\% + 109 \times 48.65\% = 107.9$，但銀在自然界不是 107amu，就是 109amu，無 107.9amu。

13. **D**

【解析】 (A) 甲在 30℃、40℃時較小；50℃時與乙同

(B) 甲 70g/100g 水，乙約 40g/100g 水

$$甲之溶解度 = \frac{70}{100+70} \times 100\% = 41.18\%$$

$$乙之溶解度 = \frac{40}{100+40} \times 100\% = 28.57\%$$

(C) 甲持續增加，乙在 50℃之後反而下降

(D) 皆為 50g/100g 水

(E) 乙在 80℃溶解度，乙在 50℃溶解度 50g/100g 水，所以不會有乙結晶

14. **B**

【解析】 反應前 $x\ell O_2$　　$40\ell CO$

反應後 $70\ell CO_2$ 與 O_2（CO 用完：限量試劑）

O_2 反應前有 $20+30=50\ell$，反應後 30ℓ

$PV = nRT \Rightarrow V \propto n$

$$
\begin{array}{ccccc}
O_2 & + & 2CO & \rightarrow & 2CO_2 \\
x & & 40\ell & & 40\ell \\
-20\ell & & -40\ell & & \\
\hline
30\ell & & 0\ell & & 40\ell
\end{array}
$$

15. **E**

【解析】 $[H^+]_甲 = 10^{-2}M$、$[H^+]_乙 = \dfrac{10^{-14}}{[OH^-]_乙} = \dfrac{10^{-14}}{10^{-3}} = 10^{-11}M$

$$\frac{[H^+]_甲}{[H^+]_乙} = \frac{10^{-2}}{10^{-11}} = 10^9$$

16. **E**

【解析】 (A) (B) (C) (D) 氧化數沒變

(E) $Zn^0 \rightarrow Zn^{2+} + 2e^-$（發生氧化）；

$Cu^{2+} + 2e^- \rightarrow Cu$（發生還原）

17. **D**

【解析】 $5 \times 3000 \times 4.2 \times 1000 = 5 \times 12.6 \times 10^6 = 6.3 \times 10^7 J$

$\frac{1}{6} C_6H_{12}O_{6(s)} + O_{2(g)} \rightarrow CO_{2(g)} + H_2O_{(\ell)}$　　$\Delta H = \frac{-2800}{6} kJ$

$2LiOH_{(s)} + CO_{2(s)} \rightarrow Li_2CO_{3(s)} + H_2O_{(\ell)}$

$\frac{3000 \times 4.2 \times 5 \times 6 \times 2 \times 24 \times 10^{-3}}{2800} = 6.48 \approx 6.5$

18. **E**

【解析】 尺度的大小，由大至小分別為星系團＞銀河系＞太陽系
＞太陽＞地球

19. **A**

【解析】 甲為近日點，位能最小，動能最大

20. **A**

【解析】 特定原子有特定的光譜，以此做鑑別

21. **C**

【解析】 弱力可使電子衰變成質子，電子，反微電子，β^- 衰變

$n \rightarrow p + e^- + \nu_e$

22. **C**

【解析】 任何波皆有

23. **B**

　　【解析】　108 km/hr = 30 m/s

$$F = \frac{\Delta P}{\Delta t} = \frac{m\Delta v}{0.15} = \frac{0.15 \times 30}{0.15} = 30(N)$$

二、多選題

24. **CD**

　　【解析】　當波浪來到岸邊，由於受到海底地形變淺影響，摩擦力降低波速；且因地形變淺，波浪無法維持原波形，故波高變高。

25. **AD**

　　【解析】　(A) 颱風中心是低氣壓中心，故氣壓值最低；雖然有颱風眼的颱風會有微弱氣流下沉，但不是每個颱風中心一定具備颱風眼。

　　　　　　(D) 颱風眼牆是氣流上升最旺盛之地，故雨勢最強。

　　　　　　(E) 颱風眼為下沉氣流。

26. **BE**

　　【解析】　(A) 地球系統包含岩石圈、水圈、氣圈、生物圈。

　　　　　　(B) 正確；如水、氣體等。

　　　　　　(C) 生態系統改變會影響地球系統平衡；如某種生物的滅絕會使得原為其天敵的生物數量大增。

　　　　　　(D) 板塊運動造成地球變動，影響地形地貌亦為地球循環的重要一環。

　　　　　　(E) 太陽是地球熱量來源之一；另者為放射性同位素的輻射熱與地溫梯度等。

27. **CD**

【解析】 「重組 DNA」是將不同生物的 DNA，藉由限制酶和接合酶的作用連結成新的 DNA。在生物技術的應用上，常將一段目標基因和 DNA 載體（如：細菌的質體、酵母菌的質體或病毒的核酸等）重組，再藉由基因轉殖將此重組 DNA 送入細菌、酵母菌或真核生物細胞中表現目標基因。

(A) 試管嬰兒為生殖醫學的重要技術，大致上的流程如下：

取出親代雙方的配子→讓精、卵在體外受精→將受精卵在體外培養至八細胞期→植入母體子宮進行著床→母體正常懷孕並產下嬰兒。

(B) 複製羊的技術和試管嬰兒不同在於需要受精作用，其流程如下：

取出白面母羊乳腺細胞的細胞核、取出黑面母羊卵細胞將細胞核去除→將白面母羊的細胞核與無核的黑面母羊卵細胞融合→在人為誘導下使融合的細胞進行細胞分裂發育成早期胚胎→將早期胚胎植入另一隻黑面母羊子宮內→桃莉羊產生，為白面母羊。

(E) 放射線誘發植物種子突變為人為誘導突變，希望藉此產生人類想要的品種。

28. **BCD**

【解析】 發酵作用可以分為兩個部分：

⑴ 糖解作用：

在細胞質進行，將葡萄糖分解為丙酮酸，並產生 2ATP 及 2NADH。

⑵ 還原作用：

　① 乳酸發酵：丙酮酸進一步得到 NADH 攜帶的電
　　子和氫質子，還原成乳酸。
　② 酒精發酵：丙酮酸利用酵素轉換為二氧化碳和乙
　　醛，乙醛進一步得到 NADH 攜帶的電子和氫質
　　子，還原成乙醇。

(A) 只有酒精發酵才會產生二氧化碳。

(B) 發酵作用過程中，可在糖解作用時淨得 2ATP

(C) 此選項敘述正確，但在高中課本中並無特別提及植
　　物種子可以利用發酵作用產能，因此此選項對同學
　　可能會造成困擾。

(D) 葡萄酒是利用葡萄經酵母作用後釀製而成。

(E) 人體的肌肉缺氧時會進行乳酸發酵，而非酒精發
　　酵。

【註】本題題幹中的「無氧呼吸」為不正確的專有名詞，
　　　目前許多課本、教師手冊及原文書已將「無氧呼
　　　吸」和「發酵作用」作區隔，分別如下：

　　　⑴ 無氧呼吸：糖解作用＋克式循環＋電子傳遞
　　　　鏈（電子接受者為 NO_3^-、SO_4^{2-} 等）

　　　⑵ 發酵作用：糖解作用＋還原作用

因此，本題對於認真區分兩種作用的同學，在作答上
會造成一定程度的困擾，但因為題目有告知應選幾項，
所以還是可以選出答案，不過若將應選幾項的提示去
除，此題將會有爭議。

29. **BCE**

【解析】(A) 透過人為復育貓熊可以延續物種，但無法有效提
　　　　高族群的遺傳多樣性。人工復育物種需要經過審
　　　　慎的流程以及避免近親交配，然而所產生的子代

　　　　　　數目並不多,因此無法有效提升基因變化和基因
　　　　　　種類。

(B)(C) 選項敘述正確,是重要的生態汙染概念。

(D) 大氣中二氧化碳濃度的增加會造成地球的增溫現
　　　象,而臭氧層破洞才會造成紫外線到達地表量增
　　　加。

(E) 生物放大效應是指一些脂溶性污染物或重金屬,
　　　因為在生物體內無法有效分解,造成此汙染物在
　　　生物體的濃度會隨食物鏈傳遞的過程而累積,越
　　　高等的消費者體內累積越多的汙染物。DDT 對環
　　　境的影響是重要的生物累積實例。

【註】 依照 99 課綱出題標準,本題部分選項出題範圍
　　　　是基礎生物第六章,應該出在試題的第貳部分。

30. **BE**

【解析】 以真核細胞在細胞核內的遺傳物質表現為例:

轉錄　　　　　轉譯　　　修飾
DNA───▶ RNA─────▶多肽鏈蛋白質─────▶
細胞核　　細胞質中的核糖體　　內膜系統或細胞質酵素

(A) 轉錄作用在細胞核內進行,由 RNA 聚合酶解開
　　　DNA 雙股螺旋,並依照模板股合成新的 RNA。
　　　此外,轉錄作用也可以在半自主胞器的基質進行。

(B) 轉譯作用在細胞質進行,進行場所可為粗糙型內質
　　　網上的核醣體、細胞質的游離型核糖體及半自主胞
　　　器基質的核醣體。

(C)(D)(E) 基因表現時,RNA 聚合酶解開 DNA 雙股螺
　　　旋,並以其中一股作為模板股,合成新的 RNA,
　　　此過程稱為轉錄作用。

31. **CE**

【解析】 (A) $\Delta H = 68kJ > 0$　吸熱

(B) $\frac{1}{2} N_{2(g)} + O_2 = NO_{2(g)}$

(C) $\Delta H = 34kJ$

(D) N_2 為還原劑

(E) NO_2 溶於水為酸性

32. **BD**

【解析】 $Na_2CO_3 + 5HCl \rightarrow 2NaCl + H_2O + CO_2$

　　　0.04mol　　　0.04mol

　+ 0.02mol　　− 0.04mol　　　　　+ 0.02mol

　──────────────────────────────────

　+ 0.02mol　　　　0　　　　　　　+ 0.02mol

(C) $0.04 - 0.02 = 0.02mol$

(D) HCl 為限量試劑

(E) NaCl 會溶於水

33. **ADE**

【解析】 (A) $2NH_{3(g)} \rightarrow N_{2(g)} + 3H_{2(g)}$

(B) $Fe_2O_{3(s)} + 3CO_{(g)} \rightarrow 2Fe_{(s)} + 3CO_{2(g)}$

(C) $C_6H_4(OH)_{2(aq)} + H_2O_{2(aq)} \rightarrow C_6H_4O_{2(aq)} + 2H_2O_{(\ell)}$

(D) $Ca(HCO_3)_{2(s)} + 2HCl_{(aq)} \rightarrow CaCl_{2(aq)} + 2CO_{2(g)} + 2H_2O_{(\ell)}$

(E) $HC \equiv CH_{(g)} + 2Ag(NH_3)_2NO_{3(aq)} \rightarrow AgC \equiv CAg_{(s)} + 2NH_4NO_{3(aq)} + 2NH_3$

34. **CE**

【解析】 (A) 為拉法第

(B) 厄斯特

(D) 由赫茲的實驗證實

35. **BE**

【解析】 (B) 光的干涉現象。

(E) 微粒說預測變快（不全）。

36. **ADE**

【解析】 (B) 愛因斯坦是第一個解釋光電效應而得諾貝爾獎的人。

(E) 與光強度（光子數）無關。

三、綜合題

37-40為題組

37. **AE**

【解析】 雷雨是因大氣強烈對流所產生的現象，也與氮的循環有關。發生時往往伴隨著閃電、狂風、暴雨，甚至冰雹、龍捲風等劇烈天氣。產生雷雨的積雨雲形成發展時，大氣環境一般具備下列三個條件：大氣處於不穩定狀態、有充沛的水汽和足夠的舉升力。(A)(E) 兩選項均為高氣壓，為下沉氣流。

38. **ABD**

【解析】 (A) 文中提及：「…空中的雷電可使氮與氧化合…」。為自然界中利用閃電能量來固氮。

(B) 文中提及：「…固氮酶可將氮氣形成銨鹽，再經由亞硝化細菌與硝化細菌轉化硝酸鹽…」。其作用方式如下：

⑴ 亞硝酸化細菌可以將銨鹽轉化為亞硝酸鹽。

⑵ 硝酸化細菌可以將亞硝酸鹽轉化為硝酸鹽。

(C) 此題硫酸銨的化學式寫錯，應為 $(NH_4)_2SO_4$。

(D) 植物吸收無機氮的形式為銨鹽 (NH_4^+) 及硝酸鹽 (NO_3^-)。

(E) 在實驗室要在高溫高壓下才能將氮氣與氫氣合成
　　爲氨，即爲「哈伯法製氨」。

【註】依照 99 課綱出題標準，本題範圍是基礎生物第
　　　六章，應該出在試題的第貳部分。此外，文中
　　　的亞硝化細菌應改爲亞硝酸化細菌、硝化細菌
　　　應改爲硝酸化細菌較爲正確。

39. **BDE**

【解析】(A)(B) 文中提及：「⋯生物中僅有固氮細菌可進行固
　　　　氮⋯」。

(C) 植物吸收無機氮的形式爲銨鹽 (NH_4^+) 及硝酸鹽
　　(NO_3^-)。

(D) 水稻田中若有共生的藍綠菌，則因藍綠菌可以行
　　固氮作用，所以可以減少施氮肥。

(E) 植物若和根瘤菌共生，則因根留菌可以進行固氮，
　　所以植物可以獲得氮源。

【註】依照 99 課綱出題標準，本題範圍是基礎生物
　　　第六章，應該出在試題的第貳部分。

40. **AB**

【解析】(D) 不需介質。

(C) 電場、磁場、傳播方向皆互相垂直。

第貳部分

41. **D**

【解析】宇宙所有星體在地球上觀測，只能看見其投影在天球所
　　　在的方位。在相同的方位中，存在許多與地球不同距離
　　　的天體；某些天體離地球較近，故看起來的形體較亮也
　　　較大；因此可能造成相同方位中距離較遠的星體看不清

楚，或因此而直接被遮蔽了。在地球上可觀測的星系必定不屬於銀河系，表距離地球位置遙遠；地球位於銀河系盤面上的其中一個懸臂上；在某些天球方位，較遠的星系可能被銀河系中密度較大、星體較多的恆星、星團或星雲等物質遮蔽了，所以無法於地球上觀測清楚。

42. **B**

【解析】 碎屑沉積岩的顆粒大小取決於外營力的搬運；沉積物越大，表搬運的營力越大。甲～丙表老～青；顆粒大～小表營力大～小。所以在沉積甲地層時應為陸相沉積（河川，直徑超過 2mm 表礫岩）；而丙的沉積顆粒極小應為深海相沉積。故此題答案應為陸地下沉或海平面上升。

43. **D**

【解析】 由甲測站資料可算出甲距離震央 $S = Vp \times Tp = Vs \times Ts$；$S = 120km$，由於 P 波波速為 6km/sec，故可算出 P 波走了 20sec；因此地震發生的時間 $T = 9{:}25{:}10$；由乙測站資料可算出乙測站離震央位置 $S = 360km$；故乙測站的 P 波須走 60sec，由於地震發生時間為 9:25:10；故於乙測站收到 P 波的時間為 9:26:10。

44. **E**

【解析】 根據題幹可以判斷 ABCD 四個選項均為正確；而上部地函位於地殼下方；所以如要鑽探應選擇地殼最薄之地。北緯 10 度、東經 15 度之地點地殼厚度較其他地區為厚。

45. **AE**

【解析】 (B) 氣體會吸收能量而產生吸收的暗線。
(C) 皆可產生。
(D) 太陽為連續光譜，但有若干吸收光譜。

46. **E**

【解析】 由於現今的自轉軸方向為 X，而北半球的夏季主要因為
地球位於遠日點，且陽光直射；而冬季位於近日點，且
陽光斜射。若當地球自轉軸進動至 Y；則表示地球在遠
日點時，北半球因為斜射所以成為冬季；故原來的冬季
會從近日點轉變為遠日點，故冬季會較原來冷。而夏季
在原來是遠日點，由於自轉軸進動，所以會在近日點時
陽光直射北半球，故夏季會比原來熱。

47. **BE**

【解析】 (A) 北風指的是從北方吹來的風。

(C) 露點的大小只能判斷在某個溫度下的飽和水氣壓；
不能進行相對溼度的判斷。

(D) 氣溫會受到溫度的影響，所以不應放置於陽光下。

48-49 為題組

48. **A**

【解析】 依照 BB 值的定義算出各動物的 BB 值如下：

小鼠：$0.5 \div 24 = 2.08 \times 10^{12}$

大象：$5000 \div 2550000 = 1.96 \times 10^{13}$

黑猩猩：$400 \div 42000 = 9.52 \times 10^{13}$

羊：$100 \div 40000 = 2.50 \times 10^{13}$

BB 值由大至小排序：小鼠＞黑猩猩＞羊＞大象。

49. **D**

【解析】 根據上題，已知 BB 值由大至小排序：小鼠＞黑猩猩＞
羊＞大象。

    (A) 黑猩猩為靈長類，但其 BB 值比小鼠小。

    (B) 以小鼠和大象為例，小鼠個體較小但 BB 值較大，而大象個體較大 BB 值較小。

    (C) 大象體重最重，但其 BB 值最小。

    (D) 小鼠和黑猩猩為雜食性，而羊和大象為草食性。由此可知雜食性動物 BB 值大於草食性動物。

    (E) 黑猩猩和大象具有高度的社會性，但大象的 BB 值最小。

50. **BE**

【解析】 植物的向地性、背地性和生長素分布不均有關，生長素濃度對根、芽和莖的影響。如圖：

    ⑴ 根：在濃度低時可以促進生長，在高濃度時抑制生長，且對於生長素濃度較敏感。

    ⑵ 芽：促進生長的濃度介於根和莖之間。

    ⑶ 莖：在濃度高時可以促進生長，在低濃度時抑制生長。

    (A) 由圖可知，根對低濃度的生長素最為敏感。

    (B) 由圖可知，1ppm 生長素對莖有最大促進生長的效果。

    (C) 由圖可知，10^{-1}ppm 生長素對芽不促進也不抑制生長，是正常生長的情形。

    (D) 由圖可知，10^{-2}ppm 生長素會抑制根的生長，但並非使根長度變短。

    (E) 由圖可知，10^{-3}ppm 生長素可同時促進根、芽及莖生長。

51-52 為題組

51. **BCD**

【解析】　(A) 此選項文中並無特別提及，是同學必須知道的生物
　　　　　知識。選項敘述錯誤，應為副甲狀腺共有 4 個，包
　　　　　埋在甲狀腺的組織內。

　　　　(B) 文中提及：「…利用碘幫浦蛋白將碘離子吸收至細
　　　　　胞內，過程中會消耗 ATP…」。此碘幫浦蛋白為膜
　　　　　上的載體蛋白，會耗能運送碘離子以累積細胞內的
　　　　　碘離子濃度，為初級主動運輸的作用方式。

　　　　(C) 文中提及：「…最後甲狀腺球蛋白中的酪胺酸與碘
　　　　　離子結合，形成甲狀腺素…」。故知需有甲狀腺球蛋
　　　　　白才能合成甲狀腺素。

　　　　(D) 文中提及：「…服用碘片的作用是讓甲狀腺細胞內
　　　　　的碘含量飽和，使放射性碘不易成為合成甲狀腺素
　　　　　的原料…」。由此可知甲狀腺細胞對碘的吸收具有
　　　　　飽和現象。

　　　　(E) 文中提及：「…甲狀腺素進入標的細胞後，會與其
　　　　　位於細胞核中的受體結合…」。由此可知甲狀腺素
　　　　　的受器位於細胞核內。

52. **E**

【解析】　文中提及：「…一般而言，碘片服用約 30 分鐘後即可
　　　　　發揮效用，而自環境中接觸到的放射性碘，則需約 10
　　　　　～12 小時才會進到人體的甲狀腺。」由此可知，若在
　　　　　3 月 21 日早上 8 點遭受放射性碘污染，最晚應在 3 月
　　　　　21 日傍晚 6～8 點前服用碘片，使甲狀腺細胞內的碘
　　　　　離子濃度飽和，以避免放射性碘進入甲狀腺細胞。

53-54 為題組

53. **BCD**

【解析】 (A) 由文章可知棉花為錦葵科（Malvaceae）棉屬
（Gossypium），但此資料不足以判斷棉花的學名。
學名由屬名和種小名構成，皆用拉丁文斜體字表
示，屬名表示名詞且第一個字要大寫，種小名表示
形容詞。

(B) 文中提及：「…其種子之種皮毛細胞形成的纖維是
紡織原料…」。此選項敘述正確。

(C) 文中提及：「…種仁則含有豐富的蛋白質與脂質
…」。此選項敘述正確。

(D) 文中提及：「…但是卻同時具有多酚類化合物『棉
酚』，只有反芻動物才能無毒消化…」。因為牛、
羊皆為反芻動物，因此此選項敘述正確。

(E) 文中提及：「…對人類則具有相當毒性而不能直接
作為食物的來源。棉花的葉、莖與花也含有棉酚，
其可保護植株避免受到病蟲害的侵襲。…」。由此
可知，棉酚對於人類和昆蟲皆為有毒物質。此選
項敘述不正確。

【註】依照99課綱出題標準，本題部分選項為基礎生
物第三章範圍，應出在試題的第壹部分較合適。

54. **BE**

【解析】 (A) 文中提及：「…棉花的葉、莖與花也含有棉酚，其
可保護植株避免受到病蟲害的侵襲。…」。由此可
知，野生種的棉花植株不只種子、花含有棉酚，葉
和莖也含有棉酚。因此本選項敘述不正確。

(B) 文中提及：「…植物學家曾利用雜交培育出不含棉酚的品種，但卻因極易受到蟲害而大幅減產。美國科學家已成功利用基因轉殖技術（核糖核酸干擾技術或稱基因沉默技術），僅減弱種子內之棉酚基因的表現，但在其他器官則不受影響，植株仍能保有抵禦蟲害的能力。…」。此選項敘述正確。

(C) 同 (B) 選項的段落可知，雜交培育出不含棉酚的品種，不具有抵禦蟲害的能力；但利用基因轉殖技術產生的種子，由於在其他器官不受影響，仍有抵禦蟲害的能力。

(D) 文中提及：「…雖然研究人員已證實這種轉基因棉花的可遺傳性，但尚未能確定其基因穩定性的維持。…」。由此可知去除棉酚毒性之基改棉花種子的基因穩定性尚未確定。

(E) 同 (B) 選項的段落可知本選項敘述正確。

【註】依照 99 課綱出題標準，本題多數選項為基礎生物第二章、第三章的觀念，應出在試題的第壹部分較為合適。

55. **BC**

【解析】　(A) 應為 C_nH_{2n+2}　　　(B) 應為 C_nH_{2n}

　　　　　(C) 應為 C_nH_{2n}　　　　(D) 應為 C_nH_{2n-2}

　　　　　(E) 應為 C_nH_{2n-2}

56. **ABC**

【解析】　(D) 葡萄糖 + 果糖

　　　　　(E) $(CH_2O)_n$ 或 $C_x(H_2O)_y$

57. **ADE**

【解析】 (A) 羧基
$$-\overset{\displaystyle O}{\overset{\|}{C}}-OH$$

(B) 鹵基 R–X（F、Cl、Br、I），並無此官能基

(C) 酯基　　　　O　　　，並無此官能基
$$-\overset{\displaystyle O}{\overset{\|}{C}}-O-R'$$

(D) 羥基 –OH

(E) 醯胺基
$$-\overset{\displaystyle O}{\overset{\|}{C}}-\overset{\displaystyle H}{\overset{|}{N}}$$

<u>58-59 為題組</u>

58. **B**

【解析】
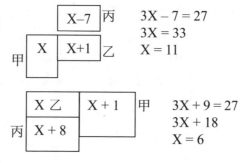

$3X - 7 = 27$
$3X = 33$
$X = 11$

$3X + 9 = 27$
$3X + 18$
$X = 6$

59. **A**

【解析】
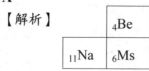

60. **AC**

【解析】 甲應為 IA 族，乙為負 2 價，丙丁輔助推答案。

61. **BD**

【解析】 C：9 個，H：13 個，O：2 個，N：1 個

(A) 9 + 13 = 22

(C) 1 + 2 = 3

(E) 9 + 1 = 10

62. **D**

【解析】 XZ 為同號電，YZ 為異號電

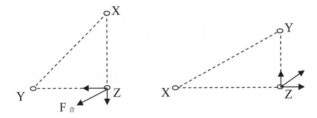

63-64 為題組

63. **B**

【解析】 曲線下面積為位移=12m，$\dfrac{1}{2} \times 2 \times 2 + 2 \times (2 + t - 2) +$

$\dfrac{1}{2} \times [6 + t - (2 + t)] \times 2 = 2 + 2t + 4 = 12$　　$t = 3$

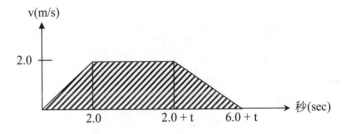

64. **D**

【解析】 加速階段 $a = \dfrac{2}{2} = 1m/s^2\downarrow$，$mg - N = ma$

$\Rightarrow N = m(g - a) = 450N$

等速階段 $a = 0m/s^2$，$N = mg = 50 \times 10 = 500N$

減速階段 $a = \dfrac{2}{4} = 0.5m/s^2\uparrow$，$N - mg = ma$

$\Rightarrow N = m(g + a) = 50(10 + 0.5) = 525N$

65. **ABD**

【解析】 (A) $f \cdot s$ 同向 → 正功

(B) 作用力與反作用力

(C) 由 M, m 系統能量守恆 → $mV = (M + m)V'$

$\rightarrow V' = \dfrac{mV}{M + m}$

(E) 部分動能變熱能

66. **BCE**

【解析】 作用力與反作用力即將施力者與受力者交換

67-68 為題組

67. **E**

【解析】 $S = \dfrac{F}{\Delta L} = \dfrac{700}{30 \times 10^{-3}} = 2.33 \times 10^4$

68. **BD**

【解析】 (B) 視力正常比視力模糊時 S 大

(D) 相同視力時，台階落差大時 S 大

103 年大學入學學科能力測驗試題
國文考科

第壹部分：選擇題（占 54 分）

一、單選題（占 30 分）

說明：第 1 題至第 15 題，每題有 4 個選項，其中只有一個是正確或最適當的選項，請畫記在答案卡之「選擇題答案區」。各題答對者，得 2 分；答錯、未作答或畫記多於一個選項者，該題以零分計算。

1. 下列各組「」內注音符號所表示的字，字形相同的選項是：
   (A) 輪「ㄈㄢ」上陣／漏鼓移，則「ㄈㄢ」代
   (B) 「ㄐㄧㄠˇ」倖獲勝／「ㄐㄧㄠˇ」俗干名
   (C) 消災解「ㄜˋ」／運會之趨，莫可阻「ㄜˋ」
   (D) 「ㄧㄢˇ」旗息鼓／土地平曠，屋舍「ㄧㄢˇ」然

2. 閱讀下文，選出依序最適合填入□內的選項：

   　　對於如樂生院這般極具保存價值的歷史遺產，首先，內政部身為主管機關，當然□□□□，應主動進行古蹟審查與指定作業；再者，過去許多年「文資法」的修訂，□□不是為了限制內政部指定古蹟的權力，而是將原先只屬於中央政府的權力釋放出來，讓地方政府有更多□□，共同為保存臺灣珍貴的文化資產與集體記憶，擔起重要的任務。（改寫自夏鑄九〈正視歷史教育，莫做古蹟殺手〉）
   (A) 責無旁貸／從來／權責　　　(B) 責無旁貸／反而／自由
   (C) 依法行政／從來／自由　　　(D) 依法行政／反而／權責

3. 桃花因顏色鮮豔美麗，故詩人常藉以比喻美麗的女子。下列詩歌中的桃花，**不具**此喻意的選項是：

(A) 一夜清風動扇愁，背時容色入新秋。桃花眼裡汪汪淚，忍到更深枕上流

(B) 每坐臺前見玉容，今朝不與昨朝同。良人一夜出門宿，減卻桃花一半紅

(C) 淺色桃花亞短牆，不因風送也聞香。凝情盡日君知否，還似紅兒淡薄妝

(D) 暮春三月日重三，春水桃花滿禊潭。廣樂逶迤天上下，仙舟搖衍鏡中酣

4. 閱讀下文，選出最接近其意旨的選項：

　　堅信一首詩的沉默比所有的擴音器加起來更清晰，比機槍的口才野砲的雄辯更持久。堅信文字的冰庫能冷藏最燙的激情最新鮮的想像。時間，你帶得走歌者帶不走歌。（余光中《青青邊愁》）

(A) 筆落驚風雨，詩成泣鬼神

(B) 不惜歌者苦，但傷知音稀

(C) 屈平詞賦懸日月，楚王臺榭空山丘

(D) 詩可以興，可以觀，可以群，可以怨

5. 某生為「先秦諸子散文」繪製便於理解的圖形如右，選出敘述正確的選項：

(A) 甲可填：《墨子》

(B) 乙可填：作者親撰與弟子對話內容

(C) 丙可填：《孟子》

(D) 丁可填：出現概括全篇主旨的篇題

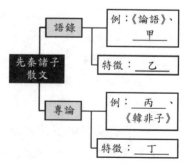

6. 閱讀下文，選出敘述正確的選項：

　　四凶之才皆可用。堯之時，聖人在上，皆以其才任大位，而不敢露其不善之心。堯非不知其不善也，伏則聖人亦不得而誅之。及堯舉舜於匹夫之中而禪之位，則是四人者始懷憤怨不平之心而顯其惡，故舜得以因其跡而誅竄之也。

（《河南程氏遺書》）

> 四凶：相傳爲堯舜時代四個惡名昭彰的部族首領。

(A) 堯知四凶不善，故意授以大位，使四凶彼此制衡

(B) 堯不因人有不善之心，即對其才幹能力全盤否定

(C) 舜得位後，四凶遭貶斥而懷恨，心性遂由善轉惡

(D) 舜認爲心懷惡念者，縱無惡行表露，仍不可寬貸

7. 右圖是兩副吟詠鄭成功的對聯，請依文意與對聯組成原則，選出最適合的選項：

甲、方知海外有孤忠

乙、稱名則婦孺皆知

丙、敢向東南爭半壁

丁、舉目有河山之異

諸王無寸土，一隅抗志，④
四鎮多貳心，兩島屯師，③
南天留祠宇，雄圖雖渺，②
東海望臺澎，風景不殊，①

	①	②	③	④
(A)	丙	甲	丁	乙
(B)	丙	乙	丁	甲
(C)	丁	甲	丙	乙
(D)	丁	乙	丙	甲

8. 下列是一段散文，依文意選出排列順序最恰當的選項：

　　千百年後凝視王羲之的〈蘭亭序〉，

甲、碰到紙上的纖維，順勢微微迴轉，

乙、單鞭蓄勢，繼續向左緩緩推出……

丙、<u>太極雲手般向右下沉去，力道隱含未盡，</u>

丁、<u>仍然可以感受王羲之筆尖每一個纖細的動作，</u>

戊、<u>永和九年歲在癸丑，那永字的一點如凌空而來風聲，</u>

光是那麼一點，可以領略的內涵，用十年時間去理解都不嫌多。

（侯吉諒〈紙上太極〉）

(A) 丁乙甲戊丙   (B) 丁戊甲丙乙

(C) 戊乙甲丙丁   (D) 戊丁乙丙甲

9. 閱讀下文，選出符合作者想法的選項：

    年紀輕的時候，倒是敢說話，可是沒有人理睬他。到了中年，在社會上有了地位，說出話來有相當分量，誰都樂意聽他的，可是正在努力的學做人，一味的唯唯否否，出言吐語，切忌生冷，總揀那爛熟的，人云亦云。等到年紀大了，退休之後，比較不負責任，可以言論自由了，不幸老年人總是嘮叨的居多，聽得人不耐煩，任是入情入理的話，也當作耳邊風。這是人生一大悲劇。

（張愛玲〈論寫作〉）

(A) 年輕人與老年人都較敢表達意見，但也不耐聽他人意見

(B) 中年人處世多權衡利害輕重，常不願說出與眾不同之論

(C) 說話者地位越高、年齡越長，越能得到聽眾喜愛與信任

(D) 「說者無意，聽者有心」的差距，形成「人生一大悲劇」

<u>10-11為題組</u>

閱讀下文，回答 10-11 題。

    不止一次有人以「博士」呼我，有的是口惠，有的竟見諸筆墨。此種善意的逾格提拔，受者是窘不堪言的。……立予糾正，顯得矯情，聽其自然，又有愧於心，說不定還給人以「無恥近乎勇」的口實，為禍為福，無待言矣。……

　　我生平第一次受類此擡舉的洗禮，是在十八、九年以前，剛當上助教不滿幾個月。夫助教者，實在是學生生活的延長。……就當此時，一位父執輩路過邊城，少不得要略盡地主之誼，這一來可引來數秒鐘的無地自容。因為，不數日，一封道謝的信來了，信封上赫然有某某教授道啓字樣。天下事那裡有天知，地知，你知，我知那樣便宜之事。那位司閽老者，平時並不把每一封信都送到每人這裡，這天卻予我以殊遇。「咯，這是你的！」說時，眼睛緊盯住我，大有要我俯首認罪之意。我想他心中一定大嘆□□□□。好傢伙，才幾個月，就□□□□若是！司閽老者當然不是具有幽默感之人，否則他大可在「教授」之旁，作一眉批：「始於何時？」（節錄自吳魯芹〈博士和博士銜〉）

10. 上文□□□□內的詞語，依序最適合填入的選項是：
　　(A) 人心不古／招搖撞騙　　　(B) 人心不古／好為人師
　　(C) 不學無術／招搖撞騙　　　(D) 不學無術／好為人師

11. 下列敘述，符合上文文意的選項是：
　　(A) 被學校破格拔擢授予博士，讓作者心裡始終懷著不安與矛盾
　　(B) 作者認為稱謂宜與實際相符，故對被冠以虛銜常感到不自在
　　(C) 作者視浮名為身外之物，故對他人奉承的尊稱並不放在心上
　　(D) 司閽老者不假辭色的批評，令作者為自己的虛榮心深感慚愧

12-13為題組

閱讀下文，回答 12-13 題。

　　王汾濱言：其鄉有養八哥者，教以語言，甚狎習，出遊必與之俱，相將數年矣。一日，將過絳州，去家尚遠，而資斧已罄。其人愁苦無策。鳥云：「何不售我？送我王邸，當得善價，不愁歸路無

賣也。」其人云:「我安忍!」鳥言:「不妨。主人得價疾行,待我城西二十里大樹下。」其人從之。攜至城,相問答,觀者漸眾。有中貴見之,聞諸王。王召入,欲買之。其人曰:「小人相依為命,不願賣。」王問鳥:「汝願住否?」答言:「願住。」王喜。鳥又言:「給價十金,勿多予。」王益喜,立畀十金。其人故作懊恨狀而出。王與鳥語,應對便捷。呼肉啖之。食已,鳥曰:「臣要浴。」王命金盆貯水,開籠令浴。浴已,飛簷間,梳翎抖羽,尚與王喋喋不休。頃之,羽燥,翩躚而起。操晉聲曰:「臣去呀!」顧盼已失所在。王及內侍,仰面咨嗟,急覓其人,則已渺矣。後有往秦中者,見其人攜鳥在西安市上。(蒲松齡《聊齋誌異‧鴝鵒》

> 畀:交給。

12. 關於本篇故事內容,敘述正確的選項是:
    (A) 八哥的主人因缺旅費,打算出售八哥
    (B) 八哥擬另謀棲身之處,設局誆騙主人
    (C) 八哥與主人合謀,利用賣身詐取錢財
    (D) 八哥與主人得手後,在西安故技重施

13. 下列關於故事的解釋,**錯誤**的選項是:
    (A) 主人將八哥「攜至城,相問答」,係為製造奇觀引人注意
    (B) 八哥對王言「給價十金,勿多予」,有助於取得王的信任
    (C) 主人「故作懊恨狀」,目的是為了讓八哥相信他萬分不捨
    (D) 八哥「尚與王喋喋不休」,係為讓王疏於防備,以便逃走

14-15為題組

閱讀下文,回答 14-15 題。

　　昌他亡西周,之東周,盡輸西周之情於東周。東周大喜,西周大怒。馮且曰:「臣能殺之。」君予金三十斤。馮且使人操金與書,

間遺昌他書曰：「告昌他，事可成，勉成之；不可成，亟亡來亡來。事久且泄，自令身死。」因使人告東周之候曰：「今夕有姦人當入者矣。」候得而獻東周，東周立殺昌他。（《戰國策·東周策》）

> 候：斥候，探子。

14. 下列各組「　」內的文字，前後意義相同的選項是：
　　(A) 昌他亡西周，「之」東周／嚮「之」來，非有取於升斗之祿
　　(B) 馮且使人操金「與」書／噫！微斯人，吾誰「與」歸
　　(C) 事久「且」泄，自令身死／今疾「且」成，已非三月不能瘳
　　(D) 「因」使人告東周之候曰／「因」人之力而敝之，不仁

15. 依據文意，選出敘述正確的選項：
　　(A) 馮且收買昌他為西周間諜，遭東周查獲而遇害
　　(B) 馮且命昌他策反東周斥候，反令昌他被捕遇害
　　(C) 馮且誣陷昌他收賄通敵，昌他逃至東周而遭戮
　　(D) 馮且故布疑陣，使昌他被東周誤為間諜而遭戮

二、多選題（占 24 分）

說明：第 16 題至第 23 題，每題有 5 個選項，其中至少有一個是正確的選項，請將正確選項畫記在答案卡之「選擇題答案區」。各題之選項獨立判定，所有選項均答對者，得 3 分；答錯 1 個選項者，得 1.8 分；答錯 2 個選項者，得 0.6 分；答錯多於 2 個選項或所有選項均未作答者，該題以零分計算。

16. 文學作品常見「悲」、「喜」並敘而「以喜襯悲」的表達方式。下列文句，含有此種表達方式的選項是：
　　(A) 這豈不正是此生不斷，反覆來襲的，熟悉，令人動心的白芒花嗎？像夢魘，但它是美麗的夢魘，美麗而哀愁
　　(B) 我已懂得，一把小小黃楊木梳，再也理不清母親心中的愁緒。

因為在走廊的那一邊，不時飄來父親和姨娘琅琅的笑語聲

(C) （秦得參）在室內踱來踱去，經他妻子幾次的催促，他總沒有聽見似的，心裡只在想，總覺有一種不明瞭的悲哀，只不住漏出幾聲的嘆息

(D) 有幾回，鄰舍孩子聽得笑聲，也趕熱鬧，圍住了孔乙己。他便給他們茴香豆吃，一人一顆。孩子吃完豆，仍然不散，眼睛都望著碟子。孔乙己著了慌，伸開五指將碟子罩住

(E) 金發伯突然奇怪的、異常的大笑起來，……秀潔聽出他是有意幽默，有意製造輕鬆，有意大笑；胸中一時千頭萬緒，五味雜陳，聽著金發伯那樣的笑聲，竟比哭聲更令人難以承受，卻也只能附和著笑

17. 「代詞」在句子中，通常指稱特定的對象，但有時亦未明確指涉特定的人事物。下列文句中的「我」、「你」、「他」，**並未**明確指涉特定對象的選項是：

(A) 同學們你一言，我一句，討論得非常熱烈

(B) 大家一窩蜂去動物園看圓仔，你推我擠，萬頭攢動

(C) 我說的那間飯店，能清楚看到黃色小鴨，包管你滿意

(D) 咱們兩個就此拆夥，你走你的陽關道，我過我的獨木橋

(E) 「他山之石，可以攻玉」，意在教人汲取經驗、見賢思齊

18. 某唐代詩人特展的宣傳看板有詩句如下，下列可作為此詩人特展解說標題的選項是：

(A) 流放夜郎

(B) 天上謫仙人

(C) 成都浣花草堂

(D) 見證安史之亂

(E) 繼承新樂府運動

> 被廷爭疏離君主／被戰爭逐出長安／蜀道這條玄宗倉皇出奔的路／你奔，就苦於上青天了／麗人行的低吟／悲陳陶的吶喊／哀江頭的吞聲／沒感動任何當局／你的詩只有酒壺聽懂

19. 閱讀右詩，選出符合詩意的選項：

(A) 「乾燥的風」和「稻草瑟縮著」凸顯農作物歉收

> 　　在乾燥的風中／一束一束稻草，瑟縮著／在被遺棄了的田野
> 　　午後，在不怎麼溫暖／也不是不溫暖的陽光中／吾鄉的老人，萎頓著／在破落的庭院
> 　　終於是一束稻草的／吾鄉的老人／誰還記得／也曾綠過葉、開過花、結過果
> 　　一束稻草的過程和終局／是吾鄉人人的年譜（吳晟〈稻草〉）

(B) 「不怎麼溫暖／也不是不溫暖的陽光」比喻人們的關懷不夠充分

(C) 「被遺棄了的田野」和「破落的庭院」皆暗示農村的沒落

(D) 「曾綠過葉、開過花、結過果」比喻老農與農村昔日的榮景

(E) 「吾鄉人人的年譜」表達對老農與農村宿命無奈的感歎

20. 關於下列甲、乙二人的陳述，敘述正確的選項是：

> 每患遷、固以來，文字繁多，自布衣之士，讀之不遍，況於人主，日有萬機，何暇周覽！臣常不自揆，欲刪削冗長，舉撮機要，專取關國家盛衰，繫生民休戚，善可為法，惡可為戒者，為編年一書，……上起戰國，下終五代，凡一千三百六十二年，修成二百九十四卷。

甲

> 予在京師，因借館閣諸公家藏數本，參校之，蓋十正其六七，……其要皆主於利言之，合從連橫，變詐百出。然自春秋之後，以迄于秦，二百餘年興亡成敗之跡，粗見於是矣！雖非義理之所存，而辯麗橫肆，亦文辭之最，學者所不宜廢也。

乙

(A) 「甲」強調該書的政治功能；「乙」肯定該書的言辭效益

(B) 「甲」所修之書可能是《資治通鑑》；「乙」所校之書可能是《戰國策》

(C) 「甲」和「乙」的陳述，皆為呈給皇帝的上書，勸諫治國應以歷代興亡為鑑

(D) 《史記》、《漢書》是「甲」用以成書的主要材料，也是「乙」用以成書的主要憑藉

(E) 〈燭之武退秦師〉可在「甲」所修之書中檢得；〈馮諼客孟嘗君〉可在「乙」所校之書中讀到

21. 閱讀下文，選出敘述正確的選項：

　　曾子寢疾，病。樂正子春坐於床下，曾元、曾申坐於足，童子隅坐而執燭。童子曰：「華而睆，大夫之簀與？」子春曰：「止！」曾子聞之，瞿然曰：「呼！」曰：「華而睆，大夫之簀與？」曾子曰：「然。斯季孫之賜也，我未之能易也。元，起，易簀。」曾元曰：「夫子之病革矣！不可以變。幸而至於旦，請敬易之。」曾子曰：「爾之愛我也不如彼。君子之愛人也以德，細人之愛人也以姑息。吾何求哉？吾得正而斃焉，斯已矣。」舉扶而易之，反席未安而沒。（《禮記‧檀弓》）

(A) 樂正子春擔心曾子睡不著，故要童子勿執燭火

(B) 曾元希望曾子換席子，以不負季孫賜簀的美意

(C) 曾子責怪曾元不懂得變通，不如季孫善體人意

(D) 曾子認為不宜逾矩，故堅持要曾元為他換席子

(E) 曾子以為：因愛而姑息對方，反可能傷害對方

> 睆：明亮。
> 簀：席子。

22. 蘇軾〈赤壁賦〉：「惟江上之清風，與山間之明月，耳得之而為聲，目遇之而成色」，此四句的文意可理解為：「江上之清風，耳得之而為聲；山間之明月，目遇之而成色」，但作者改變句子的銜接順序，故閱讀時，宜就文意調節對應關係。下列文句，與此表達方式相似的選項是：

(A) 句讀之不知，惑之不解；或師焉，或不焉

(B) 西伯幽而演《易》，周旦顯而制《禮》；不以隱約而弗務，不以康樂而加思

(C) 禽鳥知山林之樂，而不知人之樂；人知從太守遊而樂，而不知太守之樂其樂

(D) 牠們曾交錯湧疊，也曾高速接近船舷又敏捷地側翻；如在表演水中疊羅漢，如流星一樣劃一道弧線拋射離去

(E) 老和尚竟哽咽起來，掉了幾滴眼淚，他趕緊用袈裟的寬袖子，搵了一搵眼睛；秦義方也掏出手帕，狠狠擤了一下鼻子

23. 《後宮甄嬛傳》中，華妃陪皇后看戲時說：「到底是樊梨花有身家，出身西涼將門的嫡出女兒。若是換作庶出女兒，再沒有這移山倒海的本事，可真是死路一條了。」華妃表面上是評論戲中角色，實則藉以影射皇后是庶出女兒。下列文句畫底線處的文字，也在表面意義之外另有影射的選項是：

(A) 鳳姐拉過劉姥姥來，把一盤子花橫三豎四的插了一頭，賈母和眾人笑得不得了，劉姥姥笑道：「<u>我雖老了，年輕時也風流，愛個花兒粉兒的，今兒索性做個老風流。</u>」

(B) 范進想向丈人胡屠戶借鄉試的路費，被胡屠戶罵了一個狗血噴頭：「<u>你問我借盤纏，我一天殺一個豬還賺不得錢把銀子，都把與你去丟在水裡，叫我一家老小嗑西北風？</u>」

(C) 華歆勸曹丕殺曹植。曹丕召曹植入見，限七步吟詩一首，須以「兄弟」為題，但不許犯「兄弟」字樣，方可免死。曹植略不思索，即吟曰：「<u>煮豆燃豆萁，豆在釜中泣。本是同根生，相煎何太急！</u>」

(D) 虯髯客想請道士觀察李世民是否具天子之相，以決定自己是否退出逐鹿之局，乃由劉文靜邀李世民前來看棋。弈棋中的道士見李世民神采驚人，慘然曰：「<u>此局全輸矣！於此失卻局，奇哉！救無路矣！</u>」

(E) 歐陽鋒將柯鎮惡震下屋頂，郭靖、黃蓉分別以降龍十八掌、落英神劍掌對付歐陽鋒。一旁窺見的楊過，後來故意說給黃蓉聽：「<u>一個大蟋蟀跟一隻老蟋蟀對打，老蟋蟀輸了，又來了兩隻小蟋蟀幫著，三隻打一個。大蟋蟀跳來跳去，這邊彈一腳，那邊咬一口，嘿嘿，那可屬害了……</u>」

第貳部分：非選擇題（共三大題，占54分）

說明：本部分共有三題，請依各題指示作答，答案必須寫在「答案卷」上，並標明題號一、二、三。作答務必使用筆尖較粗之黑色墨水的筆書寫，且不得使用鉛筆。

一、文章解讀（占9分：第（一）題6分，第（二）題3分）

閱讀框線內文章，回答：（一）古人的「清賞」和今人的「觀光」有何不同？（二）文中「人品亦化成商品」的意思為何？

請將答案標明（一）（二）書寫，（一）（二）合計文長約100-150字（約5-7行）。

近代之觀光遊覽必廣攬遊眾，乃可贏利。故凡屬勝境，惟求通俗化，遂使群客奔波盡興，實則人看人。儻兼以歌唱舞蹈，愈撩亂，則愈活躍，心神無片刻安頓處，斯為觀光之成功。凡屬觀光，乃求動，不求靜。乃求熱鬧，不求清靜。此乃近代人心一大趨向。中國風景皆求清賞，「鳥鳴山更幽」，始覺此山中之深趣。「山中方七日，世上已千年」。儻亦男女雜沓，喧嘩擁擠，轉眼即過，則七日亦在一瞬間。此始是近代觀光客遊覽客所要求，如此才感快意。古人詩「振衣千仞岡，濯足萬里流」，今人則必在萬目睽睽下振衣，一振衣而下座，掌聲雷動，乃始快意。千仞岡上，何人得見！海水浴場，亦必人群俱集，乃始成一場面。一人濯足，則何情味可言！故千仞之岡，則必組旅行隊。萬里之流，則必組游泳團。一人閒居，必感無聊。古以窈窕乃成淑女，今則儘時髦，儘摩登，投入人群中活躍，以供人玩賞為己樂，人品亦化成商品，良可嗟矣。（錢穆〈品與味〉）

二、文章分析（占 18 分：第（一）題 9 分，第（二）題 9 分）

　　言語交際過程中，常見運用「謙遜原則」—儘量降低姿態，不彰顯自己，例如：「小弟不才，能力有限，請多包涵」。但基於某些目的，也可能刻意不採取這項原則。請就下引諸葛亮〈出師表〉的文字分析：（一）**列出並簡要說明**文中何處運用「謙遜原則」？何處刻意彰顯自己，不採取「謙遜原則」？（二）文中運用「謙遜原則」的同時，又刻意不採取「謙遜原則」，目的為何？

　　請將答案標明（一）（二）書寫，（一）（二）合計文長約250-300字（約 12-14 行）。

　　臣本布衣，躬耕於南陽，苟全性命於亂世，不求聞達於諸侯。先帝不以臣卑鄙，猥自枉屈，三顧臣於草廬之中，諮臣以當世之事，由是感激，遂許先帝以驅馳。後值傾覆，受任於敗軍之際，奉命於危難之間，爾來二十有一年矣。先帝知臣謹慎，故臨崩寄臣以大事也。受命以來，夙夜憂勤，恐託付不效，以傷先帝之明，故五月渡瀘，深入不毛。今南方已定，兵甲已足，當獎率三軍，北定中原，庶竭駑鈍，攘除姦凶，興復漢室，還於舊都，此臣所以報先帝而忠陛下之職分也。

三、引導寫作（占 27 分）

　　阿里巴巴能打開石門，是因為他知道「芝麻開門」的密語；烹飪高手能征服大家的味蕾，是因為他練就一身功夫，抓到美味的訣竅；演員能成功詮釋某個角色，必然是因為他對人生的悲歡離合有深刻的領會。對於人生的考驗，你是否也有自己的「通關密語」？**請以「通關密語」為題**，寫下你找出「密語」而得以「通關」的過程，以及其中的體會。文長不限。

103年度學科能力測驗國文科試題詳解

第壹部分：選擇題

一、單選題

1. **A**

【解析】 (A) 番
(B) 僥／矯
(C) 厄／遏
(D) 偓／儼

2. **A**

【解析】 (1) 由「應主動進行古蹟審查……」可知應選有主動、
積極意思的「責無旁貸」(自己應盡的責任，沒有
理由推卸。)
(2) 「從來不是……，而是……」在語意上才通順。
「反而……，而是……」兩個都是轉折連接，「反
而」的前面沒有相反論述，文句不通。
(3) 「讓地方政府有更多權責(職權和責任)」才能
「擔起重要的任務」。

3. **D**

【解析】 (A) 「桃花眼裡汪汪淚，忍到更深枕上流。」擬人，以
桃花喻女子。出自唐‧韓偓＜新秋＞。【語譯】一夜
清風吹來，讓人起了「秋扇見捐」的愁思，容顏也
似入秋漸漸改變。女子美麗眼裡汪汪的淚水，忍到
夜深時才任它流淌至枕上。

(B) 「減卻桃花一半紅」，指女子減卻姿容，以桃花喻女子。出自唐・施肩吾＜佳人覽鏡＞。【語譯】每每坐在鏡臺前端看自己容貌，便發覺今天與昨日又不同了。丈夫整夜外宿，讓女子如桃花般美麗的容貌減卻了一半姿色。

(C) 將桃花比爲美女「紅兒」淡妝之貌。出自唐・羅虬＜比紅兒詩＞。【語譯】淺色桃花倚著矮牆，不憑藉風吹送也能聞到花香。花兒像整日情意專注思念著意中人的女子，也像畫著淡妝的名妓杜紅兒啊！

(D) 古時在三月上巳日或三月三日，於水邊舉行濯除不潔的活動，稱爲「修禊」。此處指桃花長滿禊潭周圍。【語譯】暮春的三月三日，修禊潭中春水漲滿，潭邊桃花盛開。盛大的樂曲聲彷彿仙樂從天上降下，潭水如鏡，輕舟搖晃，恍若置身仙境般陶醉自得。

4. **C**

【解析】題意爲突顯「詩歌」可以超越時空，傳達激情與想像，能勝過一切人爲的干擾與人生的命限。

(A) 寫李白作品的感染力強。出自唐・杜甫＜寄李太白二十韻＞。

(B) 感慨知音難尋。出自《古詩十九首・西北有高樓》。

(C) 「屈原的詩歌如今仍和日月一樣大放光明，留存於世；楚王的樓閣卻早已無跡可尋，空遺山丘。」出自唐・李白＜江上吟＞。

(D) 「詩可以激發人的心志，可以觀察時政的得失，可以溝通大眾的情志，可以舒暢個人的憂怨。」指出文學的作用。出自《論語・陽貨》。

5. **D**

【解析】 (A) 《墨子》大部分是專論，非語錄。

(B) 不全然正確。如《論語》爲孔子弟子與再傳弟子編撰，而《孟子》則有一說爲孟子與弟子共同編撰。

(C) 《孟子》屬語錄體。

(D) 正確。如《荀子‧勸學》篇，「勸學」二字即概括題旨。

6. **B**

【語譯】 四凶的才能都可加以利用。堯在位時，聖人居於上位，都能依才任用，賦予他們重要職位，四凶因而不敢露出凶惡之心。堯並非不知道這四人不善，只要他們伏首聽命，聖人也不能誅殺他們。等到堯於百姓中舉用舜而把帝位禪讓給他，這四人才懷著怨憤不平的心而顯露他們的凶惡，所以舜能夠因爲他們的惡行而誅殺、流放他們。

【注釋】 (1) 四凶：堯舜時代，四個凶惡的部落領袖，《春秋左氏傳》所記爲：渾敦、窮奇、檮杌、饕餮；《尚書》所記爲：共工、驩兜、三苗、鯀。

(2) 《河南程氏遺書》：門人記載北宋理學家程顥、程頤的語錄，由朱熹編定。

【解析】 (A) 堯不因人不善而否定其才能，並非爲使之互相制衡。

(B) 由「聖人在上，皆以其才任大位」，「堯非不知其不善也」，可知(B)正確。

(C) 舜得位後，四人因憤恨不平而顯露惡行才遭誅殺、流放。

(D) 舜「得以因其跡而誅竄之」，可見是四凶惡行顯露後才行懲戒。

7. **D**

【解析】　對聯原可先由「仄起平收」判斷上下句，但選項中的下句都是平聲收尾的「甲、乙」選項，故需另由結構、文意判斷。

先判斷此四句的結構應為：(甲) 方知／海外／有／孤忠 (乙) 稱名／則／婦孺／皆知 (丙) 敢向／東南／爭／半壁 (丁) 舉目／有／河山／之異，依此可先將選項分為「丙甲」、「丁乙」兩組。

「風景不殊」句，用《世說新語・言語》：「風景不殊，正自有山河之異。」的典故，感慨政權更迭，江山易主。故知 (1)(2) 應填 (丁)(乙)。

【語譯】　望向東海上的臺澎兩島，風景和中原並無不同，但舉目望去，江山已易主。鄭成功在南方留下故國宗祠，反清復明的遠大抱負雖然渺茫難成，但一稱其名，連婦人小孩都知道。

四方鎮守疆土的將領多懷貳心，只有鄭成功忠於故國，在臺澎兩島屯聚軍隊，更敢向大陸東南爭奪半壁河山。南明諸王都空有名號而無領地，鄭成功據河山一角而志向高大，才讓人知道海外還有他忠於國家。

8. **B**

【解析】　首句「千百年後……」應接 (丁)「仍然可以……」；從末句「光是那麼一點」可知剩下幾句都在形容永字第一筆那一點，(戊) 是總括，在「甲乙丙」前；(戊)「凌空而來」接著是落筆，故接 (甲)「碰到紙上纖維」；第一筆的寫法是先向右頓，再向左收，故知為 (丙)(乙)。

9. **B**

【解析】 (A) 沒有提及「不耐聽人意見」。老年人是因嘮叨讓人
聽得不耐煩。

(B) 中年人「正在努力的學做人，一味的唯唯否否，出
言吐語，切忌生冷，總揀那爛熟的，人云亦云。」
故 (B) 正確。

(C) 老年人因嘮叨讓人聽得不耐煩。

(D) 「人生一大悲劇」是指敢說的、願意說的沒人聽；
人家願意聽的卻不敢說真話。

10-11 為題組

10. **A**

【解析】 作者認為自己僅是助教，而寫信者以「教授」稱之，
名實不符，司閽者（門房）必認為這是因他招搖撞騙，
在外以教授名號自稱，故認為他心地不淳厚，「人心不
古」了。

【注釋】 (1) 人心不古：感嘆現在的人，失去古人的忠厚淳樸。

(2) 招搖撞騙：借名炫耀，到處詐騙。

(3) 好為人師：指人不謙虛，喜歡教導別人。

(4) 不學無術：沒有學問才幹。

11. **B**

12-13 為題組

【語譯】 王汾濱說，他的家鄉有人養了隻八哥鳥，教牠說話，
人與鳥十分親近，出門遊玩一定帶著牠，彼此相伴有

好幾年了。有一天，那人到了絳州，離家還遠，但旅費已經用完。他擔憂煩惱卻想不出辦法。這時鳥說：「何不賣了我？送我到王爺的宅邸，應該可以賣個好價錢，就不用擔心沒旅費回家了。」那人說：「我怎麼捨得！」鳥說：「沒關係。主人你拿了錢就快走，在城西二十里大樹下等我。」那人聽從鳥的話，帶著牠到城裡，跟牠互相問答，圍觀的人越來越多。有個宦官見到這事，告訴了王爺。王爺傳召此人入王府，想要買下八哥。那個人說：「這鳥跟我相依為命，我不願意賣。」王爺問鳥：「你願意留下來嗎？」鳥回答說：「願意。」王爺聽了很高興。鳥又說：「給他十金就好，別多給了。」王爺聽了更高興了，馬上給了那人十金。那人故意做出懊悔遺憾的樣子而離開。王爺跟鳥說話，鳥應答敏捷。又叫著要吃肉。吃完後，鳥說：「臣要洗澡。」王爺命人拿金盆裝水，開了籠子讓牠洗澡。洗完後，鳥飛到屋簷上，梳理翅膀，抖動羽毛，還跟王爺說個沒完。不久，羽毛乾了，牠就輕快地振翅飛起。操著山西口音說：「臣走啦！」一轉眼就看不到鳥的蹤影，王爺跟侍臣抬頭張望嘆息，急忙要找鳥的主人，但已經不知去向了。後來有人到了關中，看到那人帶著鳥出現在西安市街上。

【注釋】　(1) 狎習：親近熟悉。

　　　　　(2) 資斧：資財與器用，指旅費。

　　　　　(3) 貲（ㄗ）：財貨。

　　　　　(4) 中貴：受寵顯貴的內臣、宦官。

　　　　　(5) 畀（ㄅㄧˋ）：給予。

　　　　　(6) 翩躚（ㄒㄧㄢ）：形容飛舞或行動輕快的樣子。

　　　　　(7) 鴝鵒（ㄑㄩˊㄩˋ）：八哥的別名。

12. **C**

13. **C**

【解析】 主人「故作懊悔狀」是為了讓王爺相信他萬分不捨。

14-15 為題組

【語譯】 昌他從西周出逃到東周，把西周的情資都給了東周。
東周很高興，西周大怒。馮且(ㄐㄩ，睢)告訴西周君
王說：「臣能殺了昌他。」西周君王給了馮且三十斤黃
金。馮且派人拿著黃金和書信，偷偷地傳遞給昌他，
信上說：「昌他：事情如果能成功，就盡力完成；無法
成功，就趕快逃回來。時間一耽擱事跡將敗露，會害
死你自己。」接著派人告訴東周偵察敵情的哨兵說：
「今晚會有壞人混入國境。」哨兵捉到傳遞訊息的人
而獻給東周君王，東周君王立刻殺了昌他。

【注釋】 (1) 西周東周：此處的「西周、東周」是戰國中期由
周王室分裂出來的小國，並非朝代畫分的西周、
東周。

(2) 亡：因罪出逃。

(3) 亟（ㄐㄧˊ）緊急。

(4) 候：探察敵情的人。

14. **C**

【解析】 (A) 往、到，動詞／無義，助詞。

(B) 和，連詞／向，介詞。

(C) 將要，副詞。

(D) 於是，就，連詞／憑藉，動詞。

15. **D**

【解析】 依文意，昌他出逃至東周國，想藉由出賣西周國情資而留在東周國。但馮且使東周國誤以爲昌他是西周國派去的間諜，而殺了昌他。故應選 (D)。

二、多選題

16. **BE**

【解析】 (A) 無「悲」、「喜」並敘而以喜襯悲。只是說明白芒花是作者「美麗的夢魘」。

(B) 用「父親和姨娘琅琅的笑語聲」（喜）來襯托「母親心中的愁緒」（悲）。

(C) 沒有「喜」的敘述。

(D) 孔乙己「伸開五指將碟子罩住」是寫孔乙己著慌，沒有「悲」的敘述。

(E) 金發伯「有意」製造「異常的大笑」（喜），秀潔聽了「胸中一時千頭萬緒，五味雜陳」，「比哭聲更令人難以承受」（悲）。故金發伯的大笑是反襯心中的悲哀。

17. **ABE**

【解析】 (A) 泛指同學。

(B) 泛指大家。

(C) 特指對話中的「你」、「我」。

(D) 特指對話中的「你」、「我」

(E) 泛指「別的」、「其他的」。

18. **CD**

【解析】 此詩出自大荒＜謁杜甫草堂＞。

(1) 「被廷爭疏離君主」，杜甫任左拾遺時，因營救房琯事而觸怒肅宗。

(2) 「被戰爭逐出長安」：杜甫因安史之亂而離開長安。

(3) 「這條玄宗倉皇出奔的路／你奔，就苦於上青天了」：寫杜甫帶著家人由隴入蜀時生活的困頓。

(4) ＜麗人行＞、＜悲陳陶＞、＜哀江頭＞都是杜甫的作品。＜麗人行＞諷刺楊貴妃兄妹驕奢淫逸，反映玄宗的昏庸與政治的腐敗。＜悲陳陶＞是杜甫在安史之亂時，為陳陶一場慘烈的戰役而哀。＜哀江頭＞借長安曲江的昔盛今衰，流露國破家亡的悲痛。

(A)、(B) 指李白

(C) 杜甫流寓成都時的居所。

(E) 新樂府運動由白居易、元稹發起，時代晚於杜甫。

19. **BCDE**

【解析】 此詩寫農村的沒落與農村人口老化問題。

(A) 「乾燥的風」和「稻草瑟縮著」是收割後的景象，非農作物歉收。

20. **AB**

【語譯】 (甲) 我常常憂慮從司馬遷、班固以來，史書的文字繁多，即使是未任官職的平民讀書人，也無法讀完，何況君王要日理萬機，哪有時間能都讀過！臣常不自量力的想要刪削冗長的史書，擇取精華重要

　　的部分，專取和國家興衰、民生憂樂相關的，好
　　的可以取法，不好的可引以爲戒，撰寫一本編年
　　體的書，……，時間上起戰國，下至五代，共一
　　千三百六十二年，寫成二百九十四卷。（司馬光
　　＜進書表＞）

(乙) 我在京城時，經由借閱館閣諸位大人家藏的版本，
　　參照校勘，校正了十分之六、七，……書中的要
　　旨都是以利益來立論，各種合縱連橫的政治手段，
　　機變巧詐層出不窮。然而從春秋到秦這段時間，
　　兩百多年的興衰成敗，可從這本書中看出大概。
　　雖不是義理之所在，但是文章華美綺麗，縱放恣
　　肆，是極好的文辭，學者不應該忽略它啊！
　　（王覺＜題戰國策＞）

【注釋】(1) 不自揆：不自量力。「揆」爲審度。
　　　　(2) 舉撮：擇取。
　　　　(3) 機要：精義、要旨。
　　　　(4) 館閣：掌圖書經籍與編修國史的機構。
　　　　(5) 變詐：巧變詭詐。
　　　　(6) 辯麗：文辭華美綺麗。
　　　　(7) 橫肆：形容文筆或書法的氣勢縱放恣肆。

【解析】「甲」指《資治通鑑》；「乙」指《戰國策》。
　　　　(A) 由「專取關國家盛衰，繫生民休戚，善可爲法，
　　　　　　惡可爲戒者」可知強調該書的政治功能；由「辯
　　　　　　麗橫肆，亦文辭之最」可知肯定該書的言辭效益。
　　　　(B) 正確。

(C) 由「甲」中自稱「臣」可知是上書給皇帝；由「專
取關國家盛衰，繫生民休戚，善可爲法，惡可爲戒
者」可知內容是「勸諫治國應以歷代興亡爲鑑」。
「乙」的寫作對象是「學者」，且其中無「勸諫治
國」的內容。

(D) 《史記》內容從黃帝至漢武帝，《漢書》則記西漢
一代，對照「甲」「上起戰國，下迄五代」，可知僅
能爲部分內容。「乙」《戰國策》則先於《漢書》。

(E) ＜燭之武退秦師＞是春秋時事，出處應爲《春秋
左氏傳》。

21. DE

【語譯】 曾子臥病在床。弟子樂正子春坐在床下，兒子曾元、
曾申坐在他的腳邊，童僕坐在角落，拿著燭火。童僕
說：「這席子華美而明亮，是大夫的席子嗎？」子春
說：「住口！」曾子聽到這話，驚訝地出了聲。童僕
說：「這席子華美而明亮，是大夫的席子嗎？」曾子
說：「是的，這是季孫氏的賞賜，我沒能換下來。元兒
啊，扶我起來，把席子換掉。」曾元說：「您老人家已
經病得很重了，不能更換席子。希望您可以等到天亮
的時候，我再幫您更換。」曾子說：「你愛我還不如童
僕愛我啊！君子用道德愛人，小人用姑息愛人。我還
求什麼呢？能夠合禮而死得其正，就這樣罷了。」於
是衆人攙扶起曾子而更換席子，再將他扶回席上，還
沒躺安穩就過世了。

【注釋】 (1) 睆（ㄏㄨㄢˇ）：明亮。
(2) 簀（ㄗㄜˊ）：竹席。

(3) 病革（ㄐㄧˊ）：病情危急。

(4) 細人：小人。

(A) 樂正子春深知老師個性，要童僕別再說了。

(B) 曾元希望曾子先不要換席子，因為曾子病重（病革），不適合移動。

(C) 曾子責怪曾元不如童僕善體己意。

22. **ABD**

【解析】　此為「錯綜」修辭的「交蹉語次」。

(A) 句讀之不知，或師焉；惑之不解，或不焉。

(B) 西伯幽而演《易》，不以隱約而弗務；周旦顯而制《禮》，不以康樂而加思。

(C) 由禽鳥→人→太守，為層遞修辭。

(D) 牠們曾交錯湧疊，如在表演水中疊羅漢；（牠們）也曾高速接近船舷又敏捷地側翻，如流星一樣劃一道弧線拋射離去。

(E) 摹寫。未使用錯綜。

23. **CDE**

【解析】　(A) 劉姥姥自嘲「老風流」，無影射。

(B) 胡屠戶直接罵女婿，無影射。

(C) 以煮豆影射曹丕和自己是「同根生」的同胞兄弟，何苦相逼太過。

(D) 用棋局影射逐鹿天下的戰局。

(E) 楊過用蟋蟀影射比武諸人。大蟋蟀是歐陽鋒，老蟋蟀是柯鎮惡，兩隻小蟋蟀是郭靖、黃蓉。

第貳部分：非選擇題

一、文章解讀

【引導】

（一）要分析古人的「清賞」和今人的「觀光」有何不同，就要注意文章中關於二者對立的描寫：安頓／活躍，靜／動，清淨／熱鬧，一人濯足、一人閒居／廣攬遊衆、人群俱集。

（二）「人品亦化成商品」的關鍵是前一句：「以供人玩賞爲己樂」。要注意「古以窈窕乃成淑女」的「窈窕」意爲「幽靜美好的樣子」。與前文「清賞」的幽靜之趣相通。

【範例】

（一）古人的「清賞」是在幽靜中欣賞勝境，探求其中的意趣，追求心神安頓，所以人不能多、心不能躁；而今人的「觀光」務求活躍、熱鬧，其樂趣來自投入人群，與其說是觀景不如說是觀人，故人要多、要喧鬧。

（二）「以供人玩賞爲己樂」，則把自己物化成他人賞玩的對象，一如櫥窗中之商品，任人品頭論足，貼籤標價，反而沾沾自喜，故曰「人品亦化成商品」。

二、文章分析

【引導】

（一）符合「謙遜原則」的就是諸葛亮以臣下身分，使用敬謙語氣的部分；彰顯自己而不採取「謙遜原則」，則是諸葛亮抬出先帝對他的恩寵與信任，以及描述功績的部分。

（二）文中採取「謙遜原則」的同時，又刻意不採取「謙遜原則」的目的，則須由諸葛亮＜出師表＞的寫作動機切入。

【範例】

（一）1、運用謙遜原則者：

　　　（1）「臣本布衣，躬耕於南陽，苟全性命於亂世，不求聞達於諸侯。」「先帝不以臣卑鄙」，表達自己出身卑微。

　　　（2）「庶竭駑鈍」，謙稱自己才能低下。

　　　2、不採取謙遜原則者：

　　　（1）「三顧臣於草廬之中，諮臣以當世之事。」顯示自己的才能而能得先帝青眼，禮遇備至。

　　　（2）「受任於敗軍之際，奉命於危難之間。」表達自己的才能深受先帝信任。

　　　（3）「受命以來，夙夜憂勤」顯現自己忠勤於國。

　　　（4）「今南方已定，兵甲已足。」描述自己的功績。

（二）表彰自己的能力與功績，是要後主對其北伐有信心；提出受先帝愛重，除了表達感激先帝的知遇之恩，自己將鞠躬盡瘁以報外，更是在在提醒後主勿忘先帝遺訓。這些都是為了讓後主在自己出師期間能安定朝政，以免後顧之憂。

三、引導寫作

【通關密語】

　　一顆露珠即將脫離花瓣邊緣墜落；一隻鳥兒身體微傾，側耳聆聽發表高見的同伴；一道凌厲的光芒破天而下，直擊曠野上的大樹；雲朵幻化成天馬，攢蹄奮進……，一張張精采的攝影作品，

不禁讓人對攝影家發出疑問：「你怎麼總能捕捉到這些精彩瞬間？你的運氣眞好！」「不」，攝影師從容地回答：「我比別人多的不是運氣，是耐心，沒有好鏡頭，我『等』。」我聽了不禁會心一笑，沒錯，「耐心」就是通關的密語。

　　我是個急驚風，從小就以自己反應敏捷，動作快爲榮。在課堂上我是第一個完成作業的；在餐桌上我是第一個吃完飯的；在登山步道上我把爸媽、妹妹拋得老遠；總是聽到我在呼喚玩伴「快點！快點！」。因爲性子急，事情也常常做得不仔細，作業是寫得快，卻也常粗心錯漏；打掃三兩下就完成，卻留下好幾個角落的灰塵；沒聽完講解自以爲大致了解就開始操作，因此漏了重要步驟而浪費更多時間。因爲缺乏耐心，房間裡多的是我「用情不專」、「朝秦暮楚」的證據：彈了三個月的吉他、塞在櫃子上的電子琴、還空著一大半的美麗風景拼圖、只讀了開頭一、兩本的學習套書──我總以爲，這只是因爲我沒找到眞正的興趣，不了解自己的天賦，總有一天，我會遇到讓我全心投入的事情，我會在那件事上發光發熱！──直到高二的啦啦隊比賽。

　　我一直覺得「肢體動覺」是我的罩門，同手同腳、姿勢笨拙，人家做起來行雲流水的美妙姿態，我就算練習再久也像個指令錯誤的機器人。但高二的啦啦隊比賽是班級競賽，全班都得參加，我只能硬著頭皮、厚著臉皮，向大家證明我是「非不爲也，實不能也」。在編舞同學、體育小天使輪流「個別指導」我不知多少次後，我惱羞成怒地說：「我就是學不會嘛！」同學卻無絲毫不耐煩，反而安撫我：「不是『學不會』，是『還沒學會』！來，休息一下，待會再跳一次喔！」相比於他的耐心、包容，我羞赧得不敢再抱怨，何況事關班級榮譽。我只好耐下性子在賽前一次一次又一次的練習。

　　比賽當天，我緊張得腦筋幾乎空白，只想著上場時萬一忘了動作、萬一做錯怎麼辦？唉！豁出去了，就當再練習一次！當音樂一下，我彷彿成了音符牽動的木偶，自然地隨著節拍，口號、動作，一個不漏！這怎麼可能？最後在高昂的口號聲中，我一處不錯地跳完整首曲子，同學們都激動地拍打我的肩膀說：「你做到了！」

　　這怎麼可能？我曾經以為絕對過不了的大關卡，我曾經以為是天賦的問題，這件「奇蹟」讓我反覆地想，為什麼？為什麼其他類似的事我總是應驗自己的預言，而這次卻不一樣？我想，因為這次我耐心地做了一次又一次。

　　「掘井九仞而不及泉，猶為棄井也。」如果沒有耐心，成功也只是偶然，只能碰運氣罷了。以前的我心浮氣躁，做事情總是「三分鐘熱度」，沒有耐心按部就班，紮紮實實打好基本功，打了兩三天漁，就妄想大豐收。有了這次經驗，以前左耳進右耳出的「名言佳句」都鮮活起來，羅丹說的對，「要有耐心，不要依靠靈感。」莎士比亞也說：「斧頭雖小，但經多次砍劈，終能將一棵最堅硬的橡木砍倒。」只有耐心地反覆練習，才能生巧。天賦不是縹緲不可捉摸的，它來自不斷的積累；而有了厚實的基本功，耐心等待時機，才能捕捉到人生的好風景。

　　此後，面對未來的種種關卡，我知道「耐心」，就是我的通關密語！

103年學測國文科非選擇題閱卷評分原則說明

閱卷召集人：林啓屏（國立政治大學中文系教授）

　　本次參與閱卷的委員，均為各大學中文系、國文系、語文教育系或通識教育中心之教師，共計227人，分為20組，除正、副召集人統籌所有閱卷事宜外，每組均置一位協同主持人，負責該組閱卷工作，協同主持人均為各大學中文系、國文系之專任教授。

　　1月20日，由正、副召集人與8位協同主持人，就3000份抽樣之答案卷，詳加評閱、分析、討論，草擬評分原則。每題選出「A」、「B」、「C」等第之標準卷各1份，及試閱卷各15份。1月21日，再由正、副召集人與20位協同主持人深入討論、評比所選出的標準卷及試閱卷，並審視、修訂所擬之評分原則，確定後，製作閱卷參考手冊，供1月22日正式閱卷前，各組協同主持人說明及全體閱卷委員參考之用，並作為評分時之參考。

　　本次國文考科非選擇題共三大題，占54分。第一大題為文章解讀，占9分；第二大題為文章分析，占18分；第三大題為引導寫作，占27分。

　　第一大題要求考生閱讀節錄自錢穆〈品與味〉中的一段文字後，加以解讀。評閱重點，在於檢視考生是否能解讀作者的看法。凡能解讀題旨並加評述，內容充實，理路清晰，文字流暢者，得A等（7~9分）；大致能解讀題旨並加評述，內容尚稱合宜，文字平順者，得B等（4~6分）；解讀或評述失當，內容貧乏，文字蕪雜者，得C等（1~3分）。其次，再視字數是否符合要求，錯別字是否過多，斟酌扣分。

　　第二大題要求考生閱讀諸葛亮〈出師表〉的一段文字，考生必須就本段材料回答兩個子題。兩個子題的問題重心，一在引文文字中「謙遜原則」之運用，與未採「謙遜原則」之運用的區別。一在於文中既運用「謙遜原則」，又同時不採「謙遜原則」的寫作目的，進行分析。第（一）小題針對關鍵文字，各引述兩項以上，且有得體說明；第（二）小題針對目的的說明，分析深入，文字流暢者，得 A 等（13～18 分）。第（一）小題雖引述關鍵文字而未說明，或說明欠妥當，文字大體平順；第（二）小題對目的的說明，大致能符合要求，但欠周延者，得 B 等（7~12 分）。兩小題中，僅部分符合要求，且敘述拙劣貧乏者，得 C 等（1~6 分）。另視是否分列小題作答，字數符合規定與否，及錯別字是否過多，斟酌扣分。

　　第三大題要求考生根據自己之人生體會，以「通關密語」為題，寫一篇文章，論說、記敘、抒情皆可，文長不限。評閱重點，從「題旨發揮」、「資料掌握」、「結構安排」、「字句運用」四項指標，加以評分。凡能掌握題幹要求，舉例闡析「通關密語」之意涵，緊扣題旨發揮，對通關的過程表達適當，體悟深刻，取材豐富妥適，舉證詳實貼切，結構嚴謹，脈絡清楚，字句妥切，邏輯清晰，文筆流暢，修辭優美者，得 A 等（19~27 分）；尚能掌握題幹要求，依照題旨發揮，但欠深刻，內容平實，思路尚稱清晰，取材尚稱恰當，舉證平淡疏略，結構大致完整，脈絡大致清楚，用詞通順，造句平淡，文筆平順，修辭尚可者，得 B 等（10~18 分）；未能掌握題幹要求，題旨不明或偏離題旨，內容浮泛，思路不清，材料運用不當，舉證鬆散模糊，結構鬆散，條理紛雜，字句欠當，邏輯不通，文筆蕪蔓，修辭粗俗者，得 C 等（1~9 分）。另立標題，但扣緊題旨者，至多給 A-（19~21 分）。另視標點符號之使用與錯別字多寡，斟酌扣分。

【附錄一】

103年度學科能力測驗
英文考科公佈答案

題號	答案	題號	答案	題號	答案
1	C	21	B	41	B
2	A	22	D	42	D
3	A	23	C	43	A
4	D	24	D	44	D
5	C	25	A	45	A
6	B	26	B	46	C
7	C	27	C	47	D
8	D	28	D	48	B
9	B	29	A	49	B
10	B	30	C	50	C
11	C	31	I	51	A
12	B	32	F	52	D
13	C	33	E	53	C
14	A	34	H	54	A
15	C	35	D	55	C
16	B	36	B	56	B
17	A	37	C		
18	D	38	A		
19	A	39	J		
20	C	40	G		

103年度學科能力測驗
國文、數學考科公佈答案

國　文		數　學				
題號	答案	題號	答案	題　號		答案
1	A	1	5	A	13	1
2	A	2	4		14	2
3	D	3	2		15	0
4	C	4	4		16	1
5	D	5	2		17	3
6	B	6	2	B	18	6
7	D	7	1,3,5		19	－
8	B	8	1,4		20	9
9	B	9	2,3,4	C	21	4
10	A	10	3,4		22	3
11	B	11	2,3,5	D	23	5
12	C	12	1,4		24	4
13	C			E	25	－
14	C				26	3
15	D				27	2
16	BE			F	28	1
17	ABE				29	1
18	CD			G	30	1
19	BCDE				31	3
20	AB				32	8
21	DE			H	33	6
22	ABD				34	2
23	CDE				35	2
					36	2

103年度學科能力測驗
社會考科公佈答案

題號	答案	題號	答案	題號	答案	題號	答案
1	B	21	A	41	D	61	D
2	C	22	C	42	B	62	D
3	B	23	D	43	D	63	A
4	A	24	無答案	44	B	64	C
5	C	25	A	45	C	65	A
6	B	26	D	46	C	66	B
7	B	27	C	47	A	67	C
8	C	28	A	48	D	68	B
9	B	29	D	49	C	69	A
10	C	30	A	50	B	70	A
11	C	31	C	51	C	71	B
12	D	32	A	52	B	72	A
13	A	33	B	53	C		
14	B	34	D	54	A		
15	D	35	D	55	D		
16	D	36	B	56	B		
17	C	37	B	57	D		
18	C	38	C	58	C		
19	A	39	C	59	C		
20	C	40	B	60	A		

社會考科第 **24** 題答案調整說明：

1. 在一般生活用語中，「交通違規罰金」可相當於「交通違規罰款」（根據教育部國語辭典：「罰款」亦稱為「罰金」），且此一用語在一般媒體報導或網路媒介中也常見，部分高中教科書也有相同用法，因此本中心於 103 年 1 月 19 日公布之參考答案為選項 (C)。

2. 本題測驗的主要概念為經濟學之「政府的收入與支出」，雖然「交通違規罰金」可作為如一般所理解的，而且「罰金」與「罰鍰」皆屬政府收入項目，但從法律層面嚴格而言，「罰金」與「罰鍰」兩個名詞的法律意涵有明顯差異。交通違規所繳納之款項屬行政罰之「罰鍰」而非刑罰之「罰金」，因此選項 (C) 的敘述有瑕疵。

3. 經多方考量，為避免考生因為瞭解「罰金」與「罰鍰」的差異不選答 (C) 選項，而選擇其他選項或放棄作答，因此，本題無論作答與否，均給分。

103 年度學科能力測驗
自然考科公佈答案

題號	答案	題號	答案	題號	答案	題號	答案
1	A	21	C	41	D	61	BD
2	C	22	C	42	B	62	D
3	D	23	B	43	D	63	B
4	C	24	CD	44	E	64	D
5	A	25	AD	45	AE	65	ABD
6	B	26	BE	46	E	66	BCE
7	D	27	CD	47	BE	67	E
8	B	28	BCD	48	A	68	BD
9	A	29	BCE	49	D		
10	B	30	BE	50	BE		
11	C	31	CE	51	BCD		
12	A	32	BD	52	E		
13	D	33	ADE	53	BCD		
14	B	34	CE	54	BE		
15	E	35	BE	55	BC		
16	E	36	ADE	56	ABC		
17	D	37	AE	57	ADE		
18	E	38	ABD	58	B		
19	A	39	BDE	59	A		
20	A	40	AB	60	AC		

【附錄二】

103年度學科能力測驗
總級分與各科成績標準一覽表

標準 項目	頂標	前標	均標	後標	底標
國　文	13	12	11	9	7
英　文	14	12	10	6	4
數　學	13	11	8	5	3
社　會	14	13	11	9	8
自　然	13	11	9	6	5
總級分	65	59	49	37	28

※五項標準之計算，均不含缺考生（總級分之計算不含五科都缺考的
考生）之成績，計算方式如下：

　　頂標：成績位於第88百分位數之考生級分。
　　前標：成績位於第75百分位數之考生級分。
　　均標：成績位於第50百分位數之考生級分。
　　後標：成績位於第25百分位數之考生級分。
　　底標：成績位於第12百分位數之考生級分。

【附錄三】

103 年度學科能力測驗
各科級分人數百分比累計表

	級分	人　數	百分比 (%)	累計人數	累計百分比 (%)
國 文	15	4,138	2.84	145,900	100.00
	14	11,470	7.86	141,762	97.16
	13	19,908	13.64	130,292	89.30
	12	24,330	16.68	110,384	75.66
	11	23,101	15.83	86,054	58.98
	10	18,494	12.68	62,953	43.15
	9	13,149	9.01	44,459	30.47
	8	9,380	6.43	31,310	21.46
	7	7,027	4.82	21,930	15.03
	6	5,304	3.64	14,903	10.21
	5	4,095	2.81	9,599	6.58
	4	3,053	2.09	5,504	3.77
	3	1,769	1.21	2,451	1.68
	2	632	0.43	682	0.47
	1	47	0.03	50	0.03
	0	3	0.00	3	0.00
英 文	15	7,728	5.31	145,575	100.00
	14	12,503	8.59	137,847	94.69
	13	15,359	10.55	125,344	86.10
	12	14,845	10.20	109,985	75.55
	11	12,616	8.67	95,140	65.35
	10	12,483	8.57	82,524	56.69
	9	11,291	7.76	70,041	48.11
	8	9,688	6.65	58,750	40.36
	7	9,473	6.51	49,062	33.70
	6	8,267	5.68	39,589	27.19
	5	9,036	6.21	31,322	21.52
	4	11,581	7.96	22,286	15.31
	3	8,827	6.06	10,705	7.35
	2	1,821	1.25	1,878	1.29
	1	55	0.04	57	0.04
	0	2	0.00	2	0.00

	級分	人　數	百分比 (%)	累計人數	累計百分比 (%)
數	15	6,749	4.63	145,817	100.00
	14	7,476	5.13	139,068	95.37
	13	8,352	5.73	131,592	90.24
	12	10,289	7.06	123,240	84.52
	11	11,792	8.09	112,951	77.46
	10	10,878	7.46	101,159	69.37
	9	13,413	9.20	90,281	61.91
	8	13,014	8.92	76,868	52.72
	7	10,492	7.20	63,854	43.79
	6	11,481	7.87	53,362	36.60
學	5	11,085	7.60	41,881	28.72
	4	9,413	6.46	30,796	21.12
	3	11,082	7.60	21,383	14.66
	2	7,968	5.46	10,301	7.06
	1	2,306	1.58	2,333	1.60
	0	27	0.02	27	0.02
社	15	5,975	4.10	145,792	100.00
	14	12,659	8.68	139,817	95.90
	13	24,500	16.80	127,158	87.22
	12	21,550	14.78	102,658	70.41
	11	20,466	14.04	81,108	55.63
	10	21,170	14.52	60,642	41.59
	9	13,028	8.94	39,472	27.07
	8	12,568	8.62	26,444	18.14
	7	7,215	4.95	13,876	9.52
	6	4,233	2.90	6,661	4.57
會	5	2,031	1.39	2,428	1.67
	4	358	0.25	397	0.27
	3	37	0.03	39	0.03
	2	2	0.00	2	0.00
	1	0	0.00	0	0.00
	0	0	0.00	0	0.00

	級分	人　數	百分比 (%)	累計人數	累計百分比 (%)
自	15	7,084	4.87	145,520	100.00
	14	8,305	5.71	138,436	95.13
	13	9,428	6.48	130,131	89.42
	12	10,720	7.37	120,703	82.95
	11	11,727	8.06	109,983	75.58
	10	13,735	9.44	98,256	67.52
	9	15,237	10.47	84,521	58.08
	8	15,883	10.91	69,284	47.61
	7	15,430	10.60	53,401	36.70
	6	14,417	9.91	37,971	26.09
然	5	13,134	9.03	23,554	16.19
	4	8,165	5.61	10,420	7.16
	3	2,113	1.45	2,255	1.55
	2	125	0.09	142	0.10
	1	15	0.01	17	0.01
	0	2	0.00	2	0.00

【劉毅老師的話】

　　我們出版歷屆的學測或指考試題詳解時，都會附上許多相關統計表格。不要小看這些表格，它們能讓你了解競爭者的實力，好勉勵自己要精益求精。

【附錄四】
103年度學科能力測驗
總級分人數百分比累計表

總級分	人數	百分比	累計人數	累計百分比
75	295	0.20	146,017	100.00
74	648	0.44	145,722	99.80
73	1,085	0.74	145,074	99.35
72	1,275	0.87	143,989	98.61
71	1,566	1.07	142,714	97.74
70	1,768	1.21	141,148	96.67
69	1,930	1.32	139,380	95.45
68	2,135	1.46	137,450	94.13
67	2,442	1.67	135,315	92.67
66	2,367	1.62	132,873	91.00
65	2,634	1.80	130,506	89.38
64	2,851	1.95	127,872	87.57
63	2,848	1.95	125,021	85.62
62	3,079	2.11	122,173	83.67
61	3,227	2.21	119,094	81.56
60	3,385	2.32	115,867	79.35
59	3,440	2.36	112,482	77.03
58	3,466	2.37	109,042	74.68
57	3,559	2.44	105,576	72.30
56	3,648	2.50	102,017	69.87
55	3,689	2.53	98,369	67.37
54	3,770	2.58	94,680	64.84
53	3,867	2.65	90,910	62.26
52	3,692	2.53	87,043	59.61
51	3,715	2.54	83,351	57.08
50	3,798	2.60	79,636	54.54
49	3,853	2.64	75,838	51.94
48	3,802	2.60	71,985	49.30
47	3,570	2.44	68,183	46.70
46	3,669	2.51	64,613	44.25
45	3,555	2.43	60,944	41.74
44	3,380	2.31	57,389	39.30
43	3,270	2.24	54,009	36.99
42	3,159	2.16	50,739	34.75
41	2,884	1.98	47,580	32.59
40	2,813	1.93	44,696	30.61

總級分	人數	百分比	累計人數	累計百分比
39	2,685	1.84	41,883	28.68
38	2,565	1.76	39,198	26.84
37	2,426	1.66	36,633	25.09
36	2,268	1.55	34,207	23.43
35	2,193	1.50	31,939	21.87
34	2,147	1.47	29,746	20.37
33	2,068	1.42	27,599	18.90
32	2,070	1.42	25,531	17.48
31	2,024	1.39	23,461	16.07
30	1,935	1.33	21,437	14.68
29	1,915	1.31	19,502	13.36
28	1,931	1.32	17,587	12.04
27	1,879	1.29	15,656	10.72
26	1,775	1.22	13,777	9.44
25	1,805	1.24	12,002	8.22
24	1,735	1.19	10,197	6.98
23	1,614	1.11	8,462	5.80
22	1,511	1.03	6,848	4.69
21	1,324	0.91	5,337	3.66
20	1,121	0.77	4,013	2.75
19	874	0.60	2,892	1.98
18	682	0.47	2,018	1.38
17	473	0.32	1,336	0.91
16	297	0.20	863	0.59
15	171	0.12	566	0.39
14	96	0.07	395	0.27
13	65	0.04	299	0.20
12	37	0.03	234	0.16
11	21	0.01	197	0.13
10	26	0.02	176	0.12
9	17	0.01	150	0.10
8	20	0.01	133	0.09
7	19	0.01	113	0.08
6	9	0.01	94	0.06
5	24	0.02	85	0.06
4	21	0.01	61	0.04
3	33	0.02	40	0.03
2	5	0.00	7	0.00
1	1	0.00	2	0.00
0	1	0.00	1	0.00

註：累計百分比＝從 0 到該級分的累計人數 /（報名人數 - 五科均缺考人數）

【附錄五】

103年度學科能力測驗
原始分數與級分對照表

科目	國文	英文	數學	社會	自然
級距	5.93	6.31	6.67	8.81	8.39
級分	分 數 區 間				
15	83.03 - 108.00	88.35 - 100.00	93.39 - 100.00	123.35 - 144.00	117.47 - 128.00
14	77.10 - 83.02	82.04 - 88.34	86.72 - 93.38	114.54 - 123.34	109.08 - 117.46
13	71.17 - 77.09	75.73 - 82.03	80.05 - 86.71	105.73 - 114.53	100.69 - 109.07
12	65.24 - 71.16	69.42 - 75.72	73.38 - 80.04	96.92 - 105.72	92.30 - 100.68
11	59.31 - 65.23	63.11 - 69.41	66.71 - 73.37	88.11 - 96.91	83.91 - 92.29
10	53.38 - 59.30	56.80 - 63.10	60.04 - 66.70	79.30 - 88.10	75.52 - 83.90
9	47.45 - 53.37	50.49 - 56.79	53.37 - 60.03	70.49 - 79.29	67.13 - 75.51
8	41.52 - 47.44	44.18 - 50.48	46.70 - 53.36	61.68 - 70.48	58.74 - 67.12
7	35.59 - 41.51	37.87 - 44.17	40.03 - 46.69	52.87 - 61.67	50.35 - 58.73
6	29.66 - 35.58	31.56 - 37.86	33.36 - 40.02	44.06 - 52.86	41.96 - 50.34
5	23.73 - 29.65	25.25 - 31.55	26.69 - 33.35	35.25 - 44.05	33.57 - 41.95
4	17.80 - 23.72	18.94 - 25.24	20.02 - 26.68	26.44 - 35.24	25.18 - 33.56
3	11.87 - 17.79	12.63 - 18.93	13.35 - 20.01	17.63 - 26.43	16.79 - 25.17
2	5.94 - 11.86	6.32 - 12.62	6.68 - 13.34	8.82 - 17.62	8.40 - 16.78
1	0.01 - 5.93	0.01 - 6.31	0.01 - 6.67	0.01 - 8.81	0.01 - 8.39
0	0.00 - 0.00	0.00 - 0.00	0.00 - 0.00	0.00 - 0.00	0.00 - 0.00

級分計算方式如下：

1. 級距：以各科到考考生，計算其原始得分前百分之一考生（取整數，小數無條件進位）的平均原始得分，再除以15，並取至小數第二位，第三位四捨五入。

2. 本測驗之成績採級分制，原始得分0分為0級分，最高為15級分，缺考以0級分計。各級分與原始得分、級距之計算方式詳見簡章第9～10頁。